MYTHS FROM

# THE MAHĀBHĀRATA

Vol. 1

QUEST FOR IMMORTALITY

# MYTHS FROM
# THE MAHĀBHĀRATA

## Vol. 1
## QUEST FOR IMMORTALITY

Sadashiv A. Dange

Aryan Books International
New Delhi

Myths from the Mahābhārata

Vol. 1
Quest for Immortality

ISBN: 978-81-7305-116-6



First Published: 1997

Reprinted: 2022



Published by:

Aryan Books International
Pooja Apartments, 4B, Ansari Road, New Delhi-110002 (India)
Tel.: 23287589, 23255799; Fax: 91-11-23270385
E-mail: aryanbooks@gmail.com
**www.aryanbooks.com**

Printed in India

**Books That Live!**

Aryan Books International was established in 1992. Though it began as a commercial venture, business was only a part of the whole. The primary aim was to bridge the gap between the history taught and the real history of our country, and also to present its lesser known and sometimes deliberately neglected facets. In academia, the legacy of our art, culture and ethos was being undermined to perpetuate a narrative which left us looking weak, soft and lagging behind the so-called progressive West.

It was this narrative that we sought to contest. The journey over the last thirty years has not been an easy one. However, it gives us a sense of satisfaction to have possibly made a small difference by publishing over 750 titles written by the most acclaimed authors in the field. We have specialized in publishing ingenious and outstanding scholarship, both established as also fresh. While we focus on our long forgotten history, we also bring to the fore certain extremely important aspects of Indian art, culture and traditions.

Apart from pioneering content, we also ensure that our production quality remains the best in the business, as we continue with the mission to publish books that **Live Forever**!

We are also aware that this is just the beginning of a long journey. A long road lies ahead. A lot more needs to be said. A lot more needs to be explored. We assure you that we're on it with renewed commitment!

*To*
*Revered Guruji*
*(the late) Prof. H.D. Velankar*
*Whose unique and self-practised doctrine*
शिष्यदेवो भव
*(Śiṣyadevo bhava)*
*Has always been*
*My Guide*

# CONTENTS

# PREFACE

My earlier book *Legends in the Mahābhārata* has been out of print for a pretty long time, after it was notified as 'rare' (1980), by M/s Motilal Banarsidass, Delhi, who published it in 1969. In recent years I have been receiving letters about its non-availability; and, during the last year, not knowing its exact publisher, some readers wrote to other publishers to contact me and see if the book could be reprinted; and some publishers did, indeed, approach me for bringing out a second edition. Being preoccupied with other projects, which were time-bound, I could not take up preparing a fresh press-copy of the book. Now, after perusing the book, and making additions and deletions, I decided to rearrange and widen the topic. The original book, now, forms only a part of the new plan with a modified title : *Myths from the Mahābhārata*; Vol. I, *Quest for Immortality*. Other volume(s) would follow.

I entrusted the publication of this volume to Shri Vikas Arya of the Aryan Books International, New Delhi, who recently published my book *Towards Understanding Hindu Myths* (1996); and a revised second edition of *Critiques on Sanskrit Dramas* (1994; Co-author, Mrs. S.S. Dange) elegantly and within reasonable time. I thank him for bringing out this volume also with the same elegance and sense of belonging. The cover-design is done by Mrs. Vidya Joshi, Lecturer at the J.J. School of Arts, Bombay.

Sadashiv A. Dange

Mumbai
May 19, 1997

# INTRODUCTION

Myths and folk-tales are deeply rooted in tradition. They are living monuments of thoughts, convictions, faith and fancies of people, and of tribes some of which are non-existent at the present time. They are also a sort of a key to the development of religion. They get gradually fattened up as time passes; and, sometimes, it is difficult to know what exactly was at the bottom of many of these, or, if there be any truth at the lowest level of these, what exactly it was. This gives rise to guesses and requires careful comparative investigation to interpret and understand them. The present volume is an attempt at understanding the meaning of three myths from the *Mahābhārata* (*Mb*). It is generally known that the term myth is applied to a traditional story, told in an unusual way and the meaning of which obtains rarely in the face of the account itself. Legend is a mythical account of a real person, or of a real occurrence. However, a legend has all the characteristics of a myth woven around a reality (for a detailed discussion see Dange, 1996, *Towards Understanding Hindu Myths*; ch. 1).

The study of this type of literature, apart from a mere collection of such stories, has interested scholars, both Indian and Western, for quite a long time. Such a study, obviously, drew help from collections of myths and, in the case of the Hindu myths, is seen prominently from as early as the end of the nineteenth century of the Christian era onwards in such works as *Hindu Mythology — Vedic and Puranic* (Wilkins, W.J., 1882), *Vedic Mythology* (Macdonell, A.A., 1897) and *Hindu Mythology in Outline, According to the Mahābhārata* (Fausbøll, V., 1903). Even earlier this interest is noted, as is clear from *Mythology of the Hindus* (Coleman,

Charles, 1832), *Mythology of the Aryan Nations* (Cox, G.W., 1870) and others, not to speak of works regarding the Hindu gods and their nature: *Hindu Pantheon* (Moor, Edward, 1820) and *Hindu Gods and Heroes* (Barnett, L.D., 1922). With the progress of the nineteenth century critical study of myths, and of the *Mahābhārata*, joined the efforts at collections of myths. As a more notable effort in this direction might be cited *Die Suparṇasage* (Charpentier, J., 1920). Writing more particularly about *Mb*, in his book, *The Mahābhārata* (1935) Held, G.J., gives the names of scholars who put the epic to a critical test (Ch. 1). Not getting entangled into the various theories about the text of *Mb,* he throws open an avenue of tribal organisations and their practices comparing them with accounts and details from *Mb.* Sukhthankar, V.S. (1957, *On the Meaning of the Mahābhārata*) generally follows Held's method, accepting some of his opinions. Though not directly related to the main theme of *Mb*, the study of Oldham, C.F., about the Nāgas (1905, *The Sun and the Serpent*; 1901; "The Nagas", in *JRAS)* relates to certain accounts in *Mb*. It helps the study of the myth of Garuḍa in *Mb.*, as does that by Vogel, J. Ph. (1926, *The Indian Serpent Lore*). Zimmer, H., takes the eagle (Garuḍa) and the serpent as symbolising the free aerial spirit and the fettered earth respectively (1946, *Myths and Symbols in Indian Art and Civilization*). Oldham refers to the myth of the churning of the ocean in *Mb*, while expressing his views on Vāsuki, the king of serpents, that was used as the churning–rope. Gonda, J. (1954, *Aspects of Early Viṣṇuism*), methodically similar to held presents a balanced treatment of mythical information in his interpretation of the relationship between Garuḍa and Viṣṇu, though his studies, in this book, do not relate to *Mb*.

Many myths and legends in the epics have their roots in the Vedic literature. It is noted that, in certain places, *Mb.* follows even the pattern of narration from the Veda. A separate study will be required for this; but, just as an instance may be noted the expression, *navatīr nava* (Ādi I. 32) which states that Garuḍa increased the number of his mouths to 'ninety times nine' (cf. *RV* I. 84. 13; IV. 26. 3; IX. 61. 1). The same may be said about the expression *vasavas tvā rakṣantu* etc. The *Mb.* myths take their sap also from popular beliefs. Most of the myths that have their source in the Vedic literature, assume a larger form here, fattened up by details and mixture from other myths. In the case of the myths studied in the present volume there is a common motif. All the three deal with the gain of immortality — may it be nectar, or Soma, or the lore that restores the dead to life. The 'Somāharaṇa' portion of the myth of Garuḍa has its source in the RV and later Vedic texts. The mythical story of the gain of the lore of immortality (Sañjīvanī), by Kaca, could be taken as a legend, as it serves as a prologue to the historically real account of Yayāti, whose wives were Devayānī and Śarmiṣṭhā. The account of Kaca and Devayānī is totally absent in the Vedic literature. But, the giving of Kaca to the *śālāvṛka*-s (wolves) by the demons, obtains in the Vedic myth of Indra; so swallowing and disgorging alive, amounting to a new birth, obtain. In essence, the motif is prominent in the rites relating to initiation. The Purāṇas, as a class, do not give the account of Kaca-Devayānī and the gain of the lore by Kaca. The same is the case with the myth of Garuḍa. However, the legend of Kaca occurs at length in the Matsya P. (ch : 25, which is the same as *Mb*, with very slight modifications), while most of the Purāṇas hardly refer to it, except in the context of Yayāti's marriage with Devayānī; and, that too, casually. The myth of the churning of the occean for the gain of nectar has a wider presentation.

It has been understood that the meaning of Hindu myths does not depend merely on the investigation of the Indian, or Sanskrit, sources alone. These myths have to be compared, and contrasted, with myths from other sources; for, there are parallels elsewhere. Scholars, who are not Indologists, have studied Hindu myths. Among them are anthropologists and ethno-sociologists like Andrew Lang, Tylor, D. Mackenzie and others, who went steps ahead of Cox and Max Müller. The latter's suggestion of the 'disease of the language' and the etymological method to the interpretion of Hindu myths was never fully accepted by these other scholars. Max Müller believed in the 'intellectual past' and suggested that all myths and legends were told and retold using words, the meaning of which was lost in later times. In the later period the earlier myths became obscure as the later current meaning was seen in these ancient words. Hence, according to him, etymology is the safest means to understand myths. Just the reverse of this is the view of Tylor and Lang, who do not believe in such an 'intelletual past'. According to them, and some others, myths reflect elements of savage thoughts and beliefs, meaning thereby that myths are produced by humans, all over the world, at a mental stage of the uncivilised—the savage. As against this view Lévi-Strauss, Claude (1980, *Myth and Meaning*) stresses that the intellect of the tribals (or, the so-called savages) is not less than that of the civilized man. He says that myths constituted a way of communication for the tribals in the absence of polished religious ideas and scientific expression. The modern trend is to examine myths and legends from all possible angles and using all the available 'tools' (O' Flaherty, Wendi D., 1982, *Hindu Myths*, which is of the type of internal study of Hindu myths from traditional sources; 1981, *Sexual Metaphors and Animal Symbols...*)

In the present study the myth of Garuḍa, which is of the nature of a saga, shows assimilation of two different deities: Suparṇa of the Vedic tradition and Garuḍa of the non-Vedic, though they are completely identified in the myth of the fetching of nectar. In the phase of the myth at *Mb* Nāga was a general term for a tribe, and Garuḍa was the deity of a class among them, who mastered the lore of snake-charming and that of nullifying the snake-poison. In other words, the Garuḍas and Nāgas were two phratries of the same tribe.

Among the tribals, myths and rituals involving internal conflict and reconciliation obtain. It is difficult to fall in line with Charpentier and Oldham, who believe that, the Nāga and Garuḍa were two different tribes basically antagonistic to each other. Evidence, literary and from archaeology, indicates that here we are dealing with complementary rivalry. According to Hopkins the Garuḍas were certain chieftains on the Malabar (i.e. the western) coast of India; but, he wonders how they do not have a claim to euhemeristic interpretation. His wonder is understandable; because, as against the Nāgas, who are seen as human-tribes, there is hardly any Garuḍa tribe as such. Obviously, he does not take into consideration the principle of complementary rivalry in the phratries of the same tribe. It is also to be noted, that the present-day Gāruḍīs, the snake-charmers, are to be traced to the Gāruḍas and further to Garuḍa. The Vāyu P. mentions a Gāruḍi named Sugrīva. Many references to the common abode of these two—the Nāgas (serpents) and Garuḍas obtain. The peculiar relationship between Kadrū and Vinatā, both wives of the sage Kaśyapa, and their wager reflect the unique dualism in a tribe. This characteristic of internal dualism is seen also in the Vedic period (and for Kadrū and Vinatā, it is seen in the post-RV period). Scholars, who take the Garuḍas and the Nāgas as two different tribes, do not take into consideration the note of reconciliation between the tribes. Charpentier, who treats the Garuḍa legend at length (*Die Suparṇasage*) does not dwell on the Sarpavidyā, nor on why the *vidyā*, known also as Sarpaveda and Viṣavidyā, was taught to the people called Sarpas (later identified with Nāgas), according to the Śat. Br. and other Vedic texts, and why it was called Gāruḍam. Even Śaṅkara(*-ācārya*), in his commentary on the *Chāndogya Up.*, renders the word *Sarpavidyā* as such (*Chānd. Up.* VII. 2.1; and *sarpavidyā*, as *gāruḍam*). The point to be noted is, why is it that the lore of the Sarpas came to be associated with, and named after, Garuḍa.

Father Heras (1953) contends that the episode in the *Mahābhārata*, about the carrying of the Nāgas by Garuḍa on his back, implies the invasion of Egypt by Nāgas under a ruler who belonged to Garuḍa tribe. On the test of phratry relationship, as noted above, this answers well. However, the suggestion of the invasion of Egypt is lame. His suggestion is based on his belief that the village Al Rahmania in north Egypt is Rāmaṇīyaka of *Mb.*, where Garuḍa is said to have carried the Nāgas. The identification between Al Rahmania and Rāmaṇīyaka is, obviously, based on similarity of sound; but, it is not 'sound'. Oldham's view is that Rāmaṇīyaka is on the Malabar coast. This is not corroborated by the description in the text. More authentically, Rāmaṇīyaka of *Mb* can be identified with Nicobar, the ancient Nakkavaram (Nakrapuram), known as Nāgadvīpa.

The myth of Kaca, as noted above, predominantly uses the motif of swallowing and disgorging alive. Kaca, burnt to ashes, is swallowed by Śukra, the preceptor of the Asuras, who possessed the lore of immortality. The motif is of initiation (*upanayana*), wherein the initiate symbolically enters the stomach of the preceptor, 'dies', and comes forth alive with new learning. Ritual-death and fresh birth underlie many myths—Vedic and non-Vedic, which have been noted in the pages to follow. (For more myths of this nature, but not involving swallowing, see Dange, 1996, *Towards Understanding Hindu Myths,* pp. 133ff.).

The myth of the churning of the ocean has many motific parallels. It occurs also in the Purāṇas; but, the motif goes back to *RV* in the *stūpa* of Varuṇa (I.24.7), which the god is said to have posited into the void. It acts as the support for creation and the sustenance of life in this world serving as a 'reach' to heaven— a veritable *axis mundi*. The Balenese temples, termed Meru, resemble the whole structure at the myth of the 'churning', complete with the tortoise at the base. Oldham's suggestion, that churning of the ocean with the help of the Nāga-king Vāsuki as the churn-rope, indicates commerce by the Nāgas is difficult to accept; because, the churning is not restricted to Vāsuki alone; and the churn-staff (Mandara, mountain) is centromotioned. It has to be taken as extension of the obvious motif of creation, but with the help of all existing super human forces available. Held suggests that the movements at churning, as the mountain-staff is rotated with the forward and backward movement of the rope, represent *pravṛtti* and *nivṛtti* (creation and non-creation). This is not convincing. It is against the spirit of the myth which reflects only creation (*pravṛtti*). The creation of poison is also *pravṛtti*, as it is not always associated with death. In medication minute doses of poison are help to destroy the disease and protect life. Even the myth says that at the advent of poison the gods got dazed; but, did not die. And, when Śiva drank it he simply digested it, a trait which the god inherited from the Vedic Rudra, who is acclaimed to be the best of physicians (*RV* II. 33. 4; cf. *bhiṣaktamam bhiṣajām*). After all, even poison is termed *ratna* (gem). Parallels of the myth of churning obtain from the Japanese mythology, where the churning rod is replaced by *ama-no-tama-bo-ko* (celestial jewel-spear), and Zuni American mythlogy.

The myths selected in this volume have one motif common. It is gain of immortality. Garuḍa has to fetch nectar from heaven. Kaca has to master the lore of immortality so that the gods, killed in the eternal battle of the gods and the Asuras, should spring back to life. The ocean is churned to gain nectar. Around this main motif each of the myths is woven with details that are unique to that particular myth. Further, as noted above, these details have counterparts, or parallels, elsewhere. Some of these details, which appear in the form of sub-myths here, are seen fully developed as myths later on. For example, the sub-myth of Garuḍa catching the tortoise and elephant in either of his claws, is seen developed later in the myth of Gajendra-mokṣa (release of the king of elephants from the clutches of the crocodile; Dange, 1987, *Puranic Myth and Culture*). In this later myth Viṣṇu takes the place of Garuḍa, and accepts the latter as his vehicle. The legend of Jīmūtavāhana, known to the *Kathāsaritsāgara* on which the drama *Nāgānandam* is based, has its basis on the Nāga-Garuḍa feud (Dange and Mrs. Dange, 1994, *Critiques on Sanskrit Dramas*). The myth of the metre Gāyatrīc=Sāvitrī), which is the precursor of the Garuḍa myth and a meta-myth of the hawk that fetches Soma (*RV*), appears developed later (*Mb* and the Purāṇas) in the legend of Sāvitrī and Satyavān (Dange, 1987). The swallowing motif in the myth of Kaca has its modification in such myths as show the divine preceptor suddenly assuming a huge form, the devotee (or initiate or a person on a lower stratum) appearing as a diminutive. The main motif of the gain, or the quest for immortality has been eternal; and counterparts of the bird that fetches nectar, and Kaca, are to be seen in Sumero-Babylonian Gilgamesh. This latter hero gets the plant of rejuvenation, but a snake steals it. The motif is associated also with human heroes. Thus, Alexander, the Great, is said to have discovered the secret of eternal life. Accordingly, his army reaches the spring behind Mount Oaf (that separates the earth from outer space) in the land of darkness. His commander, Khidr, drinks the buttery honeyed sweet-smelling water of life, and gains eternal life. But when he returns and takes Alexander at that spot, he cannot find it (Richard Cavandish, ed. 1982, *Legends of the World*, p. 116).

Recently, as against my proposition, it has been said that in the myth of the churning of nectar, "the action of the story does not belong to the Vedic ritual, and myth, of Soma -pressing" (Ananda, Subhash, 1996, *Story as Theology*, p.4) and that nectar does not refer to Soma (*Ib*. 5). True, nectar, in the episode as it occurs at *Mb*, is different from Soma. But, does Soma, that is said to have come out of the ocean, definitely mean 'moon' ? It is less likely. As is shown in the study of the myth (in the main body), the gems are not the same in various accounts as they occur in the later texts. The *Harivaṁśa*, which is the ancillary of *Mb*, uses the expression "Let us churn Soma-produced water" (Bhaviṣyaparvan, 30.12 *mathnīmaḥ somajam jalam*); and further on, it mentions the moon also as coming out (v 29 *śasāṅkaḥ*). This has to be taken as a gloss on the word Soma from *Mb*, retaining Soma (juice of the shoots of the Soma-plant) and giving a new dimension to the word with the later meaning of 'moon'. That the concept of nectar was fused with that of Soma (-juice) and remained so for some centuries, is clear from the *Viṣṇu Dh. P.*(I.42.46 "having taken *Soma* that remained after drinking") and from *Rām*. (I.45. 27, where the variant reading has *somo devas tathaiva ca*). This is made clear (p. 247, Ed. 1969; this Ed. p. 238). Anand does not seem to have noticed these references with care. The exact picture, of how the churning might have been suggested from the method of pressing the juice of the plant of Soma, obtains at *RV* (IX. I. 28). Here the apparatus is the mortar and the broad-based pestle (*grāvā pṛthubudhnaḥ*), standing erect in the former (*ūrdhvo bhavati*). The pestle, also called *manthā* (cf. also *manthānam* as Sāyaṇa says), was activated by a rope tied to it (cf. *vi-badhnate*). This would give the semblance of the rod that was used at the kindling of the fire, and also that of the pestle used for churning out butter from coagulated milk. The picture is compared with a person who controls a horse, or a bull, with ropes (cf. *RV*. I. 28. 1; and 4; and at the latter *raśmīn yamitā-iva*). In the legend of 'churning' this picture is transferred to the churning of the ocean, the water of which is said to be *somaja* and nectar is termed *soma* in the tradition that transpasses *Mb*. In the simile the use of the word *raśmi* with which the controller is said to fasten the horse, or the bull, indicates that the pressing stone for the shoots of Soma was moved by a rope or a strap. In another place, the pressing (or churning) of the shoots of Soma is said to be accomplished with ten *raśmi*-s. But, this can hardly refer to the ten fingers as such, with which the pestle could be held. The number ten suits the ten fingers of two hands, all right; but the *raśmi* (strap, tightened round the pestle) is a rope (cf. *rassi* in MIA and NIA, i.e. Hindi and other languages). Due to its contact with the two hands that hold it, and due to fingers, the latter are termed *raśmi*-s (Sāyaṇa). The fingers are not meant by *raśmi-s*, primarily. This would show that the 'churning' of the ocean closely follows the imagery of the pressing of the Soma-shoots. As such, Anand's contention that the churning in the myth of *samudra-manthana* came "originally from the rite of producing fire" is not convincing, because, it is not sound. It is true that the act of drilling fire is also termed *manthana*, and that the word *amṛta* is used for the fire (though Anand misses an important reference, I. 13. 5 *amrtasya cakṣaṇam*, which refers to the sight of the sacrifical fire in the sacrificial altar). However, with all the bits of myths about the fire being in water, which Anand spreads in his argument, there is hardly any Vedic or post-Vedic myth to support his hypothesis of fire being 'churned' out of water. The *Mahābhārata* mentions various gems that came out of the ocean, including 'Soma' (and nectar), sometimes Soma being the same as nectar (as we have noted above, and also in the main discussion, later); but, it never mentions fire coming out from the ocean as a result of churning. When Anand speaks about the "two sticks for *manthana*", his lack of knowledge about the two *araṇi-s* (which are not *sticks*) becomes obvious. The *araṇi-s* are slabs of wood (of the Śami tree, or of Aśvattha, or one of Aśvattha the other being of Śami). The lower slab has a dimple in the middle for the churning rod to be placed into. The rod is passed through the sizable hole in the centre of the upper slab *(araṇi)*, which is then placed on the lower slab in the dimple and held firmly. The churn-rod is activated with the help of a strong rope, set round it firmly, with the hands. The apparatus in action constitutes *manthana*. The same is the act, and method, at the churning for butter, but without the slabs. The myth of ocean-churning does not show even a speck of such an apparatus. On the contrary, all through, it speaks of water, ghee-mixed water and such liquids, from which, as a result of churning, come out the gems ; but, never Agni. (For Anand's views, *op.cit.*, pp.4-12). It is difficult to explain the name Kaca; because, Kaca does not figure commonly in Hindu myths. He is mentioned only in the mythical account as it occurs in *Mb* (as we have studied in the book), and at the *Bhāg. P.* In the latter it is subsidiary to the main legend of Yayāti, which includes his marriage with Devayāni and Śarmiṣṭhā. Devayanī was the daughter of Śukrācārya, who is said to be a brāhmaṇa; and the question is raised, "How could a brāhmaṇa girl marry a kṣatriya?". This Purāṇa does not give the whole legend of Kaca going to Śukrācārya and the gain of the lore of immortality, which is unique to *Mb*. Both at *Mb* and *Bhag. P.* the question of the *pratiloma* marriage (i.e. between a higher caste girl and a man of the lower caste) is answered by stating that Devayānī was cursed by Kaca (*Mb*.I.77.19 "no son of a sage shall accept your hand" ; *Bhāg.P*.IX.18.22 *kacasya...śāpāt*). This is why, at both the texts, there is specific mention of Yayāti pulling Devayānī out of the well *by holding her hand*, and the latter stressing this as the reason why the one who held her hand has to marry her (*Mb*.I.78.23; *Bhāg.P*.IX.18.19ff.). The position is that the myth of Kaca-Devayānī supports the real event of the *pratiloma* marriage, through the strategy of the curse. The texts, themselves, this way, explain the *pratiloma* marriage. Anand's statement, that Dange explains away the curse is, hence, misleading. Even if "Sukra is too happy at this marriage" (Anand, p.38) the specific mention of the curse in the texts, as a plea to support the changed social norm cannot be denied. Anand's suggestion, that the name Kaca might be a borrowal of the Buddhist "Kaccan" (actually, it should be Kaccāna, or Kaccayana), the disciple of the Buddha (p.44) is unwarranted. It has to be noted that Kaccāna or

Kaccayana are mispronunciations (or, Pali versions) of the Sanskrit name Kātyāyana. Why should the Sanskrit texts (*Mb* and *Bhag.P.*) borrow a mispronounced name? Kaca is said to a son of Bṛhaspati; and if the Sanskrit texts mention him as Kaca, he has to be different from Kātyāyana; and he is far, far different from Kaccāna or Kaccayana!

The association of reality with myth changes the earlier to a legend; and, in many cases simple short myths get fattened as they are ushered in to support socio-religious, or socio-historical events. Thus, the myth of the gain of Soma, or nectar, from heaven occurs first in *RV*, in a very short form (IX.77.2): "The Soma, that is being pressed here into juice was seized from heaven, earlier, by the hawk, that darted away from the hunter, Kṛśānu, with fear in mind. The hawk carried it through the mid-region; and, here it gets assimilated with the juice." This simple myth, that must have remained current in the tradition even prior to *RV*, becomes a multifaced legend with the wager and reality of the phratry and tribal beliefs combining with it. The experience of the moon being 'swallowed' by the 'demon' Svarbhānu, or by the sun as the moon slowly goes near it night after night, gives rise to the myth of the initiate being swallowed (and killed temporarily) by the preceptor, who gives him new life. The myth assumes the form of a legend with its use in the Yayāti-Devayānī/Śarmiṣṭhā relationship, which is of a historical nature. The original concept of the *axis mundi* appears in the form of the myth of churning of the ocean, getting fattened up by details in the Soma-ritual, and developing into a myth of Creation.

The association between myth and the resultant legend, with a mixture of reality and historical elements, being so intimate, I have preferred to call the lengthy accounts of the three myths presented in this volume 'legends'.

# I
## Garuḍa

*Garuḍa, in all probability, hails from a non-Vedic mythosocial context. To suppose that the Bird is only a developed aspect of Vedic Suparṇa is far from being correct. Garuḍa, the deity from a non-Vedic tradition, got a place in the later Vedic pantheon which assimilated various faiths to form a complex system of a broader religion, which is known as Hindu.*

# 1
# THE LEGEND

Garuḍa, the vehicle of Lord Viṣṇu, is quite a familiar figure in the Hindu mythology. This mythological figure does not remain closed up in the religious books of the Hindus alone. As we shall have occasion to see later, it has a universal appeal. It has served as the emblem of many royal families.[1]

Before taking up a discussion on the nature of Garuḍa, we shall do well to see the legend about Garuḍa in the *Mb.*, note the various aspects of the legend and compare them with various other accounts of the same type. The legend of Garuḍa appears in its complete form in the Ādi-Parvan of the *Mb.*, though fragments of information can be found scattered in the expanse of the *Mb*. To start with, we shall give the English version of the whole legend as it occurs in the *Mb*.

The Garuḍa-legend forms part of the 'Āstīka Parvan' in the Ādi Parvan and goes by the name of the 'Sauparṇa' (Ākhyāna). It begins with the account of the two wives of Kaśyapa—namely Kadrū and Vinatā, the daughters of Prajāpati. Kaśyapa, their husband equal to Prajāpati (himself), being pleased with them granted them a boon each. Vinatā asked for two sons — more in prowess than the nāgas, the sons of Kadrū. When five hundred years had elapsed Kadrū's sons came out of the warmed jars; but out of the two eggs of Vinatā her two sons were not seen coming out. Being disheartened, Vinatā broke one egg; and, to her great disappointment, saw her son — Aruṇa by name — with only the fore-part of his body visibly well-formed. Being angry with his hasty mother he, it is said, cursed her to be a slave to her co-wife (Kadrū) for five hundred years and also told her that her second son would set her free from slavery. Thus speaking Aruṇa flew into the sky and is seen every morning as the Charioteer of the Sun. Then at the proper time Garuḍa also was born — Garuḍa, the eater of snakes — and flew into the sky, as soon as he was born, to catch his food which was fixed for him by the creator (I. 16. 24, 25).

"गरुडोऽपि यथाकालं जज्ञे पन्नगभोजनः।
स जातमात्रो विनतां परित्यज्य खमाविशत्।।
आदास्यन्नात्मनो भोज्यमन्नं विहितमस्य यत्।
विधात्रा भृगुशार्दूल क्षुधितः पतगेश्वरः।।"

In the mean -time those two sisters (Kadrū and Vinatā) going near the steed Uccaiḥśravas, those having *penance as wealth,* saw it — the steed that was churned out of the sea while nectar was churned.[2] (I. 17. 12)

Seeing the horse, Kadrū said to Vinatā — "Tell me anon, O blessed one ! What colour is Uccaiḥśravas?" Vinatā replied, "White, indeed, is the royal steed! What thinkest thou, O auspicious one? Do thou also tell the colour of him. Then shall we have here a wager". Said Kadrū, "Methinks the horse is endowed with a black-haired tail, O thou of brilliant smile! Do thou come with me, and have a wager of salvery with me, O thou splendid one!"[3]

Thus deciding upon a wager the two went to their respective abodes saying, "We shall verify tomorrow". Then Kadrū, having an eye for deceit, ordered her thousand sons, saying, "Transforming yourselves into hair, dark like collyrium, do ye instantly enter (cover!) the horse, lest I should be a slave". Those that did not abide by her order, them did she curse saying. "In the serpent-sacrifice of Janamejaya — the scion of the Pāṇḍavas — the fire shall consume you". On hearing this extremely cruel curse of Kadrū, Pitāmaha (Brahmā) himself, along with the gods, supported it for the good of the creatures, seeing the multitude of the serpents. These serpents were endowed with deadly poison; and being mighty were habituated to bite. On account of their being endowed with deadly poison, and for the welfare of the creatures, (Brahmā) gave the anti-poison lore to Kaśyapa the great. (I. 20. 2. 11; 16).[4]

Then, when the night came to a close and after the sun rose in the morning, those two sisters — Kadrū and Vinatā, vying with one another and striking a wager for slavery, went to see the steed Uccaihśravas. There they saw the sea, the receptacle of waters . . . the beautiful abode of the nāgas[5] (I. 21).

After crossing that ocean, Kadrū, along with Vinatā flew to the horse in an instant, Kadrū — the swift one. On seeing the multitude of black hair resting on the tail, Vinatā became distressed, and Kadrū engaged her in slavery. Vinatā, vanquished in the wager, became dejected and accepted the bond of slavery. In the meanwhile even Garuḍa, when his time drew near, came forth breaking the egg even without the help of his mother. . . Garuḍa, of mighty prowess. Instantly the bird, assuming a huge form, flew into the sky with a terrible noise, fierce like another submarine fire as he appeared. Seeing him all the gods went to the fire-god and, falling prostrate before him said to him — "Do not O Agni! rise. We hope thou shalt not devour us; for this thy huge heap of blazing flames draws near." Agni said, "It is not so as you think, O gods (the thrashers of Asuras). He is Garuḍa the mighty one, and is equal to me in prowess." Being thus addressed, (the gods) went to where Garuḍa was and praised him — "Thou art the lord — the sun, thou art our best resort. Thou art endowed with the waves of strength full of great prowess; endowed with glory art thou and unvanquished in war; thou art penance, thou knowledge, O thou of unvanqished glory"[6] — Being thus praised by the gods, along with the ascetics, Suparṇa contracted his lustre. (I. 23)[7]

Then the bird, moving at will, mighty and having great

strength, went to the other shore of the great ocean — where his mother Vinatā was dejected in slavery, being defeated in the wager. Then once Kadrū, calling Vinatā who was prostrate, said to her before her son, "There lies the abode of the Nāgas, beautiful and fine to look at, O blessed one, to one side in the ocean. Take me there." Then the mother of Suparṇa carried the mother of the serpents. Garuḍa also, according to his mother's words carried serpents. When he (Garuḍa) went towards the Sun, the serpents fainted being scorched by the rays of the Sun.[8] Seeing her sons in that condition Kadrū praised Indra variously[9] (I. 25).

Indra, being thus praised by Kadrū, covered the whole of the sky with multitudes of dark clouds and ordered them thus — "Do ye shower pure water (*amṛtaṃ śubham*)". And those clouds showered forth, (I. 26; Crit. Ed. I.22).[10]

The nāgas then became quite happy, being drenched in the showers of water. Being carried by Suparṇa, they reached that island (the abode of the nāgas) and saw many attractive things endowed with rare beauty.[11] Garuḍa asked his mother why he should always abide by what the serpents said. Said Vinatā, "I have become a slave of my co-wife due to misfortune, O the best among birds, by a wager that was devised by the serpents with guile." When his mother gave this as the cause, he said to the serpents, "By fetching what, or knowing what, or by the performance of which valorous deed, shall I be free from your slavery? Speak the truth." Hearing that, the serpents said to him, "Do thou fetch nectar speedily. Then shalt thou be free from salvery, O sky-roamer!" (I. 27; Crit. Ed. I. 23).

Being thus addressed by the serpents, Garuḍa said to his mother, "I go to fetch nectar. I want to know my food." Vinatā said, "In the lap of the sea, to one side, is the abode of the Niṣādas. Thousands of Niṣādas are there. Feeding upon them, do thou fetch nectar. And thou shalt never think of killing a brāhmaṇa. A brāhmaṇa, like fire, is not to be killed by any of the creatures. The brahmaṇa, when angry, is the very fire, the sun, the poison and the weapon! Highest (preceptor) indeed is the brāhmaṇa of all the creatures." Garuḍa said, "Do tell me, O mother as I ask of thee, how and by what marks may I know a brāhmaṇa." Vinatā said, "He who, reaching thy throat, after being swallowed, is (pricks) like the fishing-hook; or might burn like the burning coal, and might not get digested in the stomach, mayest thou know him to be the brāhmaṇa". Again said Vinatā, due to love for her son, "May the wind protect thy wings; the sun and the moon (may support thee) from behind; may the fire protect thy head, the Vasus thy body from all sides; and I am always thinking about thy welfare and thy weal (peace — '*sāntiḥ*'). Go thou by thy path, my son, without any mishap, for the fulfilment of thy desire". Hearing the speech of his mother, he, spreading his wings, flew up into the sky. Then the highly one, hungry as he was, went to the Niṣādas as if he was another Death, killing those Niṣādas, and at the same time raising voluminous dust that touched the sky, causing the water in the lap of the ocean to evaporate, causing the trees that grew on the nearby mountains shake. He, the mightly bird, then, opened out his mighty beak (mouth), blocking the way of the Niṣādas. The Niṣādas swiftly entered the open mouth of him — the eater of serpents. Thousands of Niṣādas, stunned by the wind and the dust, entered, like tiny birds, the wide open mouth spacious as the sky, being distressed, as if in a forest shaken by a terrible wind. Then the mighty bird, the destroyer of enemies, closed the mouth swiftly in movement, and hungry as he was, (thereby) pounding (pressing hard) the various (Niṣādas) living by (killing) the fish (*matsyajīvinaḥ;* I. 28; Crit. Ed. I. 24).

(As Garuḍa was devouring the Niṣādas) A brāhmaṇa with his wife reached his throat, burning (it) like the coal. Him did the bird (moving in the sky) say, "Do thou go out of this mouth, that is wide open, O the best of brāhmaṇas! The brāhmaṇa is not to be killed by me even though he may be ever sinful." To Garuḍa who thus spoke, the brāhmaṇa said, "This my wife — the niṣādī — may (also) go out along with me." Śaid Guruḍa, "Taking even this niṣādī with thee do thou go out. Do thou regain life, being unharmed by my prowess." The brāhmaṇa, then, went out (of the bird's mouth) along with the niṣadī, and congratulating Garuḍa, went to his desired place. After the departure of the brāhmaṇa along with his wife, the king of birds, spreading his wings, flew up into the sky — he, endowed with the speed of the mind. He, then, went to his father, and being asked by the latter said to him, "I am, indeed, sent by the serpents to fetch 'Soma' the excellent. For breaking the slavery of (my) mother I shall fetch it even to-day. I was told by mother that I should eat the niṣādas; and I am not satisfied even after eating thousands (of them). Hence do thou suggest to me another food, O lord!, eating which I shall be able to fech nectar. Do thou tell me of the food to vanquish my hunger and thirst." Kaśyapa said, "There was a great sage, Vibhāvasu by name, of an extremely wrathful nature. His younger brother was Supratīka, the great ascetic. He did not approve of wealth in common with his brother. Supratīka always spoke of division. His brother Vibhāvasu, then, spoke to Supratīka, 'Many desire division always due to foolishness. Hence being separated they, infatuated with wealth, do not respect one another. 'Being uncontrollable, as by division thou desirest wealth, thou shalt be an elephant, O Supratīka.' Being cursed thus by Vibhāvasu, Supratīka said to the former, 'Thou also shalt be a tortoise roaming in water.' Thus cursing one another, those Supratīka and Vibhāvasu, the foolish ones, became the elephant and the tortoise respectively. Due to the vice of wrath those two of huge form, gaining animal-life and being proud of their strength and size, live in this lake with the enmity of the previous birth. One of those two, the elephant, full of prowess, approaches: and due to his roar the tortoise, residing in the depth of waters, also gets up rendering the whole water turbid, huge of form as he is. Seeing him the mighty elephant, with his trunk curled, advances into the water, rendering in rage the whole lake turbulent with the force of his tusks, trunk-tip, his tail and feet. Even the tortoise, with head up, advances for fight, mighty in prowess as he is. The elphant is three leagues in height and double the size in length. Those two infatuated (and ready) for conflict, are desiring victory over one another. Eat the twain. Accomplishing soon this deed (of eating these two) fulfil thy desire."

Hearing this speech of his father, the bird, with terrible speed, caught hold of the elephant by one claw (*'nakhena'*) and the tortoise by another and flew high in the sky. He, without halting anywhere, going to the holy place (*'tīrtham'*; Nīla glosses, *"meruśṛṅgam tīrtham"*), approached the divine trees which began to tremble, being shaken by the wind of his wings, with the thought that he may break them. Seeing those trees, the givers of the desired fruits (*'manorathaphaladrumān'*), trembling in all their branches, the bird flew near other big trees, having incomparable form, (and) having branches of gold, silver and sapphire, shining and surrounded by the waters of the sea (i.e. being in the vicinity of the sea). Thereby the great Rauhiṇa tree said to the best of birds, flying and having the speed of the mind, "This my mighty branch is a hundred leagues long; alighting on this branch do thou eat the elephant and the tortoise." Then shaking that tree that was sheltering thousands of birds, Garuḍa, the best of birds, having form (as high) as a mountain, alighting speedily, broke it (the branch) that was densely covered with leaves (I. 29; Crit. Ed. I. 25).

That great branch of the tree broke as soon as it was touched by Garuḍa with his feet; and he caught it. Looking with wonder at the great broken branch, he saw the sages Vālakhilyas), with heads down, hanging from it. Afraid lest they (Vālakhilyas) should be killed, he, the lord of birds, took the branch in the beak (mouth), thinking only about their protection.[12] Then gradually did he fly shaking the mountains with (the wind of) his wings. Thus he flew to many places, along with the elephant and the tortoise, having compassion for the Vālakhilyas; but did not find a (suitable) place. Going to the Gandhamādana — the best of mountains — with speed (Garuḍa) saw there Kaśyapa, his father engrossed in penance; and his father also saw him — the bird of divine form — endowed with prowess and lustre and having the speed of the mind and the wind, being as high as the summit of a mountain and like the curse of a brāhmaṇa set aloft (*brahmadaṇḍamivodyatam* : Nīla gives no meaning; probably it would be better to take it to mean only as 'the staff of Brahman'), beyond (the pale of) thought and not apt to be perceived, dreadful to all creatures, having great prowess, fierce, and like the very Agni rising aloft, unchallengeable and not apt to be conquered by the gods or the Rākṣasas, the shatterer of mountain-tops, and the one causing the waters of the ocean to evaporate, causing the world to get disturbed, terrible, appearing like the very Death. Seeing him arrive, father Kaśyapa, knowing his determination, spoke, "Do not, O son, perform a rash act, (for) thou shalt anon get into distress; may not these Vālakhilyas — the drinkers of the sun-rays being wrathful, burn thee." Then did Kaśyapa propitiate those great Vālakhilyas, who had destroyed sin with penance, saying, "This effort (i. e. the beginning of the efforts) of Garuḍa is for the good of the creatures, O ye ascetics ! He desireth to perform a great act. May ye grant it." Being addressed thus by the lord (Kaśyapa), those ascetics, leaving the branch, went to the holy Himavat (mountain) for penance. When they had gone, the son of Vinatā, his mouth occupied with the branch, asked Kaśyapa, "Where shall I throw this branch of the tree, O Lord! May you tell me of a place devoid of brāhmaṇas."[13] Then Kaśyapa told him about the mountain, full of snow in the caves, and unattainable by others even with mind (i. e. unthinkable). To that mountain having deep caves did Tārkṣya — the mighty bird — speed along with force with the branch, and with the elephant and the tortoise. Not a thousandfold leather-strap, (thousand-leather-piece-made) would surround the great branch of the tree, carrying which flew the mightly bird. Then, cutting in a very short time, the distance of a thousand leagues, Garuḍa — the king of birds — reaching the mountain according to what his father told, threw the mighty branch there with a loud noise — he, the sky-roamer. And the lord of mountains shook terribly under the force of his wing-wind. With the trees broken asunder, (the mountain) showered flowers, and the tops of the mountain toppled down all over![14] Then taking his seat on the top of the mountain, Garuḍa ate the elephant and the tortoise. After that he flew away from the summit of that mountain. Then terrible calamities befell the gods, who being afraid foresaw sudden destruction. The beloved Vajra (thunder bolt) of Indra began burning with fear. (In short, there were many sudden disturbances in the abode of the gods.) Then, Indra (the performer of a hundred exploits) got dejected and so did all the gods. Seeing all these sudden calamities, Indra said to Bṛhaspati, "Why O Lord, have these sudden calamities sprung up? I see not an enemy who might challenge us in war!" Bṛhaspati said, "Due to thy fault, O Indra, and thy pride, and by the penance of the Vālakhilyas — the noble ascetics — O performer of a hundred exploits! — hath the son of Kaśyapa, the ascetic, and of Vinatā, arrived to take 'Soma' away — the mighty bird (moving in the skies) who doth assume (any) form as he desireth. He is capable, the best of the mighty — the bird, who hath come to capture Soma. Everything do I think possible for him; he may even accomplish that which cannot be accomplished (by others)". Hearing this speech, Śakra spoke to the guards of nectar — "The bird of mighty strength and prowess hath arrived ready to capture Soma. Ye do I warn so that he may not take (Soma) by force. Uncomparable is his strength; Bṛhaspati, indeed, said so!" Hearing that speech, the gods were distressed and began their efforts. They stood anon concealing nectar; and even Indra — the mighty—stood ready with his Vajra. All, with their armours and weapons, got ready for the protection of nectar[15] (I. 30; Crit. Ed. I. 26).

Further, we have the purpose of Garuḍa's birth; and Sauti tells Śaunaka that the account is given in the 'Purāṇas.'

When Kaśyapa was performing a sacrifice for obṭaining a son, all the gods, Gandharvas and ascetics gave him their co-operation. Therein Śakra (Indra) was appointed by Kaśyapa for fetching faggots, and so were all the gods and even the ascetics Vālakhilyas. Śakra fetched a heap of faggots as high as the mountain quite without efforts suitable to his strength. Now (he) saw the ascetics, as short as the inner portion of the thumb, all together carrying a tiny faggot of *palāśa* along the way; they were as if concealed in their own bodies and were abstaining from food, emaciated and struggling hard in the 'cow-foot-mark' full of water. Purandara (Indra), eying them with surprise and being puffed up with pride, laughing in mockery, crossed them and went away with speed without paying any respect. Now those (ascetics), full of wrath on being humiliated, started a terrible deed dreadful for Śakra. They, of excellent penance, offered oblations to Agni with loud chants of mantras, the purpose of which do thou hear (O Śaunaka)! — 'May *another Indra* of the Gods, wandering at will and apt to make the (old) king of the gods tremble in fear, a hundred times more virtuous than Indra in prowess and strength, having the speed of the mind and a formidable one, be born as the fruit of our penance — with this thought were they resolved! Hearing that, Śatakratu — Indra — the king of the gods — being extremely perturbed, took refuge with Kaśyapa who was in penance. Hearing this from the king of the gods Kaśyapa Prajāpati, approaching the Vālakhilyas, asked about the fruit of the penance. They, having the vow of truth, said to him, "Be it so". To them said Kaśyapa Prajāpati consolingly, "This Indra (the original one) has been deputed in the three worlds according to the order of Brahmā; and for Indra alone is this effort of yours O ascetics! It does not behove you to falsify the speech of Brahmā, O best of the virtuous! This determination of yours, indeed, is not to be otherwise. (Hence) may he (the new one to be born) be the Indra among the birds — mighty and having great prowess. May this king of the gods be favoured, prostrate as he is." Being thus requested by Kaśyapa, the ascetics — Vālakhilyas — replied, worshipping the Prajāpati (Kaśyapa), the foremost among ascetics, "For Indra is this effort of us all, O Prajapati; and for a son is this effort of thine. Hence may this exploit of ours that is fruitful be accepted by thee; and do here whatever thou thinkest of benefit." In the meantime the goddess Vinatā, the auspicious daughter of Dakṣa, performing penance and having a vow, approached her husband after bath in the *puṁsavana* (rite) — Vinatā, the holy one. To her Kaśyapa said, "The plan that thou didst desire, O goddess, is fruitful. Thou shalt give birth to two brave sons, O goddess of the three worlds! With the penance of the Vālakhilyas, and according to my determination, two mighty sons, apt to be worshipped in the three worlds, will be born (to thee)." Again Kaśyapa said to her, "Do thou keep this seed (foetus) of great prowess. These two shall be the overlords of all birds. Honoured by the people, these two birds will be brave and having their form at will." Being pleased, the Prajāpati then said to Śatakratu (Indra), "These (two) will be thy help-mates, thy brothers — these of great valour. There will be no danger (*doṣaḥ*) to thee from these two, O destroyer of fortress (purandara)! Let thy perturbance be dismissed. Thou shalt be the Indra; and not again should the ascetics (*brahmavādinaḥ*) be thus insulted by thee; and not (again) should be disrespected by thee in pride these (ascetics) easily wrathful and having speech of *Vajra*." Indra, being addressed thus, went to the abode of gods without any anxiety. Even Vinatā, her desire fulfilled, became glad and gave birth to two sons — viz. Garuḍa and Aruṇa. Aruṇa, who with his limbs deformed precedes the sun (as the charioteer), consecrated Garuḍa as the king of birds. Hear the great deed of him O thou scion of the Bhṛgus!" (I. 31; Crit. I. 27).

Then, O the best of the brāhmaṇas, when it thus happened, Garuḍa, the king of birds, swiftly arrived to the gods. Seeing the mighty one, the gods, then, began to tremble and strike each other with the weapons. And there was the unsurpassable Bhaumana equalling the lightning and fire, the protector of nectar. Garuḍa killed him. (A description of the fight between Garuḍa and the gods — st. 4. 21). Killing them all (the guards of Soma), thus pushing ahead for nectar, he saw blazing fire all around, encompassing the whole sky with flames, having scorching rays (flames) and increased by the wind. Then making his mouths ninety-times-ninety, the high-souled Garuḍa, drinking rivers with these mouths, came back speedily and covered the fire with water of those rivers — he, the bird, the oppressor of the enemies. Then he again changed his form to another minute one to enter the fire after quenching it (I. 32; Crit. Ed. I. 28).

The bird, becoming golden and as bright as the heap of rays, entered (the fire) forcefully, as does a forcible current of water the sea. He saw near nectar an iron-wheel with thousand (petal-like) blades, sharp-edged and constantly circling. It was lustrous like the fire and the sun, terrible, and apt to cut those who would take away Soma. It was fierce and well-set by the gods. The bird turned (and turned) on seeing the distance (between the spokes); and through the gap of the spokes did he enter contracting his body in a moment. He saw under the wheel there two mighty serpents, shining like the blazing fire, with tongues (swift) as the lightning, powerful, with glowing mouths and blazing eyes, having poison in their glance, always full of wrath and very active. These were kept to guard Nectar, always with a fixed and an unwinking gaze. Even one of these was apt to render to ashes any one he eyed. Suparṇa (Garuḍa) closed (filled) their eyes suddenly with dust : and being unseen (by them), smote them all over, pouncing on their bodies and cutting them to pieces — Suparṇa, the sky-wanderer son of Vinatā. With force did he run for Soma and then darted speedily uprooting the machine-wheel, Vainateya, the powerful one. Without drinking nectar, the bird passed along avoiding the brilliance of the sun. Then Vainateya came across Viṣṇu in the sky. Viṣṇu — the supreme one — being pleased with his selfless task said to him, "I shall give thee a boon". The bird demanded, "May I have a position above thee" (*'upari'— "dhvaja iti arthaḥ"*, Nīla); and further said to Nārāyaṇa, "Even without nectar may I be devoid of old age and death". "Be it so", said Viṣṇu to the son of Vinatā. (Accepting the two boons, Garuḍa said to Viṣṇu, "To thee also shall I give a boon; may thou choose.")[16] Viṣṇu chose the mighty[17] Garutmat as his vehicle; and the god prepared a banner saying to him (Garuḍa), "Thou shalt have a seat upon it." "Be it so," said the bird to Nārāyaṇa, and went away speedily rivalling Vāyu. While the best of birds was thus flying away, taking *amṛta*, Indra smote him with his Vajra. In the tumult, Garuḍa said to Indra, smilingly and in a tone of frank gentleness (*ślaṣṇayā vāvā*), being smitten with the Vajra, "I shall honour the ascetic from whose bones the Vajra has been fashioned. I shall honour the Vajra and also thee, O Śatakratu. Here do I release a feather of mine, the end of which thou shalt not obtain; and no pain is there for me with the stroke of the Vajra." Thus saying, the king of birds released a feather. Seeking that feather of him that was excellent (next to none), all the creatures, being glad, named Garutmat as 'Suparṇa' — ('of beautiful wings'). Noticing that great wonder, Purandara, the one with thousand eyes, thinking that the bird was a great creature, spoke, "I wish to know thy strength that does not have a rival; and I desire to have everlasting friendship with thee, O best of birds!")

(I. 33; Crit. Ed. I. 29).

Garuḍa said, "May my friendship be with thee, O god Purandara; but know that my strength is great and unbearable. True it is that the good never relish the praise of their own self nor even the talk about their own virtues by themsleves. But, as thou hast asked me as a friend, here shall I speak, O friend. It is not proper to speak of one's own praise, without a cause! This earth, with all its forests and mountains and with its oceans full of water, I can carry on one of my wings — and also thee supporting thereon. All the worlds, as a whole, along with their static and moving objects I can carry without (the least of) exhaustion. Know this to be my strength." To the hero who said thus, Kirīṭī (Indra with the crown), the foremost among the glorious, said, "Keep thou my friendship that is excellent. If there be no purpose of nectar (Soma), return it to me; for they, to whom thou shalt give it, will surely trouble us." Garuḍa spoke, "For a certain purpose this Soma is being carried by me. I shall not allow any one to take this Soma; but where I shall place it, O thou Sahasrākṣa! (of thousand eyes!), thence do thou pick it away quickly, O lord of the heavens!" Śakra said, "By this speech of thine I am pleased, O bird; whichever boon thou desirest take it from me." Being addressed thus, (Gaurḍa) replied, having in memory the sons of Kadrū, and also the deceitful slavery to which his mother was subjected, "Lord though I am of all, I shall request thee — O Śakra! May the mighty serpents be my food." Saying, "Be it so", (Indra), the destroyer of the *dānavas,* again said, "I shall take away Soma placed by thee". Then did Suparṇa (Garuḍa) come to the side of his mother. To the serpents he said with all gladness, "Here have I fetched nectar for ye; I shall place it on the Kuśa grass. May this mother of mine be free from slavery from to-day; what had been said (by you) that have I accomplished." Then saying to him, "Be it so," the serpents went for bath. Indra (Śakra) also, again snatching nectar went to heaven. Now, the serpents, arriving with joy at that spot with the desire of (drinking) Soma, after bathing and performing the chants — the spot where nectar was placed on the spread up Kuśas — and knowing it snatched away with a counter-deceit, licked the *Kuśas* mindful of the place where Some was kept. Then, due to that act (of theirs) the tongues of the serpents became split up; and even the *darbhas* became the *'pavitrins'* (the pure ones). Then Suparṇa (Garuḍa), being greatly joyous, resided there in the forest giving joy to Vinatā — he of undiminishing fame, respected by the birds feeding on the serpents.

The man who might hear this tale or read it in the assembly headed by the brāhmaṇas, ṣhall, without doubt, go to heaven, being virtuous, by the praise of the great lord of birds (I. 34; Crit. Ed. I. 30).

## 2
# GARUḌA AND THE NĀGAS

In the whole legend the most dominant note of all is the antagonism between Garuḍa and the serpents (nāgas) and it is a unique one. Aruṇa, Garuḍa's elder brother, nowhere appears prominent in the picture, except as the one who curses his rash mother and gives a sort of a push to the whole legend setting it agoing; but the main character is Garuḍa alone, who, as a saviour of his mother, attracts our interest and attention.

More than anything else, Garuḍa is spoken of as the enemy of the nāgas or their 'eater.' He is called *'Pannagabhojana'* — (*Mb.* I. 16. 24), *'Pannagāśana'* (V. 112. 5; 15 etc.). The serpents are destined to be his food by the order of the creator himself; and as soon as he was born he flew up into the sky to grasp his prey (the serpents).[18] He is said to have asked the serpents to be his food as a boon from Indra.[19] He is called *'bhujaṅga-bhakṣyaḥ'* (I. 34. 25); also *'bhujagendrāri'* (V. 112. 1). This antagonism between Garuḍa and the serpents can also be seen from the fact that Garuḍa easily kills the two serpents guarding Soma.[20]

Now this antagonism between Garuḍa and the nāgas (the serpents) is by no means restricted only to the *Mb*. It is found also elsewhere in the Sanskrit literature, and is generally well rooted in the popular belief. The fact of Garuḍa's asking serpents as his food, as we have noticed in the *Mb.*, is also to be found in the *Sup Ad*, and is a prominent feature of the Garuḍa legend, seen elsewhere.[21] We have also references where Garuḍa gets angry with Indra and Viṣṇu for giving protection to Sumukha, the lawful food of the king of birds (Garuḍa).[22] In the Kāśī Khaṇḍa of the *Sk. P.*, we have Kadrū — the mother of serpents — herself cursing those serpents, who did not abide by her orders to change the tail of the horse (in the wager), to be the food of Tārkṣya (Garuḍa).[23] In the *Rāmāyaṇa*, we have Garuḍa coming to the rescue of Rāma when the latter is pierced by the serpent-arrows of Rāvaṇa.[24] The same can be seen from the story of Jīmūtavāhana.[25] Vogel quotes a story from the Ceylonese chronicle *Mahāvaṁśa*, where Saṅghamitrā, carrying the branch of the Bodhi tree, assumed the form of Garuḍa, and terrified the nāgas, practising magic to win the branch.[26] That this antagonism has found an important place in the popular belief can be easily seen from the fact that, the Hindu festival 'Nāgapañcamī' is supposed to be an anniversary of the deadly fight between Garuḍa and the nāgas, and on this day the image of Garuḍa at Cāṅgu-nārāyaṇa is reported to perspire regularly.[27] Examples of this hereditary enmity between the nāgas and Garuḍa can easily be multiplied, but the examples referred to above are sufficient to give an idea as to how the Garuḍa-nāga feud in the *Mb* legend is well set in a tradition that has a wide field.

## Garuḍa and Poison

Another important point to note in the context of this antagonism between the serpents and Garuḍa is the fact, that the name of Garuḍa is seen to be given to some magic stones that are a cure against poison. Thus in the Vaiṣṇava Khaṇḍa of the *Sk. P.* we have an account of Garuḍa performing penance for thirty thousand years in the Badarikāśrama, and after propitiating lord Hari getting a slab of stone bearing his name established there. By remembering this stone, so the account goes, one can get relief from snake-poison.[28] From the Prabhāsa Khaṇḍa of the same Purāṇa, we know that Vainateya (Garuḍa) established a Śivaliṅga the worship of which checks snake-poison.[29] Stones bearing the names of Garuḍa are quite a frequent occurrence in the Sanskrit literature.[30]

## The Note of Reconciliation

When we come to the Buddhistic literature, we see the Garuḍa and the Nāgas often spoken of as hostile to each other. They appear to be two different groups. Thus we know from the story of Bhūridatta, that a captured nāga looks at the crowd of bystanders, as a rule, for two reasons to see : — (i) whether any 'Suparṇa' (Garuḍa) or (ii) any kinsman is near.[31] In the stories of conflict between the nāgas and Garuḍa (or the Garuḍas), it is quite a frequent experience to see a note of reconciliation at the end. The 'Uragajātaka' has a story in which a holy hermit "in a truly Buddhistic spirit", brings about a reconciliation between a nāga and a Suparṇa.[32] In the Piṇḍāra jātaka story also we find that the Nāgas and the Garuḍas appear as real tribes having their kings. These kings come to meet a naked mendicant who is ship-wrecked. The Garuḍa king asks the ascetic about a method to catch the nāgas in water without himself being much troubled. The method is learnt by the Garuḍa who catches a nāga, but *having pity on him leaves him.*[33] The 'Uraga-jātaka' mentions a feast of the Devas, nāgas, Asuras, Suparṇas, etc., where a nāga, and a suparṇa stand side by side on the same spot. The nāga unknowingly, puts his hand on the shoulders of the Suparṇa. Being afraid on recognizing his enemy, he runs away to the bank of the river. The Suparṇa gives a chase. A recluse happens to be living on the bank of the river. The nāga takes shelter in the garment of the recluse who had gone for bath, changing himself into a jewel. The Garuḍa arrives and there follows a *reconciliation* between these two with the help of the recluse.[34] The nāgas are said to be afraid of Garuḍa and also of the snake-conjurers.[35] We have also references, where, on the occasions of royal proclamation, nāgas and Garuḍas would come together along with others;[36] and because of the influence of the Buddha, the nāgas would not be attacked by the Garuḍas.[37]

## Garuḍa and the Sarpa-Vidyā

It is clear from what has been said above that the nāgas and Garuḍa (or the Garuḍas) were often reconciled though said to be antagonistic to one another; and we can understand how at the time of the marriage of Garuḍa, the serpents got afraid thinking Garuḍa's children would eat them up; and attacked him severely.[38] We saw that Garuḍa's name is associated with the stones that are supposed to cure serpent-bite or poison in general. It is not difficult to see how this point might have been suggested from the actual antagonism between the snakes and the bird Garuḍa and the subsequent victory of Garuḍa. The serpents being poisonous, their killing on the part of Garuḍa would have naturally suggested Garuḍa as having control over their poison. It can be also seen from the fact that 'Gāruḍā-Vidyā' and 'Sarpa-Vidyā' are spoken of as synonyms. Max Müller refers to a passage from the *Śānk. Śr. Sū.* in which there is a mention of various lores that the Vedic student learnt in ancient times.[39] From it we know that the Kādraveyas, the people of Arbudadeśa, were taught the special lore called 'Sarpa-vidyā' which was to be recited on the fifth day of the horse-sacrifice.[40] The commentator of the *Śān. Śr. Sū.* renders the word '*sarpavidyā*' as '*Gāruḍa-vidyā*'.[41] The *Āś Śr. Sū.* has '*Viṣavidyā*'[42] in place of '*Sarpavidyā*'. This was taught to the *sarpas* who, according to the text, were '*the knowers of the sarpas*' ('*sarpa-vidaḥ*'), which obviously means snake-charmers, as Max Müller rightly renders, or those who know the art of controlling snake-poison. It appears that the texts referred to above make a distinction between the ordinary *sarpas* (as a tribe or clan as a whole) and '*sarpa-vidaḥ*' among them, i.e. who learnt the art of snake-charming. It is not known what exactly the '*sarpa-vidyā*' was; nor does it seem to have a definite name, as it is also called 'Viṣavidyā' by another *Śr. sūtra,* as we have noted above. Whatever may be the name of the *vidyā,* one thing seems to be quite clear that it was the 'lore of snake-charming'. In this connection it is necessary to remember a reference in the *Mb*. itself to some such lore given to Kaśyapa by Brahmā. The name of the lore is given as '*Viṣa-harī vidyā*',[43] which reminds us of the 'Viṣa-vidyā' spoken of in the *Āś. Śr Sū.* The 'Viṣaharī vidyā' was given to Kaśyapa to counteract the snake-poison for the good of the people, as the *Mb*. clearly states. Now the position is this : —

The 'Viṣa-vidyā, and the 'sarpa-vidyā were taught to the sarpas as their lore. The 'Viṣaharī vidyā' mentioned in the *Mb*. was given to Kaśyapa who was the father of the serpents (*sarpas* and *nāgas*) and Garuḍa. While commenting on the passage in question, the commentator (Nārāyana) of the *Āś. Śr Sū.* renders the words '*sarpa-vidaḥ*' as the 'knowers of the science of poison — who are the scions of the family of Kaśyapa etc.' These '*sarpavidaḥ*' are themselves from amongst the Sarpa class as the *sūtras* says. Hence, the natural step would be to take these 'kāśyapīyas' as hailing from the sarpa-clan and forming a part thereof. The peculiar context in the *Mb*. tale of the traditional animosity between Garuḍa and the serpents, wherein the gift of the '*Viṣahari*' lore comes, is significant. The possessor of the *Viṣaharī vidyā* is Kaśyapa; and Garuḍa also occurs as an antagonist and the eater of the serpents and also as the son of Kaśyapa. Now, we have seen that the antidotes against snakes or snake-poison have association with the name Garuḍa. Dubois speaks of the brahmins of South India saying their daily prayer to Garuḍa before going to bed,[44] to ward off snake-bite. The *Gaṇ. P.* refers to a *śāstra* called *Garuḍa śāstra*, the knower of which has control over the serpents.[45] The *Vāyu P.* speaks of a destroyer of the serpents living on the mountain Vikaṅka. His name is Sugrīva and he is a Gāruḍī,[46] which means 'snake-charmer'. From this it seems clear, that the mantras counteracting the snake-poison could be called '*Garuḍa-mantras*'. The Tamil lexicon actually refers to such mantras by the name 'Gāruḍā-vidyā'. The 'Viṣaharī' or the

'Viṣa-vidyā' or the 'Sarpa vidyā', spoken of in the Sūtras and the *Mb* as charm against snake-poison could be nothing else than this 'Gāruḍā-vidyā' and it is rightly so rendered by the commentators. Hence it will not be wrong to term those *vidyās* generally by the name 'Gāruḍā-vidyā' and refer to them only as such. Those who learn this lore of snake-charming could even be called 'Gāruḍas' or the 'Kāśyapeyas', though they be from the Sarpa clans. It is true that the lore of the Sarpas is not clearly mentioned in the Sūtras as the 'Gāruḍā-vidyā'; but, as we have seen, all these names indicate the lore of snake-charming. At least we could hold that the 'Gārudā-vidyā' was a name later given to the 'Sarpa-vidyā' or 'Viṣa-vidyā'. Again, when the Sarpas were identified with the nāgas, the 'Gāruḍā' vidyā would naturally be taken as the sacred lore of the nāgas. When in the *Mb.*,[47] we have references to the whole families of the Garuḍas in the same region as of the nāgas (Pātāla) it would not be wrong to suppose them to be only those from among the nāgas,[48] who were well versed in the 'Gāruḍa vidyā' and hence came to be called the 'Garuḍas' (snake-charmers), being the worshippers of Garuḍa, the presiding deity of the *mantras* conteracting snake-poison. Now let us look to the lore taught to the people of Tārkṣya, who later came to be identified with Garuḍa and hence came to be the antagonist of serpents —

> "On the ninth day he tells the story which begins with Tārkṣya Vaipaśyata (Vaipaścitya according to Āśvalāyana). As his *men were the birds,* and as these are present, he tells the 'Birds' this story."[49]

These men belonging to the Bird class are called 'Vāyovidvika'; and learn the (Vāyu) P.[50] The people — the Birds — however, are not taught the *'vidyā'* of snake-charming though Garuḍa is later identified with Tārkṣya and is sometimes mentioned as the son of Tārkṣya.[51] Nor is the name of the *vidyā* of the Birds (the people of Tārkṣya) given as *Tārkṣya-vidyā,* which could be identified later with the Gāruḍavidyā on the basis of the identification, Tārkṣya = Gāruda. On the other hand Sarpavidyā is rendered as 'Gāruḍāvidyā' by many as we have seen. We have seen that the word 'Garuḍa' is often associated with the antidotes of poison, and it generally suggests the antidotes to snake-poison. To give a few more instances. We have the 'Garuḍāñjanam' to remove the snake-poison;[52] also 'Garuḍa-dhyānam' in which the person concerned imagines himself to be Garuḍa and utters charms on a patient bitten by snake, to remove the poison. The term *'Garuḍa viddai'* also is given by the Tamil lexicon, the meaning being "(1) The *mantras* associated with 'Garuḍan', especially efficacious for snake-bites; and (ii) Art of charming away the poison of snake-bite by appropriate incantations, the charmer imagining himself to be Garuḍa for the nouns."[53] It is clear from this, that the magic-charmer who helps drive the snake-poison imagines himself to be Garuḍa; and the *mantras* that he recites are said to be presided over by Garuḍa, and come under 'Gāruḍa-Vidyā', which probably indicate the *vidyā* taught to the Sarpas. To have a clear view of the snake-charms, we shall quote from the *Agni P.* the *mantra* called the 'Tārkṣya-mantra',[54] with the deity Garuḍa. The whole *'mantra'* is as follows, and shows tantric influence.

> *Om jvala, mahāmate hṛdayāya, garuḍaviśālaśirase garuḍaviśikhāyai; garuḍa viṣa-prābhañjana prabhedana prabhedana vitrāsaya vitrāsaya vimarda vimarda, kavacāya apratihataśāsanāya humphāt.*[55]

There are other *mantras* in which, to counteract poison, Rudra is invoked; but, looking to them, we can see how even there Garuḍa could be seen to have prominence. Thus we have —

> *Om namo bhagavate rudrāya, chind chinda viṣam, jvalita-paraśupāṇaye ca; Om namo pakṣirājāya.*[56]

It could be seen that here Rudra is seen as 'Pakṣi-Rudra' thus identifying him with the 'Bird' who can be none else than Garuḍa who features in the *mantra* quoted above. It seems probable that Śiva (Rudra) and the bird Garuḍa came to be identified on the commonness of their control over poison—Śiva (Rudra) drinking poison at the churning of the ocean, and Garuḍa as an antagonist of snakes, and, thus, of poison.

It will be quite clear from what has been said above that the lore to cure snake-poison could be termed the 'Garuḍā' lore and, most probably, is not different from the 'Sārpa vidyā' or 'Viṣaharī Vidyā' given to Kaśyapa by Brahmā. This 'Gāruḍā' lore probably consists of charms that have Garuḍa as their deity; one can easily explain the term Gāruḍā as '*Garuḍasya Sambandhinī iti*'.[57] Now, the question is, how could this Gāruḍā vidyā be taught to the Sarpas? Well, when the lore taught to the 'Birds' (tribe of people named birds) was the Vāyu P., it is clear, that the 'Gāruḍā vidyā' had nothing to do with the 'Bird-clans', if really such clans existed. Secondly, Garuḍa (though a bird) being the main deity of the charms against serpent-bite of snake-poison, was auspicious to those who learnt the 'Gāruḍā vidyā'. Now, if Gāruḍā vidyā was the lore taught to the Sarpas, it is clear that those of the Sarpas (who were later identified with the nāgas, as we have seen) who learnt the 'Gāruḍā Vidyā' might *think Garuḍa to be their deity, though they themselves were of the Sarpa class*. These 'Gāruḍā-vidyā' veterans would naturally be proud of their possession and then it is not difficult to imagine the next step which is, to suppose themselves superior to the other members of their own class who did not learn this 'vidyā'.

It will not be out of place here to discuss the opinion of Oldham as regards the Garuḍa-tribe. According to him, the Garuḍas, like the nāgas, might have been a separate tribe. The solution of the whole question of their mutual antagonism, according to him, is to believe that these two were two *different tribes having two different totems.* "These tribes too were neighbours — unrelenting enemies. Both were in Pātāla." He refers to the Vāyu P. which says that the abode of the Garuḍas is Pātāla[58] which is also said to be the abode of the nāgas.[59] He thinks that the Garuḍas and the nāgas came from outside India and were engaged in conflicts with the aboriginal races here. "Kriṣṇa, when he assumed the form of Viṣṇu, appears to have adopted Garuḍa as his ensign." He believes that the people termed Asuras had various tribes among themselves according to various totems, including the Garuḍas and Nāgas; and that these Asuras were sun-worshippers. He also says, "At first Garuḍa appears to have been dependent upon the nāgas; but that afterwards he threw off their yoke and obtained from them the promise that they should be his food." It is difficult to accept the opinion of Oldham. His point about the 'totems' is not supported by the main principles of totemism; and hence it is quite rightly that Kennedy[60] objects to this point of his. As Kennedy rightly points out, the serpent and the Garuḍa are not worshipped by special sects. These two form the objects of worship for many others who could not be called to belong to these totemistic (?) societies. Another important point in this connection is, that nowhere do we hear of any killing of the nāga or Garuḍa and sharing his flesh by the people of the tribe to imbibe the totem in their own bodies (or rather to have the union of the outward and the inward soul).[61] The statement that Garuḍa was accepted as his ensign by Kriṣṇa is shown from the *Mb* and the Purāṇas,[62] but, Oldham does not examine this point (the explanation of which we have tried at a later stage in our discussion). To state that Garuḍa was dependent on the nāgas and later won freedom etc. is to state nothing more than what is given in the *Mb* and the Purāṇas. Oldham clearly refers here to the wager between Kadrū and Vinatā but gives no explanation of it.[63] But, more of it later. The most important point is that Oldham does not mention the part of reconciliation[64] between the Nāgas and the Garuḍa, which lurks in the traditional antagonism between these two. He does not, also, seem to have noticed that these two are inter related and appear to be belonging to the same family, the indications of which are to be seen at places more than one, not to say alone that these two are said to be the offspring of Kaśyapa; for, Kaśyapa is said to be the common ancestor for all the different tribes — the very Prajāpati from whom hail the gods and the Asuras. We have other indications to show how the nāgas and Garuḍa were of the same stock. The *Mb* refers to the sons of Garuḍa among whom Sumukha is one. Sumukha was also the name of the snake whom Indra and Upendra (Viṣṇu) gave shelter, but who in reality was destined to be eaten by Garuḍa, and ultimately was thrown on Garuḍa's neck by Viṣṇu, not to be eaten by him, but to be in his neck always thence.[65] Thus the two get reconciled and live together. This clearly reminds us of the Buddhistic tales where the Buddha, in the form of a recluse, brings about their reconciliation. The inner germ of truth in this story seems to be that Garuḍa and Sumukha — the one belonging to the sect of Garuḍa and the other of the nāgas (or serpents) in general — fought and were reconciled with one another. In the age of Vaiṣṇavite predominance the good act of reconciliation was attributed to Viṣṇu. Another important thing to be noted here is that these sons of Garuḍa are said to be Kṣatriyas, having lost their chance to brāhmaṇahood due to destroying *their own* kindred, who are no other than the serpents whom they ate.[66] This has a hidden suggestion to the class-rivarly hinting at the original superiority of the serpents (nāgas), and the 'Garuḍas' being criticised as inferior to the former, probably, because of the latter's *posing* as superior to their tribe-members (nāgas) by virtue of their possessing unique power — 'Gāruḍā Vidyā', and menacing their tribesmen (nāgas), by superior magical powers, the promotion of a new symbol of worship (i.e. Garuḍa) adding to the class rivalry. Vinatā, who is the mother of Garuḍa and Aruṇa, is herself said to be the mother of Surasā — the mother of Serpents — and of Kadrū — the mother of the nāgas. It is said that Śukī gave birth to Natā. Vinatā is the daughter of Natā. (*She*) *gave birth* to ten wrathful (daughters), viz., Mṛgī Mṛgamadā, Harī, Bhadramadā, Mātaṅgī, Śārdūli, Svetā, Surabhi, *Kadrū* and *Surasā* endowed with all virtues.[67]

Śeṣa says that Vainateya Garuḍa, the one that traverses the skies, is his brother; and that the sons of Vinatā and Kadrū are constantly jealous of one another.[68] But even with all this, we read that Garuḍa (Vainateya) was given as a helpmate to Ananta — the serpent — who went under the earth to support it.[69] This is very much like Sumukha being always with Garuḍa, and the point of reconciliation in enmity is the same here. Both these cases, probably, point to a real reconciliation, and the element of Viṣṇu's command may safely be considered to be a later addition when Vaiṣṇavism became dominant. Thus the strife between Garuḍa and the nāgas appears to be a strife between two sects that are parts of one whole. It must be remembered, that these two are spoken of as Brahmins and Kṣatriyas who themselves are only two classes of one whole. It will be helpful to refer here to some of the sculptures that depict the nāgas and Garuḍa in one. We have Garuḍa carrying nāgas in the human form represented in the sculptures. Vogel refers also to sculptures wherein Garuḍa and the nāgas are both represented as human beings.[70] Sculptures from Kamboja show that, in certain cases the pet theme—nāgas being devoured by Garuḍa — is set aside, giving place to the representation of Garuḍa and the nāgas connected together in one piece. Thus in the structure of Bayon Garuḍa appears for all times as attached to the nāgas.[71] The nāgas of the Balustrad style show generally in their crest little Garuḍas.[72] Garuḍa is mostly figured, with arms more or less separated, appearing in the small figures above the middle nāga. Again on the shoulders of the Garuḍas, that stand in the crests of the nāgas, are seen small figures of Viṣṇu. The constant association of the nāgas and Garuḍa in these sculptures and on the lower railings of the Bayon style[73] appears to have more meaning than the simple theme of traditional antagonism. It should be clear that here in such sculptures the usual theme of Garuḍa eating the nāgas is not to be found; and there is representation of reconciliation, the textual references to which we have already seen from the epic and the Buddhistic literature. We can infer from these that, along with the idea of antagonism, the idea of oneness and reconciliation was also working on, the germ of reconciliation being exploited by the Viṣṇuites and the Buddhists at different times to show the superiority of their own creed in establishing peace of warring sects. From the survey of these sculptures, J. Boisselier draws the conclusion that in the times of the Buddhists there was a tendency to assume the existence of two types of nāgas — one good and the other bad and hostile; and that Garuḍa is represented both as the protector of the nāgas and the destroyer of them, good or bad as they might be.[74] Will it be bold to take a step further and opine, in the light of what has been noted previously by us, that the good nāgas whom Garuḍa protects are those that form his own class or, to be clearer, those that have Garuḍa as their symbol, and the bad as those that are devoid of this symbol? Particularly interesting are the figures of the small Garuḍas on the crest of the nāgas. As Viṣṇu that rides Garuḍa can be said to be the tutelary deity of the Garuḍa-vaṁśa,[75] cannot we say, on the same analogy, that these nāgas who have Garuḍa on the crest are those that have Garuḍa as their tutelary deity? It will be encouraging to ask at this point whether the crest-Garuḍa does not resemble the sect-mark.[76] In the same style — i.e. Balustrad — among the nāgas of the lower railings are two-headed nāgas, the first of which has his neck enclosed with Garuḍa.[77] This helps us to understand the point the more; and, in all probability, hints at the point which we have already put forth, that Garuḍa and the nāgas in reality might have been sects of the same tribe, Garuḍa being the symbol accepted by those of the nāgas who learnt the 'Gāruḍa-vidyā'. Gradually these 'Garuḍas' came to be a major sect, in all probability, and were dreaded by the rest of the nāgas, as being all powerful. The antagonism between these two sects, primarily, was on the lines of superiority in the power of charm and magic; and never a political one. It was on the basis of social status. For all other practical and political purposes they were nāgas only; and this can answer well why the 'Garuḍas' are never said to have any strong claim to interpretation euhemeristically, like their antagonists — the nāgas. This solves the question as to why these two being in the same place — the Pātāla — only the nāgas are spoken of as if they were brahmins and the Garuḍas are said to have lost their claims to brāhmaṇa-hood because of their killing their own kin, the nāgas (*Mb* V.101.6). The stories of the antagonism between these two are to be treated only as the competition for the show of superiority of magical knowledge.[78] Hence, it is nearer the truth to say that these two were only two sects of the same tribe, and not actually two tribes as Oldham specifically mentions.[79] Viewing in this light, the supposed dependence of Garuḍa[80] on the nāgas and subsequently throwing off their yoke seem to be nothing but a symbolic expression of ultimately gaining superior status in the said organism. This winning of special and superior status indicates again the general respect for the 'Gāruḍā vidyā' which, later (as we shall refer to again), was joined up with the episode of the bringing of nectar (cf. the 'viṣaharī vidyā' given to Kaśyapa) which, in other words, is the nullification of Death, and in this particular context, Death by snake-poison. It is also possible that these sectarians, Garuḍas, lost their social status because of their indulgence in magic and became obsolete socially, though their tutelary deity remained long in memory with all the adventures attributed to it.

A passing reference to the Māṅgas and the Māṅga-

Gāruḍīs may not be out of place here. Both these are aboriginal tribes considered to be the Antyajas (out of the social system of the caste-Hindoos) and were called 'untouchables' in Mahārāṣṭra. These two are not on the same social status between themselves and one considers the other lower than itself in status. Although this social difference is present between them, their names betray that these might have once formed a complete whole being only two sects therein. The Māṅgas probably came to be different from the Māṅgā-Gāruḍīs because of the latter indulging in magical powers. Even now these Māṅga-Gāruḍīs are supposed to be endowed with magical powers and are often invited to protect the village from sudden out-breaks of epidemics. The Māṅgas, on the other hand, are peaceful people not associated as a caste with magical powers. Karve-Date[81] and Ketkar[82] refer to the Māṅgas. Both say that these are a sub-caste of the Māṅga-Gāruḍīs. As we have noted, these formerly might have formed two divisions of one tribe; but later separated due to different social status forming two different castes. There is another caste, as we have already noted, named 'Gāruḍī' which is different from the 'Māṅga-Gāruḍīs'.These Gāruḍīs exhibit their control over the snakes before eager spectators, who are mostly idle boys, and wander from place to place. They also exhibit their knowledge of sham magic. Now, in the Māṅgas and the Māṅga-Gāruḍīs we have a probable parallel to the nāgas and the Garuḍas; and, as the Māṅga-Gāruḍīs were separated from the main stem the Māṅgas, in the same way the knowers of the 'Gāruḍā vidyā', could be supposed to be differentiated from the other nāgas who were their tribesmen.[83]

## The Principle of Phratry

The peculiar way in which the nāgas and the Garuḍas (with their emblem in Garuḍa) fight with each other and again are shown to come to reconciliation need not surprise us when we know the peculiarities of such tribal social organizations as are based upon the principle of phratry. In this system the whole society or tribe is divided into two main sub-divisions that may be called phratries, the whole system of classification having a dual organization. These two phratries are always represented as conflicting and again coming together on occasions, thus showing *reconciliation in strife*. The relation between these phratries is generally represented as that between Heaven and Earth; Light and Darkness; Man and Woman and so on. These two, though quite different *apparently*, are, as can be easily noted, complementary to each other and are quite necessary to make a complete whole. These two phratries have fixed social status.[84] If we look to the nāgas and Garuḍa from this point, it appears that this classification well suits their relationship. Figures are common where there is a combination of a serpent and the eagle (possibly Garuḍa) — the two said to be antagonistic to one another. Thus, Vogel refers to certain winged serpents that decorate the upper terrace of the main temple of Panataram in Jāvā.[85] The mothers of these two — Garuḍa and the nāgas — are said to be sisters[86] and also wives of the same person Kaśyapa; and they are identified as Heaven and Earth.[87] Their wager and the defeat of Vinatā resulting in the nāgas being carried by Garuḍa on his back fit in well with the conception of the two sects of a dual organization competing with one another. As we have already hinted, Garuḍa's carrying his step-brothers (the serpents) on the back from place to place, most probably indicates lower position in this sytem of classification for the followers of Garuḍa — i.e. the sect who learnt the magic-charms — who probably used it for gaining a better status in the dual organization.[87a] We have probably the same hint in such passages where parties antagonistic to one another take birth from one and the same person, and the same person who gives birth is also an enemy of the one that is born. The Brāhmaṇa texts are replete with such passages;

and it is not wrong to believe that these passages in the Brāhmaṇas might themselves be due to the influence of the popular faiths existing in the country at that time. The Suras and the Asuras is such a dual. They always fight and compete with one another, join together and again fight, both being the sons of Prajapati.[88] Another interesting episode is the Indra-Vṛtra myth, which resembles the Garuḍa-Nāga legend quite closely. Indra the enemy of Vṛtra is also his eater, Vṛtra being identified with Soma.[89] Indra and Vṛtra are again brothers, Tvaṣṭṛ being Indra's direct father, and Vṛtra being produced from the residue of Soma by him.[90] From the wing of Garuḍa are produced the pea-cock, snakes, and also the ichneumon that is the deadly enemy of the serpents.[91] Now, the peacock eats the snakes which are again eaten by Garuḍa and killed by the ichneumon. These creatures, eating and being eaten, form one family as is suggested by their birth. These examples are enough to show how we have a reflection in these of the peculiar classification-system of social organisation. It appears quite probable, then, that the Garuḍas and the nāgas primarily belonged to the same social organization, and were classified as different groups. Garuḍa — the presiding deity of the 'Gāruḍā vidyā' — was the symbol of those who were initiated and got well-versed in the *vidyā*. Later these people became a class as a whole in the whole social organization but never outside it, the whole totality being the Nāgas. The idea of the eating of the nāgas by Garuḍa only indicates the superior power of the deity — probably a mystic and magical power. The same idea of superior power is, probably, indicated by the concept of Garuḍa's wing producing the nāgas in the verse from the *Sup. Ad.* we have just referred to. These two ideas can be seen to be one. The power of procreating the creatures can well go with the power of diminishing as suggested by eating — the whole idea being that of omnipotence, and assimilation.[92]

What may be the propriety of the statues that depict the

nāgas being eaten by Garuḍa? The explanation is not far to seek. The worship of a deity in the most original form springs mostly from the dread of the deity, rather than from any softer idea for it. The deity usually requires sacrifices both animal and human.[93] Instances are not wanting to show how, even in India, the tribals and other people indulge in such bloody sacrifices; and instances of human sacrifices are quite well heard of, not to speak of the Śunaśśepa-Ākhyāna[94] which hints at the fact by a repudiation of it. The highest honour supposed to be done to the deity would be the sacrifice to him of oneself, or some other thing that is like our own self.[95] We have seen how the Sarpas (or the nāgas) were taught the 'Gāruḍā vidyā', the presiding deity of which was Garuḍa. Now, as the presiding deity of the sacred lore of the Sarpas, it is not unnatural for Garuḍa to command the highest honour and the best type of sacrifice from his worshippers. The symbolization of this type of sacrifice can well be understood if we take into account the awe with which the deity would have been viewed, especially if some sort of magical halo was associated with it. Thus both ways Garuḍa could be represented as devouring the nāgas — (i) as the presiding deity of the magic-lore or charms; and (ii) also as a general terror-causing deity, which is to be propitiated. If we imagine that there would have been a Garuḍa race,[96] who, to glorify their victory, perpetuated it in these sculptures, we are confronted with the fact of the clear absence of such a race, when we have their antagonists the nāgas — even to-day. On the other hand, we are told by Risley that, practically the whole population of India before the 'Aryans' came, admitted the serpent as their ancestor,[97] and was ruled by Nāga kings.[98] The supposition of the suzerainty of the people having 'Garuḍa' as their totem over those having nāga (serpent) as their totem or symbol, lacks evidence; and, again with it, it remains to be satisfactorily answered why the *Sarpavidyā* which is rightly rendered in the commentary as 'Gāruḍā vidyā' was taught to the Sarpas.[99]

Before we close this chapter it would be interesting to examine a folk-tale noted by Oldham in his article we have referred to.[100] It runs thus — Bāsuki or Bāsade was always engaged with Garuḍa. It was decided to give one nāga daily to Garuḍa. Once the latter surprised him by an attack. So the former took refuge in Kailāsa Kuṇḍa, a mountain-lake between Chinab and Ravi. The Vazir of Bāsuki saved him by giving his own flesh to Garuḍa. In the meantime an army was raised, by which Garuḍa was defeated and killed — "at least so the legend says". The Vazir's name is given as Jībūtavāhana who is also worshipped even now at the order of Bāsuki.

Oldham states, from this, as a conclusion, "All this would seem to point to a warfare between rival tribes, rather than to any supernatural or symbolic conflict."

It is not necessary to suppose this to be the strife between two rival parties, as we have already seen above. It is clear that the tale is similar to the tale of the *'Nāgānandam'* — a drama of Harṣa, and that of the *K.S.S.*[101] In all probability the tale itself may be coined from the traditional contest between the nāgas and Garuḍa. The army that attacked Garuḍa need not be an army of a real king to attack a real person, but can very well be a later addition giving the colour of fact to fiction. Vāsukī's sending to Garuḍa a victim every day need not also be surprising; it forms a popular motif of many a folk-tale.[102] It seems more probable that Garuḍa, the dreaded deity,[103] which had control over the magical lore, was to be propitiated by daily human (nāga) offering. At the most this account of the killing (according to the tale) of Garuḍa hints at possible unpopularity of the cult of charmers (among the nāgas, as we have seen already) who were supposed to hold sway over the rest of the tribesmen.

To sum up, (i) Garuḍa, in all probability, was primarily the deity of a sect of nāga-charmers who, further on, might have developed into a separate division as such, but never outside the whole Nāga organization; (ii) This sect might have enjoyed popularity among the nāgas; but might also have suffered unpopularity at times, their deity the Garuḍa always remaining an emblem of power and of the art of magic and charms; (iii) It is not surprising for certain nāgas to have a god-head who actually is the killer of, and thus superior to, the serpents — the killer bird whom they probably revered and worshipped[104] taking into account the peculiar nature of the bird Garuḍa who kills the snakes and thus could well have offered an ideal presiding deity for the lore of 'snake-charming'; (iv) The dragon-Garuḍa was a phase in the evolution;[105] and (v) This Garuḍa had, probably, nothing to do primarily with other birds, say as their king,[106] the idea being a later and a secondary one.

# 3
# GARUḌA, THE DEVOURER

## (A) The Tortoise and the Elephant

The tortoise and the elephant are the creatures that Garuḍa was advised by Kaśyapa to eat on his way to fetch Soma. We have given the translation of the tale in the first sub-chapter.[107]

On studying the episode we get at the following points: —

(i) The Tortoise and the Elephant (i.e., the 'Kūrma' and the 'Hastin') were quarrelling with each another;

(ii) They were two brothers in the former birth and even then they were quarrelling with each other;

(iii) Both of them were eaten by Garuḍa.

The same account is given in the *Sk.P.* and in the *Padma*, P.[108] Hence, it is not necessary to review it here. The account from the *Sup. Ad.* is important as it is an earlier one; and we shall see how it stands there. There, it is not Kaśyapa (identified with Tārkṣya) that indicates the twain as food: it is Vinatā who tells Garuḍa about the two creatures—

"This is the mountain, on the top of which is the lake; therein (lives) the mighty creature. The same shall seize the elephant that enters the water. He is thy food — (nay) they both, — look O Garuḍa. The great 'nāga' (elephant?) Padmī, with a terrible noise, is huge and appears like the cloud. Him did the creator give thee (as food) in friendship. Do thou hasten to the abode of the gods, after devouring these two."[109]

Here we have a deviation in the following points:—

(i) There is no clear mention of the Tortoise here; we

have, instead, only 'the Great creature';

(ii) There is no mention of their quarrel in the previous birth;

(iii) The other creature is the *mahānāga* Padmī, and is also known as Hastin (which would mean 'elephant');

(iv) This Nāga is said to be given to Garuḍa by the creator, which is very much like the *Mb* idea, that Garuḍa, as soon as he was born, ran straight to seize his food — the serpents — fixed for him by the creator.[110]

Now to turn to another verse in the *Sup. Ad.* in this connection:—

"I have taken these two nāgas — Śuddha-Padma, that are the followers of Mataṅga and are, as it were, divided (*prabhinnau*) between themselves about the female elephant (*vāśitā*). Being glad do I fly forth along this (aerial path)".[111]

The description here concerns the same two creatures as spoken of in the passage quoted above. Now, the two creatures carried by Garuḍa are here called *nāgau* (two nāgas) while the same are spoken of as — (i) The Great creature (*bhūtam mahāntam*), and (ii) *Hastin* (Cf. VII.13.1, 2). Hence, naturally the two are of the same species, though the words used for them seem to be different. These two are only '*nāgau*'. The word 'Śuddha-padmau' could be understood to mean either— (i) Śuddha and Padma or (ii) having white (pure) lotuses. Thus we understand that the two 'nāgas' were, both having pure lotuses; or one of them was named Śuddha and the other Padma. If we take 'Śuddha-Padma' as indicating two names or even as an adjective, we are reminded of another word, 'Padmī', which is used for the '*ghoṣavān*'-'*Mahānāga*' in the previous passage. Now our position is this —

1. '*Mahānāga*' that is '*ghoṣavat*', is called Padmī.
2. The two 'nāgas' are called 'Śuddha-Padmau'.

Now, the word '*prabhinnau*'. This word is rendered by Jarl Charpentier as 'ruttish'[112] and the two 'nāgas' are taken by him to mean 'water-elephants' (*jala-hastin*). The word 'nāga' we shall discuss a bit later. The word *'prabhinnau'* means also 'divided'—'dis-united'; and here, in all probability we have the germ of the two quarrelling creatures (The tortoise and the elephant) in the *Mb.* If we take the word *'nāgau'* to mean 'the elephants', we naturally would be induced to take the word *prabhinnau* to mean 'ruttish'. But, the question is — what are these two creatures, the two nāgas? Whether both these 'nāgas' are to be taken as 'elephant' or not, one thing is pretty sure; both are spoken of as if they belong to the same species — that of the 'nāga'. Now, the tortoise and the elelphant, though apparently of different species, can be seen to belong to the same species, when we take into consideration that they both were brothers in the former birth. The idea is well rooted in the Pūraṇas, varying only as to who they were in the former birth. The *Mb* tells that they were two ascetic brothers, quarrelling over property. The *Sk.P.*[113] has the same version as the *Mb.* The *Viṣṇu-Dh. P.* mentions the two brothers as being two Gandharvas in the former birth. Their names were 'Hāhā' and 'Hūhū'; but the whole motif is used for the episode of 'Gajendra-mokṣa'.[114] They competed as regards their virtues in singing; and then they cursed each other. It can be seen, thus, how closely all the accounts resemble the 'two nāgas' of the *Sup. Ad.*,[115] who, as we have remarked, are of the same species.

Having, thus, seen how there is a clear indication in the *Mb* and the Purāṇas of the Tortoise and the Elephant as being of the same species by virtue of their being brothers in the former birth, we now go to see what exactly the elephant and the tortoise are. The word 'nāga' has a double meaning — that of the serpent and also that of the elephant. About the word 'Kacchapa' or 'Kūrma', there seems to be no doubtful meaning. Now let us again turn to the *Suparṇa A.* We have noted that it refers to the 'Great Creature' in one place and calls it 'nāga' (in 'nāgau') in another. At another place we have "Lifting the mighty *Hastin*, as high as the mountain Meru, with the *'Grāha'* in the sky."

Here the 'great creature' is called the *'Grāha'*, the crocodile. Thus we come to the various phases of the creature —

1. It is called only a *'Great Creature'*;
2. It is referred to as 'nāga'; and
3. It is referred to as *'Grāha'* which means a crocodile.

The last one reminds us of the crocodile in the episode of 'Gajendra-mokṣa', which quarrels with the elephant, its brother in the former birth. It is interesting to note how the creature that is called 'nāga' (serpent) is changed into a crocodile; but it is not quite surprising if we look into some examples which note this change. Vogel mentions a sculpture on the Gupta temple at Devagarh in which the 'Gajendra-Mokṣa' episode is depicted. In it we see a seven-hooded Cobra (*nāga*) in the place of the Crocodile.[116] The same author mentions nāgas resembling *makaras* (crocodiles) decorating the upper terrace of the main temple of Panataram and at the entrance of the Chandi Kidal near Malang in the island of Jāvā.[117] In the Chinese mythology we meet with the same interconnection of the serpents and the crocodile. The water-dragons in this mythology are said to have mixed limbs of various animals, and the neck of the dragons is that of the serpent while their appearance is like the crocodile.[118] The 'makaras' depicted on the Chandi Kidal referred to by Vogel have a jewel on the top of the head which reminds us of the nāga-maṇi, the jewel that is supposed to be in the hood of the nāgas. The winged serpents on the upper terrace of the main temple of Panataram in Jāvā can be well compared with the fantastic *makaras* that Lindsay refers to.[119] Lindsay comes to the conclusion that this *makara*-motif is of the South Indian origin and connects it with the *makara* in the Amarāvatī sculpture. The interchange of the nāga (serpent) and the *makara* might have been also helped by the fact that both these are water-animals, and have more or less the same appearance — the reptilic!

In the light of what has been said above it could be easy to understand the *Sup. Ad.* speaking of the 'nāga' and the *grāha* as the same creature. In this connection, it will be good to note the account of the Rāma-grāma-Stūpa by Hieun Tsiang, noted by Vogel.[120] According to this account a dragon came at various periods and walked round the *stūpa* changing his form into that of a nāga (serpent). According to another account, certain elephants came there and watered the relics of the Buddha. Fa-hien also mentions it in his records.[121] Vogel is perfectly right in noting the double meaning of the word 'nāga' and remarking, "Now, if we remember that the term 'nāga' has the double meaning of the serpent-demon and the elephant, we may safely assume that the second story has developed from the first, the word 'nāga', having been taken in its another sense".

Now here is a point. The word 'nāga' would give rise to a variant version of the same story, by virtue of its having another meaning. On the same analogy, it will not be hazardous to remark, that the 'Two nāgas' in the version of the *Sup. Ad.* could be primarily serpents — both of them. When this is remembered it is easy to understand how Garuḍa comes in the picture. The whole of the 'Grāha-nāga' episode turns out to be the episode of the antagonism between the nāgas and Garuḍa, only changing its form with the misunderstanding of the exact and original meaning of the word 'nāga'. The words *hastin* and *karin* need not baffle us. Even these words have double meaning — *hasta* and *kara* meaning both 'hand' and 'trunk'. We have seen that the Devagarha sculpture depicts the 'Grāha' in the 'Gajendra-Mokṣa' episode as a seven-hooded cobra. Likewise we meet with sculptures where the serpents (nāgas) are depicted with uneven hoods. Sometimes they are three, five, or seven. The head-wear of human figures depicted as nāgas are also seen to have three, five or seven hoods in it.[121] Now if we look to the meaning of the word *hastin* or *karin* we can render it also as '*having the hand*'. Now the hand has five fingers, which can very well give the idea of the five hoods of a serpent. Vogel notes this point and supports it by referring to a simile in the epic where the five hoods of a nāga are likened to the human arm ending with the palm having five fingers.[122] Of the 'two nāgas', one — the 'Grāha' — is the nāga with seven hoods as we have noted above. He quarrels with the '*Hastin*'. Might it be too bold a step to suggest here that, the '*Hastin*' could, most probably, be no other than a nāga having five-hoods, resembling the palm? We have already seen that both of them are nāgas (serpents) and it suits well in this context of the quarrelling nāgas to suppose that they represent two sects of nāgas clashing with one another — the one having the 'seven-hooded' emblem and the other the 'five-hooded'.

**Śuddha-Padmau**

The next point is that both these are associated with the word 'padma' (if we take the word '*śuddha-padmau*' to be a *Bāhuvrīhi* compound). At least one of them is so associated (cf. *mahānāgo ghoṣavān nāma Padmī*). In this connection we refer to a passage in the *Rāja Tar.*[123] In it we read of two nāgas, who, due to fear of Garuḍa, take refuge in a lake. Their names are given as 'Śaṅkha' and 'Padma', which remind us of 'Śuddha' and 'Padma' in the *Sup. Ad.* The lake in which these two took refuge, says Vogel, is mentioned in ancient chronicles by its Sanskrit name, *Mahā-padma-saras* or *Padma-nāga-saras.* Vogel remarks further that this '*Padma*' (nāga) appears to be identical with '*Mahā-Padma*', the tutelary deity of the great Vular lake which occupies a central position in the Kaśmīr Valley.[124] The *Mb* does not mention the name of the lake, nor does the *Sup. Ad.*, referring to it only as 'Great lake on the top of the mountain'. But, judging from what we have referred to, it seems quite probable that the lake mentioned in the *Mb* and the Purāṇas and earlier in the *Sup. Ad.* is the same Padma-nāga-saras, or Mahāpadma-Saras situated in the mountainous valley of Kaśmīr; and that the *Rāja Tar.* records the same ancient account which we have in the *Sup. Ad.* and the *Mb.* The account, it is quite probable, was current during ages and at various places, with a slight change in the form of it. The difference in the two accounts might be due to their being drawn from the different sources. Though the *Mb* does not speak of the nāga (elephant) as Padmī[125] we can see the idea reflected later in the 'Gajendra-Mokṣa' episode, where the elephant takes up a lotus in his trunk.[126] This motif of having a lotus in the mouth is quite common, again, with the nāgas (also *makaras*). The nāga sculptures mentioned by Vogel and the *makara* by Lindsay invariably show a lotus hanging from the mouth of the water-creatures. Vogel refers to the sculpture of a 'nāgarāja' whose feet are represented as placed upon a rock in front of which is a *lake full of lotuses*[127] which, again, reminds us of the 'māhānāga' — Padma by name — the tutelary deity of the *Padma-nāga-saras* or *Mahāpadma saras*. It is clear that the 'Two nāgas' seem really to be serpents, and with the meaning of 'Grāha' applied to one and 'Elephant'[128] to the other, these two came to be different creatures; and a separate tale — the *Gajendra mokṣa* — was coined about them, with the already forged tale of a Crocodile (grāha) and the Elephant (nāga);[129] but the undercurrent always betrayed the origin of these tales inasmuch as both these creatures, however changed they may be, are always of the same species — the brothers — the motif of reincarnation coming to their help!

It is difficult to obtain direct proof to see how 'Kūrma' or the 'Kacchapa' could come in the place of the 'Grāha' or the 'Nāga'. The 'Kacchapa' or the 'Kūrma' is not mentioned in the *Sup. Ad.* But the two epics and the Purāṇas have the 'Kacchapa' or 'Kūrma'.[130] Now, the 'nāga elephant' is the common factor in all these episodes; the 'Grāha-Kūrma' varies. But when the two creatures and the tale of their previous birth are the same, it could naturally and safely be concluded that in the 'Kūrma' we have the 'Grāha' of the 'Gajendra-Mokṣa' account (the old nāga) — in a transformed condition. Moreover, among the names of serpents the word 'Kaccha' (and also 'Hastin') are found.[131] According to the findings of Risley, the original people of the land of India believed in the tortoise and the serpent as their ancestors.[132] Rapson points out that several tribes came under the common name Nāga in ancient India.[133] This conclusion of Rapson appears to tally with Risley's account inasmuch as it helps put the tortoise and the serpent as possibly inter-related tribal divisions, the tortoise coming under the bigger group — the serpent or the nāga. Risley points out that even in the modern times there is an agriculturist caste in Orissa called 'Kūrmī'.[134] The tortoise and the serpent being accepted as ancestors, also suggests a possible competition for supremacy between these two sects. This competition might have been symbolically described on the lines of the then-current account of the two nāgas, as we have already noted, 'divided' between themselves.

Thus it appears to be the nearest approach to reality to see in the fighting twain — the tortoise and the elephant — two nāga-sects fighting for supremacy in the social organisation. Once this is understood, it is not difficult to see how Garuḍa comes in the picture as the terrible punisher who might even be thought of eating — i.e. symbolically having full control over them. The *sarpas* (nāgas) who mastered the poison-lore (*sarpa vidyā — Gāruḍā vidyā*) had, in all probability, the bird Garuḍa as their deity.[135] Hence it could easily be understood how Garuḍa could be a deity to be dreaded. This dread of the deity and the *mantras* get symbolized in representing Garuḍa as devouring the commons.[136] This dread and control of Garuḍa over the nāgas might be in the sphere of magic as we have propounded, and suggestive of a superior rank for the charmers to all the other sects.

**(B) Garuḍa and the Niṣādas**

The Niṣādas are suggested as food to Garuḍa by his mother. We shall briefly refer here to the *Mb* account, Vinatā says —

"In one side, in a part of the ocean, there is the abode of the Niṣādas, where reside thousands of Niṣādas. Devour them. But, never think of eating a brāhmaṇa; for, a brāhmaṇa is not to be killed by the creatures. He is like fire, like the poison and is the very weapon, if he is angry. He is the highest of all.' His mother tells him the characteristic of a brāhmaṇa, whereby he would know if he has swallowed a brāhmaṇa. The moment he is swallowed, and has reached the throat, the whole body of the swallower would get burning. Knowing it, the king of birds darted into the skies and reached the region where the Niṣādas lived. He expanded his mouth, and the Niṣādas got getting into it helplessly. Even the birds glided into his open mouth due to the force of his breath as if they were fluttering in a forest tormented by a speedy storm. Anon the hungry Garuḍa snapped his mouth close, grinding in it multitudes of Niṣādas, the fish-killers. But, lo! A brāhmaṇa, with his wife, unknowingly swallowed by him, reached the throat of Garuḍa, causing great burning as if he had swallowed a burning coal.

Garuḍa realised his mistake, and asked the brāhmaṇa to come out; but, the brāhmaṇa said, "This my wife, whom thou hast swallowed along with me, let she also be out with me." Garuḍa granted his wish, and the brāhmaṇa and his wife came out of his mouth. And they went away blessing Garuḍa. Garuḍa, then, went further to fulfil his task. (I. 28.1-21; 29.1-6).[137]

The analysis of the episode brings up the following points:—

(i) Garuḍa's food — the Niṣādas;

(ii) The Niṣādas are called '*Matsya-ghātinaḥ*' and live

near the sea;

(iii) The saving of the Brāhmaṇa devoured by Garuḍa.

We shall now proceed to see how the episode stands earlier in the *Sup. Ad.*[138] Garuḍa, not being satisfied with the 'nāgau' asks his mother to suggest another food, whereupon Vinatā suggests the Niṣādas.

"The kingdom of the Niṣādas stands divided variously in itself. Eat the same according to my desire (or, to fulfil my desire). These do not cause the Vedas to be recited and do not offer oblation of pure food. This do we hear, Garutman! But do never kill (devour) a brāhmaṇa that is abiding amongst the people, he — the God that is pardonful — O thou brave (son). He, indeed, is death; may it not be for thee" (*Sup. Ad.* VIII.16.2-3).

Further—

"Like a fish devouring the fish-hook, doth the eater of the brāhmaṇa get a swollen stomach; like a fire brand doth he get into the throat — he the brāhmaṇa! Do thou not kill him O Garutman!" (*Ib.* IX.17).

Then the fine-winged (Garuḍa), hungry as he was, went on eating the Niṣādas, as was ordered by his mother. Dragging them by drawing his wings together, he put in the mouth those who could be obtained. As the bird was eating the Niṣādas, pouncing upon them, he felt, as if, he was scorched by a terrible fire when a brāhmaṇa entered his throat. Being tortured (by the fire) without smoke and sparks, he, remembering the words of Śuṅgā (i.e. Vinatā — his mother), (thought) — Oh, the prowess of the twice-born that subsist merely by their birth! (He said to the brāhmaṇa) — "Get thou out of this (throat of mine); thou art not apt to be eaten by me. These (Niṣādas) are my food that I have obtained." (The brāhmaṇa said) — "I do not consider to be alive myself without my sons and wife. I, a brāhmaṇa with a Niṣādī wife and with sons, have entered thy mouth." Leaving the brāhmaṇa with his people (family) and abiding by the order (of his mother), the bird — the wanderer of the skies — obtained his goal after eating the others (Niṣādas). (*Ib.* X.18.1-6).

Analysing the above account we get the following new point:—

The Niṣādas are here spoken of as forming a kingdom. They do not recite the Vedas nor do they offer oblations. They are also divided amongst themselves.

The other points are the same as we have in the *Mb*. The praise of a brāhmaṇa is the same. We have no mention of the locality of the Niṣādas, while in the *Mb* they are said to be near the sea — or rather in one side, in the lap of the sea (*samudrakukṣau ekānte*).

The same episode occurs in the *Sk. P.* in at least two places. There the episode does not materially differ from the version of the *Mb*; but it will be interesting to note a few variations. The *Sk. P.* in one place has the Niṣādas, while in the other place Śabaras.[139] Where the word 'Niṣādas' is seen to occur, there are also other adjectives as 'the killers of the fish' and 'residing on the shore of the sea',[140] which coincide with the *Mb* version. It is interesting to note the cause for killing the Niṣādas. The *Mb* does not give any reason why they should be devoured by Garuḍa. But, as we have already noted, the *Sup. Ad.* does give a motive *viz.* they (the Niṣādas) do not perform sacrifices and are devoid of faith in Vedic learning, which makes them contrasting to those (i.e. Vaidikas) that learnt the Vedas and offered sacrificial oblations. This reminds us of an almost similar passage from the *Ṛgveda*, where it is the 'kīkaṭas' that are in question.[141] This is a point which marks a deviation from the general conception of Garuḍa seen by us thus far. It goes a step further than the traditional feud between the nāga sects and brings us face to face with a situation where the Vedic religion and the religion of the non-Vedic people is contrasted. Here Garuḍa is invoked to perform practically the same exploits as Indra is to perform as we see from the

*ṚV*. and here, in all probability, we have a strong indication of Garuḍa taking a pace forward from the original mythical environment and being accepted as a symbol of power and success by the Vedic people.[142] It appears that in this episode a factual account of the defeat of the Niṣādas by the Vedics is symbolically perpetuated. It should be noted here that there are distinct points which distinguish the Niṣāda-episode from the previous episode of the 'Tortoise and the Elephant' which falls in line with the general antagonism of the Nāgas and Garuḍa —

(i) The Niṣādas are specifically mentioned as a nation;
(ii) They are specified as a food of Garuḍa, *because* they do not follow the Vedic religion;
(iii) It is difficult to find the Niṣādas as traditionally antagonistic to Garuḍa;
(iv) The word 'Niṣāda' does not have any phase of meaning which means the nāga (serpent) in any way, unlike the words 'nāga' and 'Kūrma' which are associated with the serpents also, as we have already seen.

The *Sk. P.* adds a more didactic tinge to the episode. Vinatā says,

"There reside the multitudes of Niṣādas that kill (eat) the fish, by the shore of the sea. Do thou eat them — (O Garuḍa) — the cruel ones! Those cruel ones who sustain themselves with others' lives, are to be punished with effort. To immense good doth that punishment lead" (IV. 50.64-65).

The only point here is that the Niṣādas are said to be cruel and apt to be killed. Otherwise there is no deviation from the version of the *Mb.* There is no mention of any contrast with the Vedic religion. But, the *Pad. P.* gives this again as a reason for killing the Niṣādas.

"Many hundreds of thousands of Niṣādas — the most sinful ones — live on the shore of the ocean. Do thou eat them and be happy. They pollute the holy waters (places of holy water) — they, the crows at the holy places!" (*Pad. P.*V.

44.49-50).

Here it can be seen that the reason for killing or eating the Niṣādas is their destructive nature and troubling the followers of the Vedic faith. The *Pad. P.* goes on further to tell that the people eaten by Garuḍa were even Mlecchas, whom Garuḍa is advised by Kaśyapa to disgorge,[143] indicating that the bird ate them. The Kirātas, the Śabaras and the Niṣādas thus form a sort of a group whom the followers of the Vedic faith, probably, overran and subjugated, the distinct reason being that these were tribes not having the way of Vedic sacrifice. To this group later were added the Mlecchas and the Yavanas,[144] the symbolic success being always suggested by their being 'eaten' by Garuḍa.

It may be useful here to compare with this idea of the symbol of success, Garuḍa's exploit in subduing Bali, the king of the demons. Bali promises Vāmana the alms of the portion of his kingdom covered by the third step of the latter; but on the advice of his preceptor — Śukra — refrains from it. Vāmana then calls Garuḍa who admonishes the king of the Asuras saying, that if the latter went back on his words he would punish him, and instantly binds him with the Varuṇa-pāśas.[145] Bali is subdued and Vāmana is successful in getting his desire fulfilled. As a symbol of victoriousness Garuḍa is often represented as accompanying the king in battles in later India, the king being the incarnation of Viṣṇu.[146] Thus it is clear how Garuḍa, stepping out of the narrow limits of tribal social organism, came to be accepted even by the Vedic people as the symbol of victoriousness. This was done as early as the *Sup. Ad.* This type of symbolization is not altogether an isolated case. We meet with the same idea of symbolized success in the tale of Videgha Māthava, wherein Agni is such a symbol. There we have Agni, coming out of the mouth of Videgha Māthava and going on burning the grassy earth from the banks of the Sarasvatī, where Māthava then was, towards the East.[147]

In the version in the *Mb* and the Purāṇas the Niṣādas

are called 'Matsya-ghātinaḥ', i.e. the 'killers of the fish'. This probably means that these people were trading in fish. There are various views on the subject as to who really the Niṣādas were. Yāska derives it as 'one who has sin settled in him'.[148] Mahīdhara commenting on the *Vāj. Sam.* (*Vājasaneyi-Saṃhitā*) renders it as 'Bhil'. The ritual of the *Viśva-jit* sacrifice requires a temporary residence with the Niṣādas. Weber deduces from this that the Niṣādas were settled aborigines;[149] for, to be able to reside with them, as is required by the ritual, their close association with the Vedic Aryans, and accepting the influence of the latter, are necessary. The *Bṛhatsaṃhitā* of Varāhamīhira (XIV-10) refers to a 'kingdom' (*'rāṣṭra'*) of the Niṣādas (cf. the *Sup. Ad.*) in the south-east of Madhyadeśa. The *Manu Sm.* (X. 8) and the *Yājña Sm.*[150] include the 'Niṣāda' among the sons born of a Śudra girl and a brāhmaṇa; but the commentaries differ in their explanation of Niṣāda from the Niṣāda in our discussion (in this legend) as they state that the latter is a *pratilomaja*, maintaining himself by killing the fish.[151] Macdonell and Keith opine that the term 'Niṣāda' refers generally to all the non-Aryan tribes and *no particular* tribe as such.[152] According to the *Mb* (III.10.538), they were living beyond the place of the disappearance of the Sarasvatī. Mukherji says that they, along with the Śabaras, were the inhabitants of the South.[153] One thing seems to be pretty clear; the 'Niṣādas' were outside the pale of the Vedic Aryan civilization when it was restricted to the Madhyadeśa. Before the time of the *Kau. Br.* they lay outside the Vedic-Aryan territory proper, and later were assimilated into the Vedic fold. The ritual of the *Viśvajit* sacrifice, probably, is to commemorate this assimilation and occupation of it by the Vedic people. Some of the Vedic Aryans might already have settled there and might also have had matrimonial relations with their women. It is this fact that appears to be suggested by the brāhmaṇa in our legend living among the Niṣādas and having children from a Niṣādī. Garuḍa's attack on the

Niṣādas is, hence, a symbolic description of the Vedic Aryan advance and the destruction of the Niṣādas, except of those who were born of the Vedic Aryans. This took place before the period of the *Kau. Br.* (may be about 2000-1000 BC). From the situation of the 'Niṣāda-rāṣṭra' to the south-east of Madhyadeśa, and from their being *'Matsya-ghātinaḥ'*, it appears that these people were residing on the south-east coast of India, and had small states that were divided amongst themselves.

## The Brāhmaṇa Left Out

The next part of the Niṣāda episode is that of the brāhmaṇa. If we analyse this part of the episode we get the following points: —

(i) The brāhmaṇa lived among the Niṣādas and saved at least some of the Niṣādas;

(ii) The dread of the brāhmaṇas in general.

We have seen already that the brāhmaṇa, together with his wife and children, was allowed to go unhurt by Garuḍa. We have referred to the *Sup. Ad.*, *Mb.*, and the *Sk. P.* The *Padma P.*[154] is more elaborate on this point and deviates a bit from the other texts. Here we have Garuḍa again going to Kaśyapa and informing him of his inability to swallow the brāhmaṇa completely. Kaśyapa knows the cause of the trouble of Garuḍa, and asks him to come out, whereupon the brāhmaṇa tells that he could not come out as the people being devoured were various relations of his — fathers-in-law, brothers-in-law and his close friends.[155]

Closely resembling this part of the episode of the Niṣādas, there is another tale and quite a famous one too! It is that of the sacrifice of Jīmūtavāhana. We shall briefly refer to it. The tale occurs in the *Bṛhatkathā-mañjarī* (IX) and also in the *Kathāsaritsāgara* (XC). It forms the main plot of the *Nāgānanda* — the drama of Harṣa.

According to the tale, once Jīmūtavāhana, wandering

with Mitrāvasu, his brother-in-law, upon the Malaya mountain, comes to the shore of the sea. Seeing there heaps of bones, he says to Mitrāvasu — "Of what animals are these heaps of bones?" Mitrāvasu tells him the whole account in short, giving the account of the wager between Vinatā and Kadrū, and the deceitful victory of Kadrū over her co-wife. Because of that enmity, Garuḍa, even after releasing his mother from the fetters of slavery, starts eating the serpents (nāgas) — the progeny of Kadrū. Every day he enters Pātāla (the abode of the serpents) and eats the nāgas one by one. Some of the nāgas are themselves afraid and thus die. Seeing the imminent destruction of the whole race of the nāgas, Vāsukī lays down a condition (*samayam vyadhāt*) before Tārkṣya (Garuḍa). According to the condition Vāsukī is to send to Garuḍa every day a nāga to the shore of the southern sea; and Garuḍa is not to enter Pātāla. From that day onwards Garuḍa begins eating one nāga daily (*dine dine*) sent to him according to the agreement.[156] Jīmūtavāhana is moved and decides to save the life of at least one nāga by giving his own life. In the meanwhile he hears the weeping of an old woman; and, going there, learns that on that day the woman's son — the nāga Śaṅkhacūḍa — is scheduled to be eaten by Garuḍa. Jīmūtavāhana offers himself in place of the unfortunate nāga, but the nāga Śaṅkhacūḍa does not agree. Saṅkhacūḍa, deciding to go to Gokarṇa before being devoured by Garuḍa, leaves the place. Jīmūtavāhana stays there thinking it would be good if Garuḍa arrived in the meantime; and knowing that it was the time for Garuḍa to arrive, mounts the death-slab. Garuḍa arrives in the meantime and, pouncing on Jīmūtavāhana, carries him to the top of the Malaya mountain to eat. Now, when Śaṅkhacūḍa comes back, he is surprised to see the slab smeared with blood. Following the line of blood on the ground, he arrives at the place where Garuḍa is eating Jīmūtavāhana. Now, to the utter horror of Garuḍa, who is already confused on seeing a different prey,[157] Śaṅkhacūḍa tells him that the one the latter is eating is not a nāga. Ultimately Garuḍa leaves Jīmūtavāhana who is restored to his original form. He also promises not to kill the nāgas thenceforth, according to the request of Jīmūtavāhana; and accepts also to revive to life all those nāgas that were killed by him.[158]

The similarity between the *Mb* account of the Niṣāda-brāhmaṇa and this tale can easily be marked. In both we have the whole community saved by one man. The idea of the whole community being saved is not so much clear in the *Mb*; but we have the germ there of this idea, which gets further developed in the account of the *Pad. P.* where not only the wife and children but also the father-in-law and the friends of the brāhmaṇa are saved. The idea of self-sacrifice is not so much bright in the accounts of the Niṣāda-brāhmaṇa, as we see in the tale of Jīmūtavāhana. But, even in the brāhmaṇa who forsakes his life for his kin we have the seeds of the sacrifice of Jīmūtavāhana that has a higher level, in that he purposefully tries to give up his life for others. The only difference is that in the previous accounts we have the brāhmaṇa saving the Niṣādas and, in this one, the nāgas are saved by a Vidyādhara.[159] The tale of Jīmūtavāhana does not deviate from the traditional Nāga-Garuḍa feud; while in the Niṣāda-brāhmaṇa account the tale appears to undergo a change but for Garuḍa and for the motif of saving others' life by self-sacrifice. Oldham refers to I-tsing the Chinese pilgrim, according to whom the great Rājā Śīlāditya got this episode often enacted, himself playing the part of Jīmūtavāhana; but at these times Śilāditya used to transform himself into a 'nāga' (and not a 'Vidyādhara'). Oldham comments further that Jīmūtavāhana was considered to be a nāga at the time of Śīlāditya.[160] The same tale is given in the *'vetāla pañcaviṃ-śatiḥ'*.[161] There is practically no difference but for the fact that Jīmūtavāhana is here asked by Garuḍa if he was a brāhmaṇa. We shall quote the relevant passage —

Speaks Garuḍa —

"Who is this famous one, devoured by me — sinful as I am? Others leave their vital breath the moment they see me. This one is complacent even when being eaten. Moreover, he wears a sacred thread. O Great one, are you a brāhmaṇa?"[162]

The passage has a minute resemblance with the episode in the *Mb*, in the point of the *Yajñopavītadhārī vipra*; but the rest of the account is the same. Putting these various points together we come to understand that —

(i) Jīmūtavāhana is described sometimes as a Nāga,[163] and sometimes as a Vidyādhara with the 'aṁśa' of Bodhisattva;[164]

(ii) The Niṣāda-brāhmaṇa episode and the Jīmūtavāhana episode are similar in motif but the latter is the same traditional tale of the Garuḍa-nāga feud;

(iii) The Jīmūtavāhana tale is more current than the brāhmaṇa episode.

It seems probable that both these tales are taken from a common popular tale describing the exploit of a nāga-hero who redeemed his fellowmen from the adverse power of Garuḍa. In the age of Brahmaṇic influence it was used for the explicit purpose of glorifying brāhmaṇahood, as being higher in power and social status. The same tale was used to suit the Buddhistic setting to prove the superiority of the Buddha, by making the hero an 'aṁśa' of the Buddha. In both these versions the principle of reconciliation can easily be marked; and this falls in line with the other instances of reconciliation where the Buddha or Viṣṇu plays an important role. Thus, the Brāhmaṇa-Garuḍa-Niṣāda episode also reverts to the same Nāga-Garuḍa feud with the ultimate reconciliation. In the original tale the nāga-hero who brought about reconciliation, might, probably, be one who was himself a follower of Garuḍa, and superior to the rest of the nāgas and possessed the knowledge of magic (or the Gāruḍa-vidyā), thus symbolically winning Garuḍa — the deity.

The Brāhmaṇa-episode, otherwise, seems to be just a patchwork on the legend. Garuḍā's march to fetch nectar suddenly gets checked by his hunger which is not satisfied by the Tortoise and the Elephant. Hence he is asked to go to eat the Niṣādas; but, even then, the saving of the brāhmaṇa and his Niṣāda-family does not have any direct connection with the main exploit of Garuḍa. The bearing of the whole passage seems to be the praise of the brāhmaṇas, which seems to be the real purpose of the episode; and for it the popular tale was used on the background of the victory over the Niṣādas.

# 4
# THE VEDIC PROTO-TYPE

## (A) Garuḍa and the Bringing of Nectar

The bringing of nectar forms the main and a very important exploit of Garuḍa. Garuḍa brings nectar as a condition for his mother's freedom from the slavery of her co-wife.[165] We shall do well, here, to recapitulate the main points in the episode.

1. There is also another reason given for the seizure of nectar. *viz.*, the insult of the thumbkins-Vālakhilyas by Indra.[166]
2. When Garuḍa went to fetch nectar (Soma) and killed the gods, he saw fire around the place (*sarvato' gnim' apaśyat*). It appeared to envelop the whole firmament. He extinguished the fire with the water of the rivers that he drew by his mouth transformed to 8,100 fold *(navatyā navatir mukhānām)*.
3. He saw a sharp-edged iron disc (*cakram kṣuraparyantam*) revolving constantly around nectar. It would cut to pieces anyone trying to enter.[168]
4. There were two serpents with poison-in-eyes, below the disc. Garuḍa vanquished them by filling their eyes with dust and took nectar off.[169]
5. He did not drink nectar himself. Being glad with this selflessness of his, Nārāyaṇa, who met him in the sky, gave him two boons. Garuḍa also asked Viṣṇu to ask for a boon, and the latter asked him to be his vehicle.
6. When attacked by Indra with his Vajra, Garuḍa dropped a feather for honouring the sage (Dadhīci) from whose bones the Vajra of Indra was created. Seeing that beautiful feather of his, all creatures gave him the name

'Suparṇa'.[171]

7. Garuḍa was accepted to be his superior by Indra and they became friends. Garuḍa accepted the request of Indra to return nectar (Soma) to the gods; and Indra took it away when Garuḍa had shown it to the nāgas and set his mother free.[172]
8. (Nectar was caused to be brought by the Sarpas by deceit) and it was lost to them by counter-deceit.[173]

All these points can be grouped into the following main topics :—

(i) The bringing of nectar by Garuḍa and the return of it;
(ii) The rivalry between Garuḍa and Indra;
(iii) Garuḍa's association with Viṣṇu.

We shall deal with these one by one.

We have seen that Garuḍa is called Suparṇa[174] a number of times. In dealing with the point of the bringing of nectar — (which is also called *Soma*) — by Garuḍa, we have to go back to the Vedic texts wherein the Somāharaṇa by Suparṇa is referred to. We shall gradually examine these passages and try to see, how the *Mb* version stands in comparison with them.

## ṚgVeda: Capture of Soma

Suparṇa as the bringer of *Soma*, can be seen from the *ṚV*. In ṚV (IV-26) Vāmadeva (or Indra)[175] is said to take the form of *śyena* and bring *Soma* for Manu. The *Śyena* (hawk) is called *suparṇa*.

In the subsequent passages also Śyena is referred to as *Suparṇa*, which shows that *suparṇa* is an epithet of Śyena. (*ṚV*. IV.26.5-7). It is said, "When Śyena flying downward did utter a cry, when too (the Soma-guards) tried to snatch (from the Śyena) the brilliant (drink), rushing with mind's speed did the archer Kṛśānu fix the bow string (on the bow.)"

Śyena — the straight-darting one — snatched (*Soma*) that was in the high abode (heaven) of Indra as did (Aśvinau)

Bhujyu. At that time the feather of the bird in the middle (of the wing) fell down, when charged in the fight" (*ṚV*. IV.27.3, 4).

*ṚV*. (I.93.6) has Śyeṇa churning Soma from the mountain; (V.49.7) that Śyeṇa went forth to fetch Soma.[176]

From the above two points are clear.

(i) Śyena, who is called, 'Śuparṇa', brought Soma;

(ii) Kṛśānu, the archer, shot an arrow which clipped a feather from Śyena's wing.

**Taittirīya Saṃhitā**

*Taittirīya Sam.* VI.1.6.1ff.

"Kadrū and Suparṇī, indeed competed as to their form.[177] That Kadrū defeated Suparṇī. She said, "In the third heaven is Soma; fetch it. Therewith do thou set thyself free." This (earth), indeed, is, Kadrū, that (sky) Suparṇī. The metres are *sauparṇeyās*. She (Suparṇī) said (to her children), "For it (Soma) indeed, do the parents hold (give birth to) the sons. In the third heaven doth *Soma* lie. Fetch it; therewith do thou set thyself free, thus said Kadrū to me". The Metre Jagatī flew forth with fourteen letters. Without gain she returned; two of her letters were lost in exchange. She came back with the sacrificial animals and consecration. Hence is Jagatī, of all the metres, the most endowed with (bestows on the sacrificer) cattle. Hence, consecration falls to the one who has beasts for sacrifice. The metre Triṣṭubh flew forth with thirteen letters. Even she returned without gain. Two of her letters were lost (in exchange). She came back with the sacrificial gifts and with penance. Hence, indeed, in the world of Triṣṭubh, during the *mādhyandina savana* — (Mid-day pressing) the sacrificial gifts may go. This indeed is the penance (i.e. the gifts) of one who gives, so they say. Gāyatrī flew forth with four letters. She fetched *Soma* and also the four letters (left by the two previous metres). She became endowed with eight letters. The Brahmavādins say, "wherefore did Gāyatrī, being the youngest of the metres, circumambulate the head of Sacrifice? She did bring that Soma; hence she went round the head of sacrifice. Hence is she the most brilliant of all". She took two pressings in her feet and one in the beak[177a] which she carried (held) in the mouth that did she milk. Thence the two pressings of *Soma* — the morning-pressing and the mid-day-pressing. . . Viśvāvasu, the Gandharva, stole Soma that was being brought."[178]

From the Ṛgvedic passage, the point that is common with the bringing of nectar by Garuḍa is that Kṛśānu shot at the bird which caused the feather of the bird to fall down.

From the passage in the *Tait. Sam.*, just quoted, we get the following points in addition to the one noted in the *ṚV.*

(i) Kadrū and Suparṇī had a competition as regards their form, and Suparṇī was defeated;
(ii) Identification of Kadrū with the Earth, Suparṇī with the sky and of the metres with Sauparṇeyāḥ (Suparṇī's issues);
(iii) *Soma* was in the third heaven.
(iv) *Soma* was taken away from Gāyatrī (Sauparṇeyā) by Viśvāvasu, the Gandharva;
(v) Two metres were defeated in the attempt while Gāyatrī was successful; and
(vi) Gāyatrī is 'Sauparṇeyā';

In comparison with the *Mb.* we see that the idea of Garuḍa fetching Soma and it being taken back is faintly present here. While here it is the Gandharva Viśvāvasu that takes it back and Kṛśānu that renders the blow, in the *Mb.* both these are the same person i.e., Indra. Indra deals the blow; but that does not cause the feather to fall off, the actual cause being the desire of Garuḍa to respect the sage from whose bones the bolt was made. Though it is so, it could well be taken as being caused to fall by Indra, as it is he who gives the impulse for it and is indirectly the cause. It is Indra, again who takes nectar back.

One important variation from the *ṚV.* in the above passage can be seen in the fact that here we do not have Śyena that is being identified with Gāyatrī (or the metres in general). It is '*Sauparṇeyāḥ*'. This sounds similar to *Suparṇa*, the Ṛgvedic epithet that was given to Śyena. Here it has become a regular appellation, but definitely formed from the word Suparṇī.[178] We do not have the word 'Suparṇa' here. Unlike the *Mb* we have no trace here of the fact that Kadrū gave birth to nāgas. There is no mention of the birth of Suparṇa.

**Kāṭhāka Sam. XXIII.10**

"Kadrū and Suparnī argued as regards their form. That Kadrū defeated Suparṇī. This (earth) is Kadrū; heaven, Suparṇī."

The rest of the account is the same as we have seen in the *Tait. Saṃ*. One thing can be noted here. The metres are called '*Sauparṇāni*' — not yet '*Suparṇa*'. The word looks like '*Sauparṇeyāḥ*' but the shade of meaning is obviously changed. There is a definite word '*dyauḥ*' (sky; heaven) in place of simply '*asau*' (she) as we have in the *Tait. Sam.* In another place the *Kāṭh. Sam.* identifies Gāyatrī with Śyena.

"Gāyatrī, indeed, fetched *Soma* being (changing into) Śyena. The guardian of Soma, following him, cut his (i.e. of Śyena) nail" (*Kāṭh. Sam.* XXXIV.3).

**Aitareya Br. III.25.**
**Tāṇḍyamahā-Br. VIII.4**

"Soma, the king, indeed was in the other world. Upon him did the gods and the sages meditate (as to) — 'How might this king *Soma* come to us?' They said to the metres, 'Do bring this king *Soma* to us.' Saying, 'be it so', they (the metres), transforming themselves into '*Suparṇas*', flew up. As they flew up becoming Suparṇas, hence it is said to be the

*'Sauparṇam Ākhyānam'.*"

The following points are worth noting here :—

(i) It is the gods who asked the metres to fetch Soma;
(ii) The metres are not 'Sauparṇāni' or 'Sauparṇeyāḥ', but '*Suparṇas*' (in plural);
(iii) There is no mention of one '*Suparṇa*' going to bring Soma;
(iv) The '*Suparṇākhyāna*' is named so because the metres changed themselves to 'Suparṇas'
(v) There is no mention of the wager between Kadrū and Suparṇī,

The fact that 'Sauparṇākhyāna' is named so because the metres became 'Suparṇas' indicates the existence of a '*Suparṇa*-tale' in which the chief character to bring Soma was 'Suparṇa'. This Suparṇa, again, as we have already seen, was Śyena who had the epithet 'Suparṇa'. It is with this principal character Śyena, that the metres are constantly identified.

### Śatapatha Br., III.2.4.1. ff.

"Soma was, indeed, in the heaven, and here the gods. Those gods desired — may Soma come unto us. With him, come to us, shall we sacrifice. They created these two illusions — Suparṇī and Kadrū. That is described in the Brāhmaṇa of the Dhiṣṇyas, the '*Sauparṇī-Kādravam*' as it was."

1. This passage has the same note as in the *Ait. Br.*, i.e., it is the gods who desired Soma; but here we have one more variation; and an important one. *The gods created the twain* Suparṇī and Kadrū, which are said to be illusions.
2. The name 'Sauparṇī-Kādravam' seems to be a variant of 'Sauparṇam Ākhyānam' mentioned in the *Ai. Br.*

From closely observing the passages quoted above we can jot down a connected line of points:—

(i) *Soma* was in the heaven and was brought by Gāyatrī who is identified with the bird Śyena; the metres as a whole are called variously, viz. 'Suparṇāni', 'Sauparṇeyāḥ';

(ii) The motives for bringing Soma vary — (a) The Gods and the sages wanted *Soma* for sacrificial purposes according to one view; and (b) the competition between Kadrū and Vinatā according to the other;

(iii) These differing views are joined up, as it were, in the version of the ŚB. by suggesting that the gods themselves created Kadrū and Suparṇī as two illusions;

(iv) Suparṇī is identified with Vāk (Speech, *Mait. Sam.* III.7.3) and also with the sky, while Kadrū is identified with the earth;

(v) *Soma* is brought and retaken.

The gods and the sages wanting Soma for sacrificial purposes can be understood without much difficulty, Soma — the drink of Indra — being an important constituent of the sacrifice. The competition between Kadrū and Suparṇī as to the beauty of form leading to the bringing of Soma seems to be a thread quite different from the original idea and seems to have got mixed with it from some other source. This hypothesis gains support from the fact that, in certain other texts (as we have quoted above), there seems to be a regular effort to get these two competing parties mixed into the idea of bringing Soma by saying that they were created by the gods themselves. It is quite clear that the original idea was the bringing of Soma for sacrificial purposes; and then the account of the competing Kadrū and Suparṇī was attached to the original account. Most probably the account of the competition is borrowed from another popular tale which flourished independently and these two were joined up together to give colourful appearance to the simple Ṛgvedic idea of Somāharaṇa by Śyena.[179] But more of it later.

The Ṛgvedic Śyena is completely identified with Gāyatrī in the Brāhmaṇas, as we have just noted. The Brāhmaṇa-stress on the metres, headed by Gāyatrī can well be understood in the light of the sacrificial atmosphere of the Br. s., and the importance of the *mantras* therein. Once the importance of the *mantras* is taken for granted, the next natural step would be to join them with something already reckoned as lofty; and this would be done by the process of identification. It is usual to find in the Br. s. the metres to be the bringers of immortality, or the way to get free from the fetters of death. Thus, the Gop. Br. has it that, Indra cleft fear of death with the help of the metres.[180] The Mait. Sam. has that the metres protected the gods from the fear of death.[181] The gods are said to go to heaven by means of the metres.[182] These metres are themselves said to be the heaven.[183] The metres saved Agni and Indra from sin — the death! They '*covered*' (*acchādayan*) them (protecting) against death, hence they are called '*Chandāṁsī*'. These again cover (shelter) from death him who thus knows.[184] It should be clear from these passages that the metres were of great importance in the sacrifice conferring immortality (i.e., lack of death) and even heaven upon the sacrificer. Passages, again, are not wanting, to point out that Gāyatrī — the best of the metres — carried the sacrifice itself from heaven. *Soma*, necessary for the sacrifice could easily come to be thought of as carried by Gāyatrī — the best of metres. This importance of Gāyatrī in bringing the heavenly world and freedom from death to the sacrificer and the gods could naturally help the identification of Gāyatrī and Suparṇa (Śyena) who was the bringer of Soma — the immortal juice. Gāyatrī easily could be supposed to bring the immortal juice from heaven (Cf. 'third heaven') when she herself was thought as capable of leading the sacrificer to heaven. Thus, we see Gāyatrī carrying *Soma* and also the sacrifice. A few examples would go well to clarify the point.

### Mait. Sam. III.7.8

A new point is seen here — the Sacrifice.

'Soma, indeed, was there (in heaven). The gods sent Gāyatrī (saying), "Bring that Soma". She saw the sacrifice fully spread. She thought — 'If I enter the sacrifice I shall enter my ownself.' Here it could be seen that Gāyatrī is completely identified with the Sacrifice on the one hand; and on the other, performs the exploit of Suparṇa in bringing Soma.[185] We have already noted from the passages quoted how Gāyatrī is said to carry the two pressings.[186]

Thus from the idea of the sacrificial importance of the metres and Gāyatrī, their importance in controlling the whole sacrifice and leading the sacrificer to heaven, making him free from the fetters of death,[187] to the identification of Gāyatrī with Śyena-Suparṇa was a steady progress. The bringing of Soma by Suparṇa and the freedom from death given by the metres was an idea that helped a lot in this identification; and, as we have seen that the gods got themselves freed from death by the help of metres, so we have also this idea of getting free from death creeping in the tale of Suparṇī and Kadrū in at least one instance.

### Ś.B. according to the Kāṇva Recension, V.6.2

That Kadrū said to Suparṇī, "I have defeated you. *Soma* is in heaven. Fetch it for the gods. Thereby free yourself from Death".[188]

In the same passage we have, "Suparṇī gave it to the gods. Thereby she freed herself from death. Hence it is said, as soon as he is born man gets birth for death; when he sacrifices, he releases himself from death."

Here we have the identification of the idea of bringing Soma and being free from death — the first originally associated with Suparṇa Śyena, the latter with Gāyatrī and the metres.[189]

In all these cases it is Gāyatrī that is being identified

with Śyena-Suparṇa and it is not that Suparṇa himself takes the form of Gāyatrī. We have already seen passages to the effect that it is Gāyatrī who, becoming Śyena, carried Soma. It is the metres that are called variously 'Sauparṇāḥ', 'Sauparṇāni', etc., showing their closeness with Suparṇa.

It is thus clear that Gāyatrī (and metres) and Suparṇa are *different* and are being identified, though further on we meet with such comments where the word 'Suparṇa' is often rendered as '*Pakṣi-rūpā Gāyatrī*'[190] making, as it were, the circle complete! The same reversed identification can be seen when in the *Sup. Ad.* we have *Garuḍa-Suparṇa* saying,

"We indeed, are the metres, O Vinatā-Suparṇī! we, who support the spread up sacrifice."[191]

"**I am**, O Vinatā-Suparṇī!, *these very metres*! —the four best ones — that carry the spread sacrifice. Me *did the gods send* to Soma (to fetch it)."[192]

It could be noted how in the Br. s. Gāyatrī was sent by the gods to fetch Soma, while here it is Suparṇa who is sent by the gods and is called metres—Gāyatrī included. Thus the course of identification runs to be: — Suparṇa (Śyena) — superimposed on Gāyatrī and Gāyatrī again superimposed on Suparṇa. Here the popular legend serves ritual need.

We are now to see where *Garuḍa* comes in the picture. The *Sup. Ad.*, the *Mb* and the Purāṇas describe the bringing of nectar (Amṛta or Soma) as one of the exploits of Garuḍa. We have also seen that Garuḍa is called Suparṇa. Hence it is easy to understand how the exploit of Suparṇa — that of bringing Soma—was transferred to Garuḍa. Whether Garuḍa and Suparṇa of the Vedic literature were one and the same shall be seen later; but it is sufficient here to say that they being constantly referred to as one and the same being, the bringing of nectar by a bird is deeply rooted in the Vedic (including the Brahmanic) literature — may he be Suparṇa or, later, Garuḍa.

We have noticed that in the Somāharaṇa episode, as depicted in the Brāhmaṇas, two motives for bringing Soma are found which got fused into one. The *Sup. Ad.* also has the same indication when Garuḍa says to his mother that he was sent by the gods to bring nectar. In the *Mb*, however, only one motive, i.e. of the competition, defeat and release of Vinatā is given.

Thus far we have noted that the capture and the retaking of Soma that we have in the *Mb* are pretty well found in the *ṚV.* and the *Br.s.* But, therein the element of Indra-Garuḍa competition is not to be yet found. We now turn to certain other details that have their part in the Somāharaṇa account.

### (C) The Cutting of the Wing of Garuḍa

We have seen that the Ṛgveda mentions Kṛśānu as shooting an arrow and cutting the feather (*Parṇa*) of Śyena (*cf. ṚV.* IV.27.3, 4). The *Mait. Sam.* also has the feather cut; but here Gāyatrī is identified with Śyena.[193] The *Ś.B.* has also a feather of Gāyatrī cut; but we have an additional point there, that it was cut by a footless archer.[194] The *Ai. Br.* (III.25) has the same thing; and it mentions the name of the archer as Kṛśānu. The *Kāṭhaka Sam.* as we have noted already, has the nail cut.

### (D) The Fire around Soma and the Poisonous Serpents

The *Mb* speaks of there being fire all around the place where Soma (*amṛta*) was kept. This point we do not get in the account of the Somāharaṇa in the Brāhmaṇas; but probably the fire in the *Mb* and before that in the *Sup. Ad.* has been suggested by such passages wherein we have Gāyatrī seeing the Sacrifice (*'vitatam yajñam'*) — indicating the sacrificial fire. Kṛśānu (*ṚV.* IV.27.3) itself means 'fire'. It is in the *Jai. Br.*[195] that we get more points similar to our present legend —

"*Soma* was in the heaven of Indra. The fire-gandharvas guarded it. They, for sure, were the serpents (*āsīviṣāḥ*). It was in the golden covers, constantly falling on each other".[195]

This passage gives definite new points which are: —

(i) Soma was in the heaven of Indra;

(ii) It was guarded by fires. These fires were called Dhiṣṇyas.[196] They themselves were the gandharvas;

(iii) These (gandharvas) themselves were the poisonous serpents;

(iv) *Soma* was between two golden covers (two halves) (*kuśis*) which were constantly closing up with each other.[197]

In this passage we have an indication of the future tussle between Indra and Garuḍa. The clear mention of Indra in the possession of *Soma* in the passage is a step further than the other ones (except *ṚV*, IV.27.4) where we have simply that Soma was high up in the third heaven. The presence of fire also is to be marked here. While in the *Mb* the two serpents and the guards of *Soma* are different, here both these are combined into one. In the *Mb* the guards of Soma are the gods themselves. The Gandharvas as the guards of *Soma* are mentioned in the *Mait. Sam.* (III.7.3) and also in the *Ś.Br.* (*Mādh.* III.2.4.9); and in Viśvāvasu — the gandharva — who takes back Soma from Gāyatrī we can have the glimpse of the gandharvas as the guardians of Soma; but the *Jai. Br.* takes a clear step ahead in suggesting the presence of fire and the serpents around Soma, thus coming closer to the later *Mb* account. The fire and the gandharvas could both have been suggested from the word kṛsānu — (*ṚV*. IV.27.3).[198] But it should be noted that even in the *Jai. Br.* we find no trace to the fight between the two poisonous serpents and Gāyatrī, the bringer of Soma, nor do we have any actual fight between Indra and Gāyatrī (as we have in the *Mb* between Indra and Garuḍa!), though there is a suggestion of the rivalry between Gāyatrī and Indra inasmuch as Gāyatrī is sent to heaven from where she has to seize *Soma*, which is in the custody of Indra.

A word about the *disc-machine* that Garuḍa breaks before finally bringing the pitcher of Amṛta. Though we do not get the exact disc in the Brahmanic passages, it is not at all an idea foreign to the Vedic literature. We have referred already to the two half covers in which Soma was kept; and how the two (sharp and) golden halves were constantly joining up and opening again. These two halves joining and being apart could be compared with the one full disc constantly rotating before the entrance to *amṛta*. The *Jai. Br.* speaks only of the two cups; but does not specifically say that they were sharp-edged. This attribute is supplied by the *Ś.B.* For a better comparison we shall put side by side these passages and also the one from the *Mb*.

*Jai. Br.* (I.287), *sa hiraṇmayoḥ kuśyor āsa*;

*Ś.Br.* (III.6.2.8), *sa . . . āsa, te ha sma kṣurapavī* (sharp-edged); *Mb.* I.33.2, *cakram kṣuraparyantam . . . paribhramantam aniśam*.

The *Jai. Br.* passage, it can be seen, has the idea faintly, while the *Ś.B.* goes a step further and comes nearer the *Mb* in stating that these '*Kuśis*' were '*Kṣurapavī*'. The close similarity in the idea of speed can be marked from the words *pari-bhramantam (Mb)* and '*abhisampatataḥ*' (*Jai. Br.* and *Ś.B.*).

The passages from the *Jai. Br.* and the *Ś.B.* just quoted mark a point which seems altogether different from the other passages from the *Br. s.* On comparing both these passages, we can have the idea that *Soma* was kept under a thorough guard. The old guard Kṛśānu or the gandharva Viśvāvasu was not sufficient to protect Soma; and it was thought necessary to have a mechanical device and also the serpents to guard it. The more important for us of these two, viz. the poisonous snakes and the *Kuśis*, are the snakes. The trend of the passage is to identify the poisonous snakes with the gandharvas. The sentence 'They, indeed are the fire-altars (Dhiṣṇyāḥ) and 'they (Dhiṣṇyāḥ) verily are the poisonous snakes' indicates the following:—

(i) That the gandharvas and the snakes were the guardians of Soma is an original idea; and

(ii) that these two are interpreted in the ritual context as the fire-altars.

Now the gandharvas, as we have seen, could be inferred as the guards of Soma from references to the gandharva Viśvāvasu who steals Soma back. Kṛśānu — spoken later as gandharva — also is known from the *ṚV*. as the shooter of an arrow; but nowhere did we notice serpents[199] as the guards of Soma, except at *Jai. Br.*, in the Vedic passages.

Now here is a point. We have seen how Śyena-Suparṇa is identified with Gāyatrī, the most important of the metres. Suparṇa (Śyena) is not spoken of as Gāyatrī in the *Ṛgveda*, where we have the first references to the tale of Somāharana. Gāyatrī steps in the later Saṃhitās and *Br. s.* and the old account is adapted to suit the sacrificial setting. Generally speaking in the *Br.* passages we have no identification of the gandharvas and the serpents, in the Somāharaṇa episode; nor do we have the serpents as the guardians of Soma. Hence when the 'Dhiṣṇyas' (fire-altars) are said to be the gandharvas and the serpents, it clearly shows that the fire-altars and the serpents are different in origin, and, like the Suparṇa-Gāyatrī identification, here we have a point where these serpents are being interpreted in the light of the sacrificial set-up! In other words, the serpents do not seem to belong to the sacrificial ritual or even the original tale of Somāharaṇa. They are borrowed from certain other sources and are ushered to fit in the Somāharaṇa account. This is not the case only with the serpents; there are other points also which seem to belong to a different tale altogether and were mixed with the account of Somāharaṇa. This will be clear from the following account from the *Ś.B.* (*Kāṇva* — V. 6.2 ff.).[200]

'Kadrū and Suparṇī had a wager involving sharpness of sight. Kadrū said, "The white horse stands on the pillar beyond the *Suparṇya*[201] waters. Him I see. His tail is loose; the wind causes it to move. I see it'. (Now)! what is beyond the waters, as she said, that is the altar; as much is the altar (*vedi*), only so much is the earth.. . . The pillar is the sacrificial post (*yūpa*). Agni (fire in the altar) is the white horse . . . the trail dangling in the wind is the binding cord (*raśanā*) at it (ie. at the *yūpa*)."

The portion that follows informs that one of the half-covers (*kuśī*) was cut away by Gāyatrī; she gave it to the gods. That was *dīkṣā* (consecration). The other one which was cut and seized was *tapas* (penance).

The portions that are important are—

(1) What she spoke as 'beyond water', it is only the sacrificial altar she spoke of;

(2) The whole horse rests on the pillar, i.e. the sacrificial post is that pillar. Agni is the white horse;

(3) As to what Kadrū said, "Down hangs the tail of that horse. The wind shakes it. That I see." It is only the cord (fastened to the sacrifical post) that she spoke of.

In the instances above, it could be noticed how the sacrificial things are zealously being identified with the things that are originally different. It is certain that the *Br.* passages speaking of *Somāharaṇa* used the 'Somāharaṇa' to glorify the sacrificial ritual. It also is quite clear that the 'Somāharaṇa' of old was not an elborate tale; but gradually got fattened as various threads of different accounts got mixed into it. It is in this way, that we can explain how certain points are noted in certain passages and in certain others they are absent. When gradually the account of the 'Somāharaṇa' grew into a tale — (it took years and years!) — the Brs. took it to glorify the ritual of the sacrifice; various new shades were gradually mixed with this account giving occasion to identify the new shades with certain other important things in the sacrifice. These new shades were obviusly from the popular versions then current.

Now, to come again to the 'poisonous serpents' — the guards of *Soma*. We have seen that they are not spoken of in the Vedic account of Somāharaṇa, nor are they so spoken of in many Br. passages concerning Somāharaṇa. In this case the only possible explanation is that they have been borrowed from some other source; and this source, most probably, was the popular tale or faith. Serpents as the guards of *Soma* need not surprise us; as instances are not wanting to show that in popular belief serpents are often considered as the protectors and guards of wealth;[202] and when *Soma* was an essentiality for sacrifice, it is not surprising to find that, gradually the serpents crept into the time-old 'Somāharaṇa' tale and found their proper place as guards. When the serpents thus found way into the 'Somāharaṇa' account, the next step that could be naturally expected would be to identify them also with certain important factor in sacrifice. Thus the equation would be: serpents (= gandharvas, the guards of *Soma*) = the fire altars (*dhiṣṇyāḥ*).

We now go to see briefly the account at the *Sup. Ad.* as regards the bringing of *Soma*. In the *Sup. Ad.* we have *Soma* brought by Garuḍa Vainateya, and it is said to have been brought as a price for the freedom of Garuḍa's mother. Kadrū says to Vinatā —

"Soma is guardedly kept in the cave in the third heaven of Indra. Fetching it with speed, with it, O auspicious one, do thou free thyself and roam at will;

"Soma do the serpents desire to drink, (after), being brought by us from the heaven; and difficult to fetch is the shining (*Soma*) from heaven; and (lo!) that is the price (of freedom.)"[203]

Then follows the fight with the guards of *Soma*, that are mentioned in the following verses. Indra is at a loss to understand the sudden uproar in the heaven and resorts to

Bṛhaspati who tells him about the advance of Garuḍa and his terrible deed of killing the guards of *Soma.*[204] Indra is perturbed and asks in despair where his guards went. Bṛhaspati replies that they are all killed by Garuḍa. Among these guards, in addition to the 'Apād astā' — (the footless archer) (i.e., the Vedic Kṛśānu), we have the following names — Arbuda, Nahuṣa, Kādraveya.[205] In reply to what Indra has asked we have further the words of Bṛhaspati,

"On noticing the speed of the bird — Garuḍa — the Sarpas and the Pannagas (serpents), being touched by him with full prowess, got afraid and hung down their heads along with their bodies, O Śakra!"

Here we have the following points to note : —

(i) Arbuda, Nahuṣa and the Kādraveyas are the nāgas; and they are also said to be the guards of Soma;
(ii) Even in the next verse they are said to be the serpents;
(iii) These are defeated by Garuḍa.

This could very well be compared with the serpents mentioned in the *Jai. Br.* It is sure that the idea of the serpents as the guards of Soma is the same in the *Jai. Br.* and the *Sup. Ad.* We have already hinted that the serpents as the guards of Soma, probably, was an idea taken from popular faith, and also seen that these serpent-guards are quite a new point in the whole episode of Somāharaṇa. While the *Sup. Ad.* follows the idea of the *Jai. Br.* as regards the serpents as the guards of *Soma*, it should be clearly noted that, very rarely it gives the word 'Suparṇa' or 'Gāyatrī' in the passages quoted above, though the whole book is named Suparṇādhyāya. It is considerably late in the speech of Bṛhaspati that we have the note of Garuḍa's identification with the metres — nay — even with the Vedas; but there the same old *epithet* 'Suparṇa' is used, reminding us of the Brahmanical identification between Suparṇa and Gāyatrī, though Garuḍa is still predominant a figure as *'Tārkṣyaputra'* (The son of Tārkṣya).[207] Previous to this also *Sup. Ad.* refers to the bringing of Soma where Garuḍa says that he is none else than the metres;[208] but it should be noted that even there, just in the previous verse, we have a reference to the guards of *Soma* that are not all gods; some other creatures are also told to be among the guards;[209] and Garuḍa says he would kill the *demons* that are guarding Soma.[210] To clarify the whole discussion we shall lay down the points that are important in this connection.

(i) In the Vedic-Brahmanical account of Somāharaṇa the serpents as the guards of *Soma* is not a feature that is common;

(ii) The serpents as the guards of *Soma* are noted in the *Jai. Br.*, and this is a point where the account takes a new turn;

(iii) The *Sup. Ad.* (which is a work written towards the end of the Brahmanical period),[211] speaks not only of serpents among the guards of *Soma*, but also gives their names which are the names of the well-known nāgas and sarpas;

(iv) The *Sup. Ad.* speaks of Garuḍa Vainateya as identified with Suparṇa and the metres; but Garuḍa[212] never appears in connection with the Somāharaṇa episode in the Vedic and the Brahmanical literature.

We have already seen that the *Mb* begins with the traditional animosity of the Nāgas and Garuḍa. The *Sup. Ad.* also begins with the wager of the mothers of the serpents and Garuḍa, i.e., the traditional animosity between the serpents and Garuḍa preceding the act of Somāharaṇa. Garuḍa's main characteristic is, as we have already marked, the killing of the serpents or nullifying the effects of serpent-poison. The fact that Garuḍa is never mentioned in the old accounts of Somāharaṇa, and is mentioned only when the account of Somāharaṇa has already adapted the serpents as the guards of Soma, seems to have a special significance and we are obliged to halt and think about the matter. The question that presents itself, 'Is the Suparṇa of the Vedic — Brahmanical fame, the same as Garuḍa? or, were these two different personalities originally, and later identified?' It seems that *Garuḍa and Suparṇa are not one and the same,* as is generally supposed. The traditional animosity between the serpents and Garuḍa being a fact well set in popular faith, Garuḍa seems to have found his way into the Somāharaṇa episode when the serpents as the guards of Soma was an established part thereof. It is difficult, otherwise, to account for Garuḍa's advent in the account only in the later Brahmanical period (at the time of the *Sup. Ad.*) when many nāgas are said to be the guards of *Soma*. To say that Suparṇa himself got transformed into Garuḍa, would be to deny the natural course of development. We have already seen the zealous efforts on the part of the Brahmanical writers to level up Gāyatrī to the position of Suparṇa, who, in reality, is Śyena. As the sacrificial metres — with Gāyatrī as the leader — were raised to the level of Suparṇa, we naturally expect Garuḍa, the later one — really of the popular faith — to have risen to the level of Suparṇa, the crossing bridge being the serpents among the *Soma*-guards, Garuḍa's control over snakes also helping the idea of his control over Death and giving immortality. Once we have the serpents as the guards, it is easy to see how Garuḍa, the avowed enemy of the serpents, would step in. The *Sup. Ad.*, as also the *Mb*, have the whole Garuḍa legend beginning and ending with this note of the traditional antagonism between the serpents and Garuḍa; for, at the end, Garuḍa asks for, and gets, the nāgas as his food, when asked to choose a boon by Indra whom he defeats in prowess.[213] When Garuḍa destroys the serpents, who are the Soma-guards, it should naturally be taken as his primary characteristic, the Somāharaṇa being only the secondary one.

In all probability the Garuḍa-serpent antagonism from popular faith was attached to the account of the Vedic

Somāharaṇa, the serpents having already found a suitable place in it. Garuḍa's entry even in this account is, thus, primarily as the destoryer of snakes, the killing of the snake-guards itself making Garuḍa the hero of the Somāharaṇa. Thus Garuḍa could come to be identified with Suparṇa both ways:—

(i) As the destroyer of the serpent-guards of *Soma* and the victor who took Soma *away like* Suparṇa, and

(ii) As the deity of the *mantras* to nullify serpent poison, and hence as restorer of life. The second point would make him the giver of immortality; as was the case with Gāyatrī.

Even if it may be said that Suparṇa — (Gāyatrī) — the hero in the Somāharaṇa comes to assume the characteristic of Garuḍa in killing the serpents posted near Soma, it is quite clear that Suparṇa — the 'Soma-bringer' — and Garuḍa, the 'serpent-killer', are here fused together into one, but in reality are two different personalities. But, as we have noted pretty well in the case of Gāyatrī, it seems more natural to suppose Garuḍa to have been connected with Somāharaṇa, though originally independent of it.

# 5
# GARUḌA AND OTHER DIVINITIES

## (A) Garutmān and Suparṇa

We have said that Garuḍa and the nāgas are only two divisions of one nāga whole according to the principle of phratry. We have also noticed how Garuḍa is the presiding deity of the *mantras* meant to remove snake-poison. Now, it is not difficult to see how Gāruḍa could have been brought to be associated with the Somāharaṇa. We have opined that Garuḍa might have come in the picture of the Somāharaṇa when the serpents as the guards of *Soma* was a belief pretty well fixed. Looking from a different angle also we see pretty well how Garuḍa could have got to be the hero of the Somāharaṇa exploit. Suparṇa-Śyena, being the bringer of the immortal juice (*Soma*), was in other words the giver of immortality. Gāyatrī, formerly a different entity, got identified with Suparṇa by her power to give immortality to the sacrificer and the gods. We have seen how the metres are said to be useful in *protecting the gods from death*. The idea of the *nullification of death* gradually got identified with the idea of immortality; and on the basis of this idea the metres in general (and Gāyatrī in particular) and Suparṇa could get identified. We have also seen how in the Kāṇva recension of the *Ś.B. Suparṇī* is actually said *to be free from death* by the advent of *Soma*. So, the point is this: To be free from death is like conquering death or, in other words being immortal. In this light, Garuḍa's antagonism with the serpents and his power to remove serpent-poison could very well give the idea of the nullification of death from serpent-bite primarily, and secondarily the freedom from death. The next step would be to suppose Garuḍa to be the giver of immortality. When this is done, naturally all the three — Garuḍa, Gāyatrī and Śyena-Suparṇa—would be on the same level and be spoken of as if they were one. It is precisely in this double capacity of (i) primarily killing the snakes that guarded *Soma*; and (ii) automatically controlling death by possessing the ancient *Soma*-juice that Garuḍa gets a place in the later phases of the Somāharaṇa account. Thus he acquires the name and exploit of the ancient Suparṇa, at the same time retaining his character as the Killer of Serpents. When he gets the name Suparṇa, he also becomes heir to other attributes and identifications of Suparṇa. Hence he is said to be the metres and is identified with Gāyatrī, and is said to be *'Yajña-taṇuḥ'* etc. in the *Sup. Ad.* In this connection, notice should be taken of a few passages from the *AV.* that speak of Suparṇa-Garutmat in the context of the antidotes of poison.

> "The eagle Garutmat did, O poison! first devour thee. Thou didst not bewilder him, didst not injure him; Yea, thou didst turn into food for him"[214] (*AV.* IV.6.3).

But here the animosity between the serpents and Suparṇa is nowhere to be seen. The word 'poison' is a general term and we have no indication of its being serpent-poison, leading us to the surmise as to the antagonism between Suparṇa and the serpents; and again, it is a question why in the general trend of the Brāhmaṇas there is no indication of the antagonism between Suparṇa (Śyena) — Garutmat and the serpents — especially in the account of Somāharaṇa! Sāyaṇa, commenting on the word 'Garutmat' takes it as an epithet of Vainateya thus meaning 'Garuḍa'. There is another passage wherein the antidote of 'poison' is addressed as follows:—

> "Suparṇa was born first; O him (Of antidote of poison) wert thou the bile" (AV. I.24.1.).

Here Sāyaṇa renders the word 'Suparṇa' as 'Garutmat.[215] In yet another passage the word 'Suparṇa' is rendered by Sāyaṇa again as 'Vainateya'.[216]

It should be noted, however, that Sāyaṇa renders 'Suparṇa' as 'Vainateya' (giving the semblance of Garuḍa) *only* where Suparṇa has reference to the antitode of poison; but in the other places he *does not* render it as Vainateya.[217] This clearly shows that while rendering the word 'Suparṇa' in the context of 'poison', Sāyaṇa is guided by the popular belief about the antagonism between Garuḍa-Vainateya and the serpents, and the cure of serpent-poison by Garuḍa. Though he does not specifically speak of Garuḍa, the word 'Vainateya' leaves no doubt about his meaning 'Garuḍa' by it. Now, while Sāyaṇa renders 'Suparṇa' here as Vainateya (Garuḍa), it is interesting to see that he does not render the word 'Garuḍa', when it occurs for the first time in Sanskrit literature (which is in the *Tait. Ār.*) as 'Suparṇa', though 'Garuḍa' has there the attribute *'suvarṇapakṣa'* which would naturally suggest its being so rendered![218] He flaty says that the praise therein (*Tait. Ār.* X.1.6) refers to the "god who took the form of the *King of birds* famous in the Purāṇas and so on", rendering the word *'suvarṇa-pakṣa'* as 'having beautiful wings as the means for flying'.[219] This clearly shows that — (i) Sāyaṇa takes the help of the later Purāṇic-idea about Garuḍa Vainateya to render passages about Suparṇa wherein the point of poison comes in; (ii) does not think definitely 'Garuḍa' and 'Suparṇa' to be the same, or else, we expect him to have rendered the word *suvarṇa-pakṣa* and Garuḍa as 'Suparṇa', when he has actually rendered the word Suparṇa, in the context of poison in the *AV.*, as 'Vainateya'; and (iii) it is also clear that he takes Garuḍa to be famous only in the Purāṇas etc. as the King of birds, and does not connect it with the Vedic Suparṇa, the hero of the Somā-Haraṇa exploit.

It is clear that the antitode of poison referred to in the *AV.* has nothing to do strictly with the serpent-poison and its antitode; for, as Suparṇa is said to have found the antidote, we have also the Sūkara (pig) who dug it out of the earth,[220] with his snout. So, to make it all short, it is clear that the Suparṇa-Garutmat of the *AV.* as the remover of poison should not be confused with Garuḍa, the nāga-destroyer and especially in the account of the Somāharaṇa the advent of Garuḍa is a point that does not depend on Suparṇa's[221] being the healer of poison. At the best it could be said that, Suparṇa the bringer of the immortal juice might have been thought of as presiding over the antidotes of poison, as one who would stand for the nullification of death thereby, much in the same way as Garuḍa, the destroyer of snakes and snake-poison, signifying the nullification of death, would be connected with the exploit of Somāharaṇa. But it is clear that these two were different from each another. In *AV.* VI.56 we have *mantras* for 'Protection from serpents'; but the deity there is not said to be Suparṇa or Garutmat. The deity is Rudra (who is invoked with Garuḍa against snake poison in the *Agni P.*). In verse 2 of the same hymn we have, 'Bow to the line of birds.' It is difficult to believe that this line of birds refers to 'Suparṇa' or 'Garutmat'. In the same verse we have 'Bow to the black one (*asitāya*)' which has hardly anything to do with 'Suparṇa' or 'Garutmat'.

It is quite clear that there was no clarity of views about the oneness of Suparṇa and Garuḍa. It is almost impossible to find passages where we get mention as to why Suparṇa is called Garuḍa. On the other hand there are definite indications of trends to show how Garuḍa *came to be called* 'Suparṇa'. We have already referred to the *mantras* meant to nullify serpent-poison[222] and also seen how Garuḍa was identified with Śiva. There is also a passage in which we have the words *'suvarṇa-pataṅga-rudra'* with a variant reading *'Suvarṇa-patan Garuḍa'*.[223] This epithet *'Suvarṇa-patan'* should leave no doubt as to the trend in speaking about Garuḍa as if he was the 'Golden-winged' Suparṇa. It is difficult to believe that Suparṇa himself took these forms

— i.e., of Rudra and of Garuḍa. The more natural way is to suppose that these are being identified with Suparṇa. It is not difficult to understand how Rudra-Śiva and Garuḍa are identified. Garuḍa, the bird, as the natural enemy of the serpents could well be compared with Śiva who drank the poison and mastered it.[224] The efforts for giving sorts of explanations as to how Garuḍa came to be Suparṇa show that he was constantly being levelled up to the Vedic Suparṇa, who was different from him. Thus we have the *Sup. Ad.* starting with '*sauparṇāni pavitrāṇi sūktāni*', giving a semblance of the praise of the ancient Suparṇa; but the very next verse is full of praise of '*Vainateya*' who is referred to as 'the golden-winged' etc.[225] As the epithet Vainateya is commonly applied to Garuḍa in the later literature and never to Suparṇa previous to the *Sup. Ad.*, it is clear that here Garuḍa (Vainateya) is the one who is praised *as if* he were Suparṇa. Further on, he is called *Vinatā-putra* (the son of Vinatā) and also 'Suparṇa'.[226] The whole Ākhyāna is called 'Suparṇākhyāna' in which the Ṛṣi is Vāmadeva, and the deities are Garuḍa, Indra, Tārkṣya, Vinatā, Kadrū and the serpents.[227] The name of Suparṇa is not given among the names of the deities. The appellation 'Garutmat' is also used for Vainateya (in I.1.3). But, though both the words Suparṇa and Garutmat are found in the Vedic literature, they are not associated with the name Vinatā, which does not occur in the Vedic literature. The *Mb* also tries to stress the point of Garuḍa's getting the name 'Suparṇa' by stating that he released his beautiful wing at his own will after Indra's futile blow with his Vajra, and seeing that 'beautiful wing', the gods and Ṛṣis said that he should be named 'Suparṇa'.[228] The *Sk. P.*[229] has a long and elaborate account of how Garuḍa came to be called Suparṇa. According to it, Garuḍa takes on his back a Brāhmaṇa friend and his beautiful daughter Mādhavī and wanders in search of a suitable husband for her. Ultimately they all go to where Viṣṇu is, being helped by Nārada who meets them on the way. When all are admitted into Viṣṇu's presence, Garuḍa sees there an old lady—Sāṇḍilī by name — observing the vow of celibacy. Garuḍa laughs at her jeeringly and says that it is difficult for women to practise strict celibacy. Śāṇḍilī, getting angry, curses Garuḍa in her mind, as she was observing the vow of '*mauna*', in which speech is taboo. Thereby Garuḍa loses his wings, seeing which Viṣṇu requests Śāṇḍilī to help Garuḍa gain his wings back. Śāṇḍilī asks Garuḍa to propitiate Lord Śiva. This done, Garuḍa gets his wings back and they become golden![230] The episode of Śāṇḍilī occurs also in the *Mb*, and even there we have the indication of Garuḍa becoming Suparṇa, being cursed and favoured by her.[231] In another place in the *Sk. P.* we have the 'Suparṇa'-hood bestowed upon Garuḍa in the Garuḍa-Indra fight in the same way as in the *Mb.*[232] The *Viṣṇu Dh.P.* also gives a short account of how Garuḍa (Tārkṣya) lost his wings and regained more beautiful wings when his pride of strength was set at naught by Viṣṇu.[233] The account occurs in connection with Sumukha's getting protection from Viṣṇu. It need not be objected here that in some of these accounts the Suparṇahood is not a new thing, for the bird is already addressed as 'Suparṇa' and is said to gain 'Suparṇa'hood only *again* ('*bhūya eva*'). It should be noted that the main source for all these accounts is the gaining of the name 'Suparṇa' by Garuḍa in the Indra-Garuḍa fight, after first losing a wing! That is the point which formed the main motif for all the other accounts having different purposes to serve.

This brings us to consider a few etymological explanations of the word Garuḍa.

## Etymology of the Word Garuḍa

1. One of the recensions of the *Mb* itself tries to solve the knot by the explanation of the word from '*Guru*' + *ud* + *ḍī* (*gurum bhāram āsādya uḍ-ḍīnaḥ*). *Mb.* I.30.7. "The greatest of Birds — the *eater of snakes* — is Garuḍa, as he flew aloft with the heavy weight".[234] It is

difficult to understand how the word '*guru*' became '*garu*'.

2. The dictionaries of Apte and also Monier Williams derive the word from = *gṛ* + *uḍac* = "swallower". We have noted how Garuḍa is a swallower of the Tortoise and the Elephant and also of the Niṣādas. Monier-Williams opines that Garuḍa was, perhaps, originally identified with the all-consuming fire of the sunrays.[235] The surmise that Garuḍa might have been identified with the *fire of the Sun-rays* is not well founded on references. It presupposes Garuḍa being first identified with the sun's rays. Though the association of fire and the sun is a common belief,[236] Garuḍa's complete identification with sun-rays is doubtful. To say that Garuḍa is the sun ray-fire that consumes all, seems to be far-fetched and a laboured explanation.
3. Hopkin's explanation seems to be based on the characteristic of Garuḍa. He derives the word from *gara* + √*ad* — i.e., 'the eater of Poison'.[237]
   This sounds quite well looking to the nature of Garuḍa; for Garuḍa is said to be the remover of serpent-poison, as we have had ample opportunity to see. But, here also there is a difficulty. Hopkins does not explain how the root √*ad* could give the form '*uḍa*' as we have in the word Garuḍa (*gar*(a) + *uḍa*).
4. The best way possibly will be to derive the word from *gara* and the causal of *ud* + √*ḍī* meaning 'one who takes off or removes the poison, or makes the poison fly away' — ('*garam ud* + *ḍāyayati*').

In any case while giving the etymology of the word 'Garuḍa', notice should be taken of the general character of the bird; and, it is the removal of poison. Hopkins caught the point though the root (√*ad*) suggested by him is unacceptable for the reason given above.

All these efforts at giving the exact meaning of the form 'Garuḍa' show the independent importance of the bird. In none of these do we have any trace of the characteristic of Suparṇa. We have seen how the explanation given by the *Mb* edition we have referred to, harps on the bird's quality of destroying the serpents. The other explanation which makes Garuḍa a swallower does not apply to Suparṇa whose swallowing nature is doubtful. The explanation based on the 'anti-poison' characteristic (or strictly speaking the anti-serpent nature) of Garuḍa[238] appeals particularly in the wake of the many references to the serpent-antidotes that are named after Garuḍa, as we have already seen in an earlier chapter. The point gains additional support from the fact that there is another word in the Lexicon for 'Garuḍa'; it is 'Garuḷa'. This word, it can be seen, has two parts, the first being *gara* (poison) and the other *'ula'*. The second part can be derived from the root √*ul* = to burn, the whole word meaning — 'the one who burns poison'.

When the word 'Garuḍa', thus, could be derived in accordance with the exact nature of the bird, it is easy to see how 'Garutmat' could not have given the word Garuḍa; for, what has the word Garutmat to convey except for the meaning 'possession of the wings'? *Garut* is the 'wing' and *Garutmat* conveys nothing special. It is also important to note that the word was not favoured by the explanations we have seen. We have already seen while discussing the passage from the *AV.* where the word *gurutmat* occurs in connection with the antidote of poison, how, to render it, Sāyaṇa took help of the word *Vainateya*. This shows that the *Garutmat* could not of itself be explained as being an antidote of poison, from *gara*. Now, when we see Garuḍa and Garutmat identified[239] in the *Mb* and in *Sup. Ad.*, and in the literature later than that, two questions stand before us —

(i) Could Garutmat, being the one who is spoken of in the *AV.* as eating the poison, give rise to the whole idea of the conflict with the nāgas, himself being called Garuḍa? In other words — is Garuḍa nothing more than an evolution from the *Garutmant* of the *AV.*?

(ii) Was Garuḍa, the antagonist of the nāgas (serpents), identified with Garutmāt of the Veda, by virtue of his being thought to be the controller of the poison of snakes particularly, and of all poison generally? In other words, was Garuḍa different from Garutmat and came to be identified with the latter?

The answer is the same as we have already given, i.e., Garuḍa was a separate entity and was later identified with Garutmat. It seems improbable that the single idea of Garutmat's power over poison should build the whole later story of the feud between Garuḍa and the serpents. The probability is the other way. Examples of this type are not wanting. When a new deity gets identified with the older one, it is usual to suppose it to be the form of the older one, while in reality it is a separate deity. We have already noted how the metres, being separate, were identified with the *Soma*-bringing bird. The similarity of sound between the word 'Garutmat' and 'Garuḍa' need not beguile us, for we have seen how the word *Garut* + *mat* has a different connotation altogether. It is to be noted that Suparṇa and Garutmat are *not generally* associated with poison in the *Ṛgveda,* and other Saṁhitas. The same is the case with the Brāhmaṇa texts. Hence the references to Suparṇa-Garutmat as a vanquisher of poison in the *AV.* (which is on a different footing than the three Vedas), might themselves have been due to the influence of the fusion of Suparṇa-Garutmat and Garuḍa.

We have propounded that Garuḍa and the nāgas probably belonged originally to a class-organization having a social system based on duality, and that Garuḍa was auspicious to a class of the nāgas who learnt the 'serpent-lore' — (or the 'poison-lore').[240] The name of the Vidyā is given variously, as we have seen, 'Sarpa-vidyā', 'Viṣa-vidyā', 'Garuḍa-vidyā' etc. The name 'Gāruḍa vidyā', might have been suggested from the fact that the bird Garuḍa kills the snakes and is immune to the effect of serpent-poison. The presence of this bird can be seen even to-day; and to this day this bird is respected both as the cure for serpent-bite and as the vehicle of Viṣṇu.[241] The Viṣṇuites worship it on every Sunday and there is mention of a class of temple-girls, dedicated to Viṣṇu — called '*Garuḍa-basavis*',[242] who have the figure of this bird tattooed on their breasts.[243] All this goes to prove that Garuḍa is firmly rooted in tradition as a definite entity. It is difficult to find such a thing about 'Garutmat', which is not the name of a definite bird, but only an attribute like Suparṇa, the original bird being the Śyena, which is different from Garuḍa (the '*Malabār eagle*' according to Dubois).[244] It may be noted in this connection that Macdonell and Keith do not give the word 'Garutmat' among the Vedic names and subjects,[245] though 'Suparṇa' and 'Śyena' are given by them, which fact would indicate 'Garutmat' to be, according to them, only an attribute of Śyena and Suparṇa. We have already seen how Garuḍa and Suparṇa are different from one another, and, it requires no special argument to prove that '*Garutmat*', (coming as the attribute of Śyena– Suparṇa) cannot be originally the same as Garuḍa. Let us have a further examination.

The word *garut* (with '*mat*') occurs only twice in *ṚV*., i.e., at I.164.46 and at X.149.3, respectively:—

> *indraṃ mitraṃ varuṇam agnim āhuhr atho divyaḥ*
> *sa Suparṇo garutmān /*
> *ekaṃ sad viprā bahudhā vadanti-agniṃ yamaṃ*
> *mātariśvānam āhuḥ//*

and,

> *paścedam anyad abhavad yajatram amartyasya*
> *bhuvanasya bhūnā /*
> *suparṇo aṅga savitur garutmān pūrvo jātaḥ sa u*
> *asyānu dharma//*

Sāyaṇa renders the word *garutmān* in the first place as "*garaṇavān pakṣavān vā*"; and at the second as "*somasya apahartā tārkṣyaḥ*". To understand 'tārkṣya' by the word '*garutmān*' presents difficulties, and this requires a later idea to understand a word in the ṚV. and also we do not have the word '*tārkṣya*' in the famous account of Somāharaṇa as it occurs in the ṚV. (IV.26 & 27). It is customary to understand by the word *garut* a wing; but as the word does not occur in the ṚV. it is doubtful if we can take it to mean so. Yāska renders the word *garutmān* as *garaṇavān*, which Durga further renders as *stutibhis tadvān*, thus connecting it with 'praise' (*Nir.* VII.18). It should be noted that in both the places where the word *garutmān* occurs in ṚV., it does not appear to denote a particular deity but, rather, comes as an adjective. In the first citation it appears that one supreme deity is being praised in various ways. The word *suparṇāḥ* is also rendered by Sāyaṇa as *supatanāḥ ādityaraśmayaḥ* (fast-flowing sunrays), or *supatanāḥ*, thus signifying a bird. Now, the word *garutmān*, at the only two places as it occurs in *ṚV* necessarily comes with *suparṇa*. If the word *suparṇa* itself could give the meaning of a bird, what propriety would be served by the word 'garutmān', if it again is to signify only 'winged' (bird)? The one deity that is being praised is conceived as a divine bird as well as Indra, Mitra etc. In this context the rendering given by Yāska, viz., '*stutibhis tadvān*' would help throw some light. This would require us to go to the root of the word *garaṇavān*; which is √*gṛ*, 'to sing' or 'to praise.' A comparison of other words from the same root would make the point clearer. Thus we have the forms—*gūrti*, (√*gṛ*) and '*gūrta*' (√*gṛ*). In the same way '*garut*' is derived from √*gṛ* with '*uti*' (an uṇādi suffix, cf. Apte's Dict.) and *garaṇa* from √*gṛ* with '*lyuṭ*'), both meaning praise. Hence, the word *garutmān* would mean 'the praiseful one' in the first instance. In *ṚV*. at least, the word does not seem to have any other meaning, and the rendering connecting it with the idea of 'bird' is to be taken as being influenced by the meaning which was attached to it later on under the influence of the word *suparṇa*.

We may compare a similar word from the Avesta — viz., *'garo-demān'* or *'garo-nmān'*. The word means, "house of Hymns", and the name of the residence of Ahura-Mazda (*Mihiryaśt*, VII.32; XIII.57.) The word *'garo'* means hymns and can be compared with the word *'garut'* (fr. √*gṛ* to praise) which, with the termination *'mat'* gives the word *garutmān*. On the analogy of the Avestan word *'garo-nmān'*, we would not be wrong if we take the word *garut* to mean the hymn. And the word *'garut-mān'* would suggest 'one with hymns', i.e., 'the one that is praised'. The meaning would then be, that the one principle is being called variously; but, it is the one *'divine Suparṇa that deserves praise* — the very master of hymns. This also hints at the Ṛgvedic conception of the supreme divinity in the form of a bird which has been suggested in the account of the Somāharaṇa, as we have already seen. It is this conception of the supreme bird who is the master of the hymns — nay, who is the very embodiment of the hymns, that is further seen to be developed in the idea of the sacrificial hymns and metres, themselves being called the 'birds' (*suparṇāḥ-sauparṇeyāḥ*).

Suparṇa does not occur as a separate deity in the *ṚV.* but it is to be noted that imprtant deities are associated with this term even in *ṚV.* (Sun, I. 35.7; Moon I. 105.1; Indra VIII.100.8). Suparṇa gets elsewhere identified with the *'chandāṁsi'* (the metres) that are said even to save the lives of gods, as noted earlier. In the Atharva V. Suparṇa is invoked to wipe off the poison (IV.6.3): but there again he is said to be 'garutmān'. The whole idea in 'Suparṇa' *garutmān* seems to be that of a supreme deity that can be *roused to power by means of the hymns*, as is the case with other deities in the *ṚV*. Thus, Indra is said to wax in power by his praise (VII.31.12; 19.11 etc.). Agni is, likewise, said to grow with praise (I.31.18; 93.6). As hymns are said to be very efficacious in rousing the power of the deity, the concept of the ONE DEITY *endowed with praise* (*garutmān*) aptly fits in with the thought of Ṛg-Vedic seers. The association of the word *garut* implying the meaning 'praise' (though not found in *ṚV*. clearly) with the concept of the bird might have given it the meaning of the 'wing' in the later literature, which rendered the confusion (identification?) between *garutmān* and Garuḍa possible, which we find, for the first time in the *Taitt. Ār.* (X.1.6):—

> *"tatpuruṣāya vidmahe suvarṇa-pakṣāya dhīmahi*
> *tanno GARUḌAḤ pracodayāt."*

Here the supreme principle *'tatpuruṣa'* is called the "golden winged", thus retaining the Ṛgvedic idea of the Supreme BIRD, its epithet *garutmān* changing into 'Garuḍa', giving rise to a new divinity, which, originally, had nothing whatsover to do with the concept of 'GARUTMAT'.

Whence came Garuḍa if not from the Vedic settings? In Tamil the word for Garuḍa is Kazu.[246] The peculiarity of the Tamil language as regards pronunciation is apt to give the pronunciation of the word *'Kazu'* sometimes as 'Gazu' (K > G). Now 'Zh' is only the English spelling of a pronunciation which is typical to the Tamil language. 'Zh' gets turned mostly into ಌ (ḷ) or the Sanskrit 'ल' (l).[247] Hence the word gets to be 'Galu'. This word closely resembles 'Galaṅ' — the Necobari word for the sea-eagle.[248] 'Galu', or 'Galan' applied to the bird that eats serpents, could easily suggest the Sanskrit word 'Garuḍa' or 'Garula', from the bird's capacity to overcome the serpents and, hence, their poison, as we have seen.

'Garuḍa' appears to be a Sanskritised form of some aboriginal word — may be *'Galan'* or *'Galu'* (*Kazhu*) or the like, meaning a definite bird of prey. Let us see the case of Suparṇa. We have seen how it was an epithet of Śyena — the bird. But that is not all. The term 'Suparṇa' is not only applied to a bird or certain gods, but to so many other things.

The one 'Suparṇa' enters the sea and pervades the whole world (*ṚV.* X.114.4)— Samvatsara (year) is Mahāsuparṇa.[249] Agni is Suparṇa (*ṚV.* I.79.2).[250] The moon and Soma are Suparṇa.[251] The fire altar is Suparṇa.[252] The Mahāvrata is the bird (Suparṇa!).[253] Sacrifice is Suparṇa.[254] The name of a fire-altar (*citi*) is 'Śyena-citi' which is said to lead the sacrificer to heaven, as Gāyatrī, becoming Śyena.[255] Indra is Suparṇa.[256] The sun is called Suparṇa.[257]

From all these examples it seems that 'Suparṇa' — the embodiment of swiftness[258] —became a favourite deity in the Vedic period. All other deities were only forms of Suparṇa; and anything that meant to the Vedic poets as great and endowed with powerful activity came to achieve the state of 'Suparṇa'. The epithet became prominently applied to Śyena and later became a separate name in connection with the exploit of *Soma*; for *Soma* — the most important of the elixirs — would naturally be conceived of being brought by a great bird, very swift in flight, and when Garuḍa got associated with the exploit (the associating point being the snake-guards of *Soma*), he also came to be known as Suparṇa.

## (B) Garuḍa (Eagle) in Other Mythologies

The idea of a big bird as an important figure in mythology is not, a speciality of the Vedic literature. Examples are quite numerous in pointing its presence even among the beliefs of the tribals as also in the mythologies of civilized races. Greek mythology speaks of an eagle,[259] who attends on Zeus as his minister, and is said to have carried the boy Ganeymede — the cup-bearer of Zeus — to heaven. The Australians believe that birds were the original gods and that the *Eagle* is a great and procreative power.[260] The Mexican mythology has a humming bird called *Huitzilin* as the leader of the Aztecs. The statue of the god 'Huitzilopochtli' wears a bird on his left foot. This case is taken by A. Lang. as one where the totem — the bird — got mixed with the later god-head, or where the totem became a god. This bird is also said to be a form of the sun.[261] A big bird is supposed to cause thunder and rain.[262] The Southern Australians believe in an *Eagle-hawk* by name *Bun-jel* (or Punjel).[263] The aborigins of the north part of Victoria believe in an *Eagle,* which, with the help of the cow, separated the Murry Black into two divisions and created everything. These two divisions are called 'crow' and 'Eagle'.[264] Guatemalan people believe in an *Eagle*-Hawk sent by the gods from heaven to ask the couple — Citalatonac (a man) and Citalalicue (a woman) — to help them produce human beings.[265] Out of the above examples, the nearer one to our Garuḍa is the Mexican war-god (i.e., of the Aztecs, the crude hunting people who entered Mexico to conquer it), Huitzilopochtli. His description[266] shows that from his mouth protrudes the Beak of the *Eagle*, his head is covered with Eagle-feather; his forehead is smeared with blood; on his breast are two *Eagles tearing out a serpent.* The coat of arms of these people and their flag symbolized Eagle, Serpent and Cactus. Chakrawarty deduces from it that the war-god represented Aquila and Serpents, both those animals being revered. The author goes on to state that serpents were also worshipped in Mexico, as serpent-stone-sculptures are found near the lake of Mexico City. A. Lang notes that this bird-god carried a green branch of plumage upon his head.[267] It is very difficult to say definitely anything about the similarity between the Eagle-serpent of Aztecs on the one hand and Garuḍa-serpents (nāgas) on the other. For the present we can only say that the similarity is a marked one. The plea of borrowing ideas is a dangerous weapon as is rightly shown by A. Lang.[268] With him we may admit that similar ideas could often be found in lands that are wide apart, and in races that are quite separate from one another. We have here two points from the Garuḍa-serpent account: (i) Garuḍa eating the nāgas and (ii) Garuḍa carrying the branch of a tree in his mouth. The worship of a god who represents the snake and the eagle in combination probably represents a duality of social organization in its original nature, having no deep hostility between the two groups, but most probably, only a sort of competition for superiority in magical power. The Zapotecs[269] of Southern Mexico also seem to have been the worshippers of the serpent-eating eagle, as is known from the stone-idols of the first century A.D. unearthed in Columbia, Andes. The creator god of the Mayas of Central America was Kukulkan, a combination of '*snake-bird*' (*Kukul* = bird; *Kan* or *Can* — snake). He was a winged serpent.[270] This winged serpent reminds us of the two-headed serpents with Garuḍa on the head represented in sculpture in Khmer, and the winged Makara-motif in the Chinese sculpture, we have already referred to.[271] Garuḍa — the killer of the snakes—resembles this *snake-bird motif* distributed throughout the world and it is not necessary to believe that he hails from Suparṇa or the Garutmat of the Vedas. It is more approximate to the truth to say that Garuḍa hails from the aboriginal popular faith of the land. Andrew Lang is perfectly right in saying —

> "Absurd as it may seem, the Vedic metres, like the Gāyatrī, have been personified and appear as active heroines of stories *presumably older than this personification.*"[272]

The same seems to be true of Garuḍa, who with his peculiar nature as an antagonist of the nāgas, appears to belong to an older faith than the Vedic-Āryan; and the epithets 'Suparṇa' and 'Garutmān' were applied to him when he got associated with the exploit of *Somāharaṇa* and became the bringer of *nectar*. But it must also be remembered that Garuḍa is not only a symbol for certain abstract power. On the contrary, the bird is a definite deity presiding over the 'Serpent-lore' and as such, has more of a social basis than simply a mythological one.

## (C) Garuḍa and Indra

Garuḍa and Indra appear in *Mb.* as rivals of each other, only to be friends at the end. *Mb*[273] follows only the *Sup. Ad.* in this respect. The root of this antagonism is said to be the insult inflicted on the Vālakhilyas by Indra when the gods and the Ṛṣis were engaged in a sacrifice performed by Kaśyapa for obtaining a son. We shall note the important points.[274]

(i) The birth of Garuḍa is a *subject of the Purāṇas,* i.e. it is a subject quite old, traditionally;

(ii) The insulted Vālakhilyas strive for producing a son that would be far *superior to Indra*; i.e., he would be another Indra.

The account further goes to say that Indra, being afraid, went to Kaśyapa who requested the ascetics — Vālakhilyas — to desist from that effort of theirs; for Indra was deputed as such by the Creator himself, and that they should not act in such a way as would make the words of the Creator false. Let the new one then be the Indra of birds. The Vālakhilyas gave the fruit of their penance to Kaśyapa himself who was performing a sacrifice for a son. Kaśyapa accepted it and told Vinatā that she would get *two sons* who will be kings of birds. Vinatā, in the course of time, gave birth to two sons and Garuḍa became the lord of birds, the other being the fore-runner of the sun. Here we get the following additional points:—

(iii) Garuḍa became the Indra, but of birds;

(iv) Garuḍa was destined to become a friend of Indra.

The whole purpose of this account seems to be nothing other than *to level Garuḍa up to the position of Indra.* That Garuḍa became the king of birds has a mark a bit lower in the levelling up; and this could be seen from the fight between Indra and Garuḍa at the time of the Somāharaṇa both in the *Sup. Ad.* and the *Mb.*

Now let us turn to the *Sup. Ad.* where the same account is given. After the verse laudatory to Vainateya Garuḍa, the *Sup. Ad.* says that Garuḍa was born from half the prowess of the sages, Vālakhilyas (I.1.3). The account goes on further to say.

"While bringing home the stalk of Palāśa for making sacrificial faggots, certain two ascetics (Vālakhilyas) got stuck up into a cow-foot (impression of a cow-foot) full of water. Seeing the ascetics (thus) stuck up in mud, Indra mocked at them who, thence, went to sage Tārkṣya and said (to him), "We shall give thee half of our penance; do thou beget a son born of an egg, — *who might crush the pride of Indra,* the self-styled one." Drinking half of the penance of the Vālakhilyas, Tārkṣya — the great-famed one —deposited in Vinatā the foetus, which there was none else to excel" (I.2.3-6).

The points that are to be noted are —

(i) It is Tārkṣya here and not Kaśyapa who begets Garuḍa.

(ii) The Vālakhilyas are two, (*ubhau ṛṣī*) and only want to crush the pride of Indra; there *is no mention of creating a Second Indra;* yet, there is mention of many Vālakhilyas.

(iii) Garuḍa is *straight to be born aṣ a bird* and the argument between the Vālakhilyas and the sage Tārkṣya (— Kaśyapa) is absent.

Thus it is clear that the *Mb* develops an elaborate account of Garuḍa's birth from a shorter one from the *Sup. Ad.*; but the germ of the competition between Garuḍa and Indra is the same. The final stage of the competition, as we have already seen, is the *supremacy of Garuḍa over Indra* inasmuch as the former robs the latter of his treasured juice— *Soma.* There is another phase of this competition which also we have noticed — and that is the *reconciliation* between Garuḍa and Indra who, at the allowance of the former, takes Soma back to the abode of the divine. This reconciliation is clearly indicated at *Mb.* when the two birds (Garuḍa and Aruṇa) are destined to be Indra's own brothers helping him anon.[275] It is not necessary to quote here this particular account as it occurs in the Purāṇas,[276] which only follow the account of the *Mb.* We shall only turn back and see whether in the literature previous to the *Sup. Ad.*, we have any glimpse of this Garuḍa–Indra competition for supremacy. We have seen how in the *Jai. Br.* there is a glimpse of competition between Indra and Suparṇa, though there is no actual fight.[277] There is another passage in the *Jai. Br.*, which hints at the conflict between Suparṇa and Indra, where Indra deputes Suparṇa to bring the news of the cows stolen by the Paṇīs. The relevant passage is below :—

"Now, indeed the Asuras called Paṇis were the Cow-guards of the gods. They ran away with them. Penning them under the earth they concealed them in a cave. The god said to the clarion-bird, 'Suparṇa, do thou search after these cows of ours.' 'Be it so'. (said Suparṇa). He, indeed, flew after them. He came up to them, under the earth hidden as they were in the cave. They (Paṇis) placed before him, when he did arrive, clarified butter, milk, coagulated milk, and sour curds. His was the perfect weal (with it all). They said to him, "Suparṇa: this shall be thy offering, this food; do thou not betray us". He (Suparṇa) again flew away. They (the gods) spoke to him. "Hast thou found out our cows, O Suparṇa?" "What be the news of the cows!", spoke he. "This is the news", said Indra, "of the cows". Squeezing his neck, he said (again), "I be the mouth (i.e. even if you do not speak, I shall speak the truth) of thine that didst stay among the cows." He (Suparṇa), indeed, threw out (vomitted) a speck of curds and coagulated milk."[278]

It is surprising to see Suparṇa, the bird who brought *Soma*, thus falling from his high pedestal. The task of searching the cows is generally given to Saramā, the bitch of the gods.[279] Whatever may be the implication in giving Suparṇa[280] the task and humiliating him in the end, it helps score a point on Garuḍa's side. It is like this: —

(i) Suparṇa is humiliated by Indra by twisting the bird's neck;
(ii) Suparṇa is later identified with Garuḍa, who, as we have pointed out, was separate from Suparṇa;
(iii) It shows the superiority of Garuḍa to Indra and also to Suparṇa, that the victor — Indra — in this account was later defeated by Garuḍa, in capturing Soma.

Leaving aside these points which acutely suggest the superiority of Garuḍa to Suparṇa and Indra, we now turn to instances where Garuḍa definitely comes nearer to Indra in his exploits to suggest equality between these two,—the equality that has been hinted at in the *Mb.*[281] as in the *Sup. Ad.*[282] inasmuch as Garuḍa vanquishes Indra only again to be his friend later. As we have seen, this trait of the actual fight of Garuḍa with Indra is rarely to be found in the Vedic literature where Suparṇa dominates in the account of the Somāharaṇa. This trait of Garuḍa's character, i.e., forcibly taking Soma away can be compared with the forcible capture of *Soma* from the house of Tvaṣṭṛ on the part of Indra.[283] Indra, as the drinker of *Soma* helps the Brahmanic idea of Indra drinking the moon which is *Soma.*[284] Though Garuḍa does not actually drink *Soma*[295] (the moon?) his power over the moon could be seen in his concealing the luminary by his wing.[286] Indra is said to have given his flag- staff to Vasu-Uparicara to gain success in battles;[287] and Garuḍa also is connected with this episode when he is said to carry Vasu Uparicara to heaven at the orders of Viṣṇu.[288] Close similarity between Garuḍa's and Indra's exploits also could be seen from the fact that Indra himself, in the form of a bird, is praised in a Ṛc. by the poet who wishes him not to be hurt by (an arrow of) an archer.[289] We know of Suparṇa (Śyena) being shot at by an archer (as we have already referred to

—*Ṛ.V.*, IV.27.3). When Suparṇa was identified with Garuḍa later, the archer, Kṛśānu, gave place to Indra, who hit at the bird. Suparṇa and Indra (in the form of a bird) thus faintly share the trait which, later on, was transferred to Garuḍa. *Ṛ.V.* (IV.27) has Indra escaping as Śyena when imprisoned.[290] The watchman Kṛśānu shoots an arrow at the bird, but it passes through his feathers letting one feather of the bird fall. The same account is transferred to Garuḍa later. Thus Indra, being identified with Suparṇa (Śyena) came to be equal to Garuḍa: but, in a step further Garuḍa gets to be superior to Indra who himself is identified with the archer, in that the latter deals the stroke of Vajra to Garuḍa who is unvanquished. In the *Ṛ.V.* passage (RV IV.27) Indra's (Vāmadeva's) going suddenly out of the *garbha* (womb) to fetch Soma can be compared with Garuḍa's having to rush for *Soma* soon after he was born, to release his mother from slavery. Like Indra again, Garuḍa's power over the mountains is always hinted at. He cuts their tops;[291] makes them tremble with the wind of the wings.[292] Indra is credited with the shattering of the nine times ninety fortresses of Śambara (cf. note 290). Curiously, according to the *Sup. Ad.* Garuḍa is said to have shattered equal number of Indra's fortresses before capturing Soma,[293] plus six thousand. From the above observation the following points suggest themselves to us :—

(i) Garuḍa is being made equal to Indra; and some times he is shown to be superior to the latter, which reflects a known pattern;

(ii) The account of the *Sup. A.* and the *Mb* support the first point laid down above;

(iii) Garuḍa is made the king of birds — which indicates that, probably, formerly he was not so.

Garuḍa being the emblem of great power, the controller of death and so on, in the non-Vedic faith, it is not at all surprising to see him being levelled up to the position of Indra — the war-god of the Vedic Āryans. It appears most probable that in the account of the fight and the ultimate friendship between Garuḍa and Indra, the two faiths have a tale of assimilation, which is just in keeping with socio-mythological development. Garuḍa might have been for long popular, and with the contact of the faith of the Indra-followers, it was socially necessary to adjust both these into the mixed faith, both having their own importance, with ultimate friendship as the result. Another thing to be noted in this connection is that Indra is always the one to be conquered to achieve eminence. Thus, the kings perform hundred sacrifices to equal Indra. Indra's seat is supposed to stir with the excellence of the penance of ascetics. It is Indra who puts all sorts of impediments in the way of those who want to achieve heaven, and even reach far above that. Nahuṣa gains tha post of Indra. Hopkins[294] thinks Nahuṣa's supremacy over Indra as an indication of the Nāga-power on the Ganges. This only suggests that Indra stood as a symbol of prowess, and hence in myth or legend was to be defeated by those who wanted to achieve glory. Indra's lordship over *Soma* (rather his covetousness!) was his special trait, and hence, Garuḍa's fighting Indra to take the same — especially when one bird (Śyena) is said to have brought Soma (RV IV. 18. 13). It is interesting to note here that Indra himself is equal to Garuḍa in the act of carrying Soma, as he *re-takes* it to heaven, but only at the express admittance of Garuḍa. All this forms a pattern. Garuḍa is being levelled up to the position of Indra. The sophisticated faiths respecting Indra could not completely set the nāga deity Garuḍa aside, the result being that both these became equal.[295] This is clearly seen in the last verses of the *Sup. Ad.* which, for the first time, mention a clear rivalry between Indra and Garuḍa. Garuḍa's words show that he was not the Vedic deity; he was probably a non-Vedic one; he is to be admitted into the Vedic fold; but, at the same time, with his original trait unchanged. This will be clear from the *Sup. Ad.* Says

Garuda :—

"The serpents do I choose for my food, O Lord of Śacī! May I carry the sacrifice, *may I enter the Vedas; may the Brāhmaṇas, desirous of heaven meditate upon me*; may those (Brāhmaṇas) obtain in heaven our assembly."[296]

The equality of Indra and Garuḍa will be clearer from the *Indra-dhvaja* and *Garuḍa-dhvaja.*

In the account of Vasu Uparicara Garuḍa takes the King to heaven (*Mb.* XII. 337.32 and earlier 1. 63. 17 ff.). Indra gives him the pole for victory. According to the account of the *Bṛhat Saṁhitā*, it is Viṣṇu who first presented the staff to Indra and Indra then presented it to Vasu Uparicara. The staff is said to be prepared out of the lustre of Viṣṇu, and by it Indra had defeated the host of enemies. It was borne on an eight-wheeled car, as if it were the Sun.[297] If the standard of Viṣṇu has Garuḍa on it, (as we have in the *Mb.* 1.33.17) it comes to follow that, in giving his own standard to Indra by Viṣṇu to vanquish the enemies, there is an implication of Garuḍa helping Indra. In the *Tait. Br. the mantra* to be uttered to ward off fear is —

"Imparter of blessing, lord of the people, the slayer of Vṛtra, the vanquisher of the enemies, may the 'bull' (mighty) *Indra* go before us — he the bestower of blessing, the subduer of fear."[298]

With this *mantra,* later the Garuḍa-dhvaja, or the Viṣṇudhvaja, was erected. The flag of it showed the figure of Garuḍa in Vīrāsana.[299]

There are laudatory stanzas about the '*śakra-dhvaja*' in which Garuḍa is praised. The '*dhvaja*' is said to be attended by Garuḍa[300] This is sufficient to see how Indra (the mighty warrior god) and Garuḍa are equated in vanquishing the enemies of gods. It is this idea of the unvanquishable prowess of Garuḍa that probably made him accompany the King —

the incarnation of Viṣṇu, and of Indra, on compaigns.[301]

## (D) Garuḍa and Viṣṇu

*Mb*(Ādi) describes how Garuḍa became the vehicle of Viṣṇu. Viṣṇu is said to have been pleased with the bird's unselfishness in taking away *amṛt* and asked him to choose two boons whereupon the bird chose —

(i) To be 'upon' (the flag of) Viṣṇu; and
(ii) That he should be immortal even without nectar.

In *Sup. Ad.* this account of Viṣṇu and Garuḍa is totally absent. The Purāṇas give it and follow *Mb.* in this respect. The *Mb.* account which describes how Garuḍa became the vehicle of Viṣṇu, when viewed minutely, suggests that —

(i) The Viṣṇu-Garuḍa account is added later to the Somāharaṇa episode;
(ii) This shows the superiority of Viṣṇu to Indra; for Indra is only the equal of Garuḍa, while Viṣṇu is superior to Garuḍa inasmuch as the latter becomes his vehicle.

This note of Viṣṇu's superiority to Indra sometimes becomes more prominent in the same context in certain Purāṇas. Thus in the *Sk. P.*, in one account of the Somāharaṇa (the bringing of nectar), Indra does not come in the picture at all, his place being completely taken by Viṣṇu, though in other places the Somāharaṇa account in the *Sk. P.* closely resembles *Mb.* Thus we have :

"Then the gods (drinkers of nectar) went to the lord of Vaikuṇṭha and said, that nectar was being seized. Having heard this, Hari (Viṣṇu) assured them. He suddenly challenged Garuḍa and fought with him for twenty *ghaṭikā*-s. Going near Garuḍa he said to him, 'I am pleased with you, choose a boon; you have earned it.'[302]

It could be seen how the Indra-Garuḍa fight at the occasion of the fetching of *amṛta* and the giving of boons by

Viṣṇu are here combined into one, Viṣṇu playing both the roles.

Noteworthy also is another variation that occurs in the *Padma P.* where Viṣṇu comes in the picture in the account of the Nāga-Kacchapa. Garuḍa, taking the two animals, sits on the branch of a Jambu-tree (not Rauḥina!) which gives way under his weight[303] and Viṣṇu asks Garuḍa to perch on his arm and eat the twain.[304] It will be interesting to note that the passage further has Viṣṇu asking Garuḍa to eat the flesh of his arm, and Garuḍa eats it, without any injury to the arm.[305] Then the Purāṇa has the usual account of Garuḍa's subservience to Viṣṇu who shows him his own real form.

After seeing this tendency to give higher positions to Viṣṇu and to give Indra less importance in the scene of the Somāharāṇa, we turn to the next point of interst, which is that Viṣṇu's superiority to Garuḍa is not always avowed. In other words, there are traces to indicate Garuḍa's superiority to — or at least equality with — Viṣṇu. In the account of the Somāharṇa itself, *Mb* smartly hints at it, when it has Garuḍa also telling Viṣṇu to choose a boon.[306] Viṣṇu chooses him as his vehicle. This is sufficient to indicate equality between Garuḍa and Viṣṇu. From the passage in the *Sk. P.* quoted above it could be seen that Garuḍa is not to be subdued by Viṣṇu easily and the latter has to fight for some time with the bird. The same account also gives interesting details of the 'choosing of boons'. According to it, when Viṣṇu asks Garuḍa to choose a boon, the latter smiles (mockingly! — or with confidence) and tells Viṣṇu flatly to choose not one but two boons; for, he himself was pleased with the god.[307] The same under-current of Garuḍa's importance and prowess and the conflict between Garuḍa and Viṣṇu can be observed in the account of Sumukha, where Sumukha is given shelter by Viṣṇu (and Indra) and Garuḍa challenges it. True it is that the whole account later indicates to have been told to emphasize the prowess of Viṣṇu, but it cannot be denied that there is also a note of Garuḍa's equality, in prowess and confidence, to both Indra and Viṣṇu.[308]

It is hazardous to see in these instances anything of the sort of a competition for supremacy between Garuḍa and Viṣṇu; but even knowing the hazard, will it not be worthwhile to note the possible implication underlying these accounts? The implications are as follows : —

(i) For some time at least Garuḍa's subservience to Viṣṇu was not quite an established fact;

(ii) It seems that Garuḍa had his own importance before, and the Viṣṇuite religion tried to assimilate the Garuḍa faith (i. e. the faith of the followers of Garuḍa), which was a different one;

(iii) In the period of assimilation the note of Garuḍa's equality was predominant, and later gave place to his subservience to Viṣṇu indicating complete fusion of the faiths.

When we understand the undercurrent of this tussle leading to complete assimilation, we can know the real implication of such words which show Garuḍa's superiority to Viṣṇu viz. — 'May I be above you' — [309] (which Nīlakaṇṭha renders as — ' Above i.e. on the banner'). Gonda doubts the meaning of these words and admits that he does not know "whether any importance must be attached to the passage"; and suggests (obviously influenced by Nīlakaṇṭha) that it should refer to 'Garuḍa's position on the staff.'[310] There is another instance where Garuḍa is definitely said to be superior to Viṣṇu. It is their fight at the time of the bringing of nectar.[311] Garuḍa is to Viṣṇu in the post-Vedic literature what Viṣṇu is to Indra in the Vedic literature.[312] In all probability Garuḍa, the deity from popular faith (that of a section of the nāgas, as we have already propounded), was gradually assimilated by the Viṣṇuite religion. This seems to be the implication of such passages as describe Viṣṇu giving shelter to the nāgas. The serpent and Garuḍa, both got assimilated into the Viṣṇuite faith and Garuḍa, already a deity, suggesting great power and speed, could well be thought of as the vehicle of the other God, who also suggests swift pervading, without however losing his own personal eminence. Garuḍa is called Indra (*Mb.* I. 23. 16) and also Viṣṇu (I. 23. 17). Indra himself is called Viṣṇu (I. 25. 13), thus keeping all the three on equal level. Gonda rightly says that when the bird is called Viṣṇu, it does not mean that originally he was *that divine being* (Viṣṇu), or that Viṣṇu originally was a bird and that one Being split into two.[313] Taking a step further we may add that Garuḍa was a separate divinity, from the popular faith, and was later levelled up to Viṣṇu, before finally he was made the latter's vehicle, suggesting both the servitude of the bird and also his aptness in flying swiftly through the three worlds which Viṣṇu pervades; and it is here that it is difficult to agree with Johannson who simply identifies the bird with Viṣṇu.[313a]

## (E) Garuḍa, Amṛta and the Machine-wheel

*Mb.* mentions a sharp-edged wheel (disc) revolving constantly near *amṛta*.[314] which Garuḍa broke and entered. The *Sup. Ad.* has the disc (*cakram*)[315] and we have noted before that the *Ś. Br.* and the *Jai. Br.* speak of the two half-cups (Kuśis) that constantly join and separate.[316] Garuḍa is identified with the metres who are the vanquishers of death and givers of immorality. Thus Garuḍa who brings the immortal juice is the one who leads to immortality. The machine-wheel revolving constantly seems to be the symbol of the sun; and Garuḍa, going through the wheel to fetch immortality, closely resembles the virtuous reaching the world of the immortals by breaking through the disc of the sun, which is referred to as the circle of the sun (*Sūrya-maṇḍala*). The abode of Viṣṇu is said to be beyond the circle of the sun, where immortality dwells. Thus the *Kaṭh.-Up.* calls the abode of Viṣṇu the goal of the virtuous,[317] the access to it being through the disc of the sun which is pierced through by the virtuous,[318] who ascend to it by a special ray of the sun. Garuḍa, also is *śara*[319] (arrow) and 'Suparṇa' (the fast moving ray of the sun).[320] The sun, which is said to stand right above the navel of the earth, is said to be the gate of the path leading to the gods. The sun is also said to be the circle at the other end of the axis.[321] The *Bṛhad. Ā. Up.* speaks of an opening like *the hob of a wheel* of a chariot through which the virtuous go;[322] and beyond this is immortality.[323]

The *Mb* (I. 23. 16)[324] has Garuḍa being praised by the gods variously, identifying him with various gods. Nīlakaṇṭha's comment on this is that there Garuḍa is being praised as if he were the 'Brahman'.[325] It seems to be correct and it is also natural. We have seen that the particular exploit of bringing Soma (nectar) was transferred to Gāyatrī. Garuḍa gets to be identified with Gāyatrī when he is identified with the metres as a whole in the *Sup. Ad.* Now Gāyatrī is said to be the highest principle, the 'Brahman'.[326] The metres, themselves, are called the 'Brahman'.[327] It is not unnatural then, that Garuḍa be said to be the Brahman.

### (F) Garuḍa, Vālakhilyas and Viṣṇu

The Vālakhilyas come in the legend of Garuḍa twice. Once providing the motive for the birth of Garuḍa to rival Indra in prowess[328] and secondly as the *thumbkins* that were resting *with head downwards*, on the branch of the Rauhiṇa tree, broken and carried in the beak by Garuḍa.[329] They are said to be '*marīcipāḥ*'.[330] The word 'Vālakhilya' really seems to be derived from the word *vāla*, which means "hair". They are actually said to have been born out of the hair of Prajāpati.[331] The *Sk. P.*[332] has a queer account of the birth of the Vālakhilyas. According to it, Brahmā — the grandfather of the worlds — saw, at the time of a sacrifice, the feet of Pārvatī, whereupon, his passions getting suddenly roused, he let his semen fall to the ground. Being ashamed of the act, he rubbed it with his feet and thence came out the Vālakhilyas — thousands of them. Nārada asked them to go to the mountain Gandhamādana. These two accounts are different apparently but the common factor in both is that the Vālakhilyas are produced from the body of Brahmā.

Jarl Charpentier thinks that these are originally 'seelenwessen' dwelling in the sun;[333] and Barnett, going a step further, opines that these thumbkins have grown in popular fancy out of the old 'Puruṣas' or tutelary gods who reside in the hearts of men, and on death pass into the sun where there is the great Puruṣa.[334] Barnett further identifies them with the Maruts and the vital airs (Prāṇas) and suggests that in the quarrel between the Vālakhilyas and Indra (as given in the *Sup. Ad.* and the *Mb*) there might be an echo of the Vedic legend of the quarrel between Indra and the Maruts.[335]

## The Vālakhilyas and their Relation with Viṣṇu

The size of the Vālakhilya-sages is that of the thumb and in this they give the idea of the soul that dwells in the hearts of beings.[336] Now Viṣṇu himself is said to have the size of a thumb. At the time of *Śrāddha* the Yajamāna thrusts his thumb in the boiled rice and the thumb represents Viṣṇu.[337] When Viṣṇu came to be identified with the highest soul these thousands of thumbkins, who represent the lower souls (i. e. those who dwell in everybody's heart), being thought to be of the same size as that of the thumb,[338] could very well be associated with him. Thus we have the Vālakhilyas as the counsellors of King Pṛthu who is said to be the form of Viṣṇu.[339] The Vālakhilyas are said to be on the Rauhiṇa tree. The Rauhiṇa is the *Aśvattha* tree, on which dwell the two souls.[340] The *Aśvattha* tree is itself identified with Viṣṇu.[341] Thus the Vālakhilyas represent the souls that dwell in the highest soul. It is this fact that seems to be symbolised in the *Mb* account where the Vālakhilyas are said to be dwelling on the Rauhiṇa branch — the branch of the tree that is only a form of Viṣṇu — the highest soul. The fact that the Vālakhilyas dwell on the Rauhiṇa tree is prominently seen in the *Mb.* The *Sup. Ad.* is not quite clear on the point; and appears to suggest that the Vālakhilyas were in the sun in the east and not directly on the Rauhiṇa. In the *Sup. Ad.* (VII. 24. 4-5) we have that Garuḍa carried the broken branch only in fear lest it should kill the brāhmaṇas on the earth. We have also seen that it is in the *Mb.* that Viṣṇu occurs first in the picture in the episode of Somāharaṇa. When the *Mb.* mentions the Vālakhilyas to be on the Rauhiṇa (Aśvattha), the identification of Viṣṇu and the tree is clear.

In the Rāmāyaṇa (III.35. 30) the account occurs in short and the Vālakhilyas are called '*māṣāḥ*' which are tiny seeds and the tree is called '*Nyagrodha*'.[342]

## (G) Garuḍa and the Sun

It is usual to think of Garuḍa as the sun-bird, and scholars have been calling him so.[343] He, being the younger brother of Aruṇa (who reduces the excessive brilliance of the sun)'[344], could well have been imagined to be the sun coming after Aruṇa, the defused light of the morning. He is addressed as the 'Sun';[345] but in the same passage he is addressed variously, even as Indra, Viṣṇu and Agni — what more, as the Prajāpati himself! We may have, in the *Sk. P.*, an indication of his being called the sun, in the speech of Kadrū to Vinatā.[346]

When Vinatā is called '*Pataṅgī*' and the sun also the *Pataṅga*, it would apparently seem that the son of Vinatā, Garuḍa, could be taken as identified with the sun who also is a bird; but here also, it should be noted that the passage simply says that both the sun and Vinatā are birds; and nothing more; for in the very next verse we have, "He is the swan in the lake of the sky; you are having the gait of the swan".

This leaves no doubt that here the identification is completely nullified and the passage hints only at similarity.

It simply should mean that Garuḍa, the son of Vinatā (the female bird) is a bird and that the sun also is a bird. There is another passage which might appear to suggest that Garuḍa is the sun. It is where Garuḍa is said to have taken up the waters from the rivers with his mouths as many as ninety into ninety;[347] but observed minutely it appears that even in that passage Garuḍa comes nearer rather to Indra than the sun; for his bringing the waters to quench the fire round nectar suggests his having control over rain which is the prominent trait of Indra.[348] Thus, it seems more correct to say that in *Mb.* Garuḍa does not inherit the traits of the sun. But, this is not to uttlerly deny his association with the sun. His association with the sun can be seen from the fact that he carries the sages Vālakhilyas who are said to be residing in the sun and are called the protectors of the orb of that luminary. He is asked by the Rauhiṇa tree to dart to the Eastern direction — of the sun where the Vālakhilyas are said to dwell (Cf. *Sup. Ad.* noted earlier). Garuḍa's association with the sun can also be seen from the fact that he takes the nāgas towards the sun on his back and is quite at ease.[349] The association of Garuḍa with the sun probably has a base in his real identification with the sun somewhere; and this trait of Garuḍa in the *Mb* probably, is reminiscent of that identification. Elsewhere we do have such identification. Thus Ahura-Mazda is represented as an eagle with wings, his body enclosed in a circle. The Assyrian god Ashur and Ahur Mazda have their bodies enclosed in a ring.[350] The ring represents the disc of the sun, and it can be seen how the sun is identified with the Eagle (Garuḍa). We have already seen instances of eagle-gods identified with the sun.[351] The older sculptures from Khmer also represent Garuḍa in human form in a circle.[352] This coincides with the statement of Oldham who says that Garuḍa (with the nāgas) belongs to a solar race.[353] That the original war-god in most cases was the sun-god, in some form or the other, is stated by W. J. Perry, who takes the Assyrian war-god Ashur as an example,[354] and Ashur himself was the sun-god always represented in a circle with wings. The sun is also called a bird,[355] not only in the Hindu mythology, but even in the mythology of other people. The Maoris mention a sacred mountain that is the haunt of the Bird of the sun.[356] Perry comes to the conclusion further, that the sun-gods give place later to the warrior gods with the impact of warring foreign tribes. The case of Garuḍa, most probably, is the same. Garuḍa might have retained the sun-bird character in very remote times; but when the original tribes — the solar tribes — came into contact with the Vedic Āryans, gradually the Bird left the form of the sun, gradually taking on himself the form of the war-god and, in the assimilation that followed, came gradually close to the Vedic war-god, Indra. The references to Garuḍa's going to the sun, or to the East, are, thus, the oldest traits of his being the sun-god; but apart from these the bird seems to have no other traits of the Sun in the *Mb*.

# 6
# THE WAGER

The name Kadrū is known to the Samhitās and the Brāhmaṇas, but Vinatā is absent therein. However, the wager between them can be traced in the Brāhmaṇas, *Suparṇī* standing there in place of Vinatā. About the identification in the case of Kadrū and Suparṇī we have the following account in the Brāhmanical literature:

Kadrū is said to be this Earth, while Suparṇī is sometimes identified with '*Vāk*' and sometimes with heaven.[357] 'Suparṇī' often comes as the name of Garuḍa's mother in the *Sup. Ad.* (1. 2. 1, VI. 11. 3); but along with it, the appellation Vinatā also occurs. In *Mb,* however, Vinatā completely obscures the name Suparṇī; and the same is the case with the Purāṇas. We have already observed that the identification of Suparṇī with Vāk is particularly suited when Suparṇa and the metres were identified. When Suparṇī came to be identified with Vinatā, it is natural that Vinatā and Vāk should be identified.[358] Kadrū, the mother of the Sarpas, is later the same as the mother of the nāgas. She is 'Sarparājñī, who is said to be the Earth.[359] She is also identified with Surasā who is also the Earth.[360] Vinatā, identified with Suparṇī — who is 'heaven' (Dyauḥ) — also came to be identified with heaven, and thus 'Heaven' and 'Earth' came to compete with each another. It is this final identification of Kadrū with the Earth and of Vinatā with Heaven that we find in the *Sup. Ad.*[361] *Mb.* does not indulge in this identification and straightaway gives the story as if of two real sisters who gave birth to the serpents and the birds. According to other opinions, Kadrū means 'tawny', and Vinatā means 'bent'.[362] It probably is suggestive of the colour of the earth and the 'curve' of the vault of the heaven. It is difficult to contribute to the interpretation of Barth who suggests that Kadrū is 'darkness' personified;[363] for, in the face of the textual passages that give the identification as given above it is hardly sound to interpret in some other way than Kadrū = Earth and Vinatā = Sky.

Leaving these interpretations a bit aside, let us see now the other epithets of these two. Kadrū is also said to be Kāṇā,[364] (because?) her eye had been lost due to the (smoke of the) offerings.[365] Surpaṇī is called by another name — 'Śuṅgī' — and sometimes as 'Śuṅgā', from which Garuḍa gets to be called Śauṅgeya (*Sup. Ad.* IV. 8. 2. : V. 10.2 : IX. 17. 5). Charpentier[366] notes these names, but does not give a definite interpretation. These names rarely occur elsewhere, but probably hint at an inner implication, which becomes clearer when we think of the peculiar wager they had between themselves. The Vedic literature has, in most cases, these two competing as regards their form.[367] Hence the epithet 'Kāṇā' (of 'Kadrū') (*Sup. Ad.* III. 5. 4; 6. 2), and 'Suparṇī' (of Śungī or Vinatā) should suggest that, Kadrū was deformed and Suparṇī was well-formed. Kadrū, thus having a deformed eye could naturally be understood to feel the drawback; and, to prove herself superior to her sister Suparṇī (Vinatā), it is not surprising that, she would resort even to deceit and have a wager in which the eyes play an important part. Hence it is easy to understand that the wager rests on the strength of eyes[368] in marking the colour of the tail of the horse. This defective personality of Kadrū is discernible in the very name Kad + rū, the first part of the word meaning 'deformed'.[369] It is possible that the other part ('rū') retains in itself dormantly the original sense of *'rūpa'*, which is constantly to be seen in the words *'ātmarūpayoḥ'* or *'svarūpayoḥ'*. The wager between Kadrū and Suparṇī is well rooted in the Brāhmaṇa texts and Charpentier seems to be right in stating that the wager between these two might have originally been a saga in which two contesting personalites were involved, who were identified with Heaven and Earth. But, whereas it is possible to agree with Charpentier here, it is not possible to take in entirety his view that the saga originally came from the 'wagering animals'.[370] It more naturally resembles such numerous folk-tales where two wives of the same person — one defective and wicked, and the other attractive and sober (or evil-minded and well-minded) — compete for supremacy and the evil one wins with deceit, only to be retaliated by a counter-blow.[371]

It is not quite clear whence the name Vinatā came and when Vogel holds it to mean 'bent' he does not give any plausible explanation suitable to her association with Garuḍa. Charpentier identifies Vinatā with Vāk and is obstructed by the word, 'Śuṅgī' or 'Śuṅgā' which is another name of Vinatā. It is also to be noted that 'Śuṅgī' or 'Śuṅgā' means the 'Indian fig tree' which is Nyagrodha or Aśvattha. The Nyagrodha is itself called 'Suparṇa' in the Rāmāyaṇa[372] in the context of this very tale of Garuḍa that is given there in a nutshell. The branch of the tree is said to be *Parṇabahulā*.[373] It seems important that Garuḍa particularly rests on the branch of Rauhiṇa to eat the tortoise and the elephant. Putting all these together we get: —

(i) Śuṅgī = *Suparṇī* = Vinatā — (according to the *Sup. Ad.*).

(ii) Rauhiṇa (Nyagrodha) = *Suparṇa* — (according to the *Rām.*).

(iii) Garuḍa = *Suparṇa* (according to almost all texts).

Can we hazard a step further and suggest that 'Śuṅgī' originally might be the fig-tree (Rauhiṇa) the usual haunt of the big birds called Garuḍas? Rauhiṇa is identified also with Vaṭa.[374] This Vaṭa is the haunt of big birds that are called Gṛdhras.[375] Now this big tree, as the haunt of big birds, might have given the idea of its being the mother of these birds, as the earth is the mother of the serpents; for, it is in the earth that the serpents generally reside (in holes or in ant-hills). The mother of the serpents being called 'Surasā', the earth, Kadrū's identification with Earth supports this. The next step is simple. With the Garuḍa birds residing on the trees and the serpents residing in the earth, having eternal enmity, we could well understand how the earth and the big tree could be said to compete with one another for superiority; and this idea of vying with each other is not difficult to be connected with the already existing tales of wager; and to speak of these two as real persons is easy. The Śuṅgā tree with its beautiful leaves can well be called 'Suparṇā' and it could be identified with the Brahmanical 'Suparnī'. It may, however, be noted that the name 'Suparṇī' — the mother of Gāyatrī (identified with Suparṇa) — is suggested from the word 'Suparṇa', the Ṛgvedic Śyena, while the name 'Suparṇī' in the case of Śuṅgī seems to be suggested from the great tree Rauhiṇa (the Vaṭa or Nyagrodha, the same as Śuṅgī) '*having beautiful leaves.*' The word *parṇa* is the same in both, but has two different meanings —

(i) feather and
(ii) leaf.

In *Mb,* and later, the word 'Śuṅgī' is completely lost in the wake of the other word 'Vinatā' which means (i) Bent by the birds; and (ii) simply Bent,[376] or coming down, the first meaning suggesting the haunt of birds as the tree Rauhiṇa (Nyagrodha) is, while the other being practically the same as the Nyagrodha.[377] Of particular importance in this context is the episode where the brāhmaṇa Kāśyapa nullifies the effect of snake-poison. There also we have the tree *Nyagrodha* which is burnt to ashes by Takṣaka, the nāga. The brāhmaṇa is warned by Takṣaka, "That excellent prowess of thy *mantras* do thou show and try. I shall burn this Nyagrodha tree even as thou dost look on, O best of Brāhmaṇas." And Kāśyapa replies, "Do thou sting this tree if thou so desirest O Lord of the Serpents. I shall cause it again to live, O Bhujaṅga, when thou hast stung it . . ."(*Mb*. I. 43. 2-3).

Nyagrodha is Śuṅgā and in this particular account when any tree would have served the purpose, the mention of Ṇygrodha seems to be important. It hints at the underlying idea of the possible enmity of the tree with the serpent and resembles the enmity between Śuṅgī (Vinatā) and the Nāgī (Kadrū). The Earth and the Heaven were probably a later identification on the lines of the Brāhmaṇa texts, the original one being the Tree and the Earth, this itself being suggested from the Śuṅgī-Nāgī or the Nyagrodha-Serpent conflict. Garuḍa, as an antagonist of the serpents and having a possible haunt on the Nyagrodha, came to be the son of this tree and called 'Śauṅgeya'. From another point, he was called 'Kāśyapeya',[378] the remover of snake-poison — being himself the son of Kaśyapa. The term 'Kāśyapeya' is rarely applied to the sons of Kadrū, though even they are said to be Kaśyapa's sons.

We have already noted that the knowers of the 'lore of snakes' — i.e. of the antidotes of snake-poison — are themselves called *'Kāśyapīyas'* according to the commentator on the *Āśv. Śr. Sū*. The mention of the brāhmaṇa Kāśyapa in the Nyagrodha – Takṣaka episode thus seems meaningful. Garuḍa's close association with Śuṅgī (ā) (the Nyagrodha), and his being the presiding deity of the *mantras* against snake-bite place him on par with the Kāśyapīyas. The idea in the brāhmaṇa, Kāśyapa, saving the Nyagrodha tree from the poison of Takṣaka and that in Garuḍa saving his mother Śuṅgī (Nyagrodha-tree) are similar. It is possible that the Kāśyapīyas, were the snake-charmers with Garuḍa as their deity, and having the Śuṅgā as their sacred tree.

The closeness of association between the Nyagrodha (Śungī) and Garuḍa can be seen from the fact that the latter is said to have killed the Niṣādas with the *Nyagrodha* branch (*Rām*. III . 53. 33.)

Garuḍa is called sometimes Tārkṣya and sometimes 'Tārkṣyaputra'.[379] But while in *Mb* he is said to be the son of Kaśyapa, in the *Sup. Ad.* he is said to be the son of Tārkṣya, in both born of the penance of the Vālakhilyas. Hence Tārkṣya and Kaśyapa get to be identified.[380] Charpentier notes this identification and is satisfied with it. By quoting various passages, he tries to show that Garuḍa and Tārkṣya are also identified.[381] One thing is to be borne in mind in this context. Garuḍa — the bird who could nullify the poison of the serpent — was the deity of the *mantras* used as cure against serpent-bite; also that these *mantras* (or the *poison-lore*) were specially taught to the Sarpas, people of Arbuda Kādraveya. Charpentier does not take note of this fact though he quotes passages just next to those that speak of the special lore of the Sarpas. This is because Charpentier's aim seems to be to identify Garuḍa, as the king of birds, with Tārkṣya who is also said to be the king of birds, thus indicating that Tārkṣya was only the former name for Garuḍa. Now the first reference to Garuḍa occurs in the *Tait. Ā.*[382] Charpentier notes the reference without, however, examining the quotation.[383] It should be borne in mind that the word Garuḍa when it occurs for the first time — as Charpentier also says — has nothing of the epithet that qualifies himself for the kingship of the feathered tribe. It occurs just after the praise of Rudra-Śiva, and it is clear that the reference to Garuḍa there is nothing more than as a bird that is equal to Śiva in nullifying poison.[384] It is clear then that, here, Garuḍa is not the king of birds. But in the *mantras* from the *Agni. P.* he is definitely referred to as the king of brids.[385] (as also in the *Sup. Ad.* and the *Mb*) and the *mantras* also are named after Tārkṣya who alone is mentioned as the king of birds in the *Aśv. Śr. Sū.* and the *Ś. B.*[386]. The accounts of Garuḍa's birth as given in the *Sup. Ad.* (I. 2. 3. ff.) and the *Mb* (I. 31; Crit. I-37) strive to show that Garuḍa is to be made the 'Indra' of birds which presupposes that Garuḍa, who was an ordinary bird formerly, is being made the king of birds. Probably this is what is suggested in the episode in the *Sup. Ad.* when Garuḍa is born to the ascetic, Tārkṣya, as his son. Here is an indication of the bird Garuḍa being assimilated with the original king of the birds. To put down more clearly —

(i) Garuḍa was a bird different from Tārkṣya;
(ii) Tārkṣya was the king of the birds (i. e. bird-tribe);
(iii) Garuḍa was the bird — not from the 'bird - tribe', but only as the one — who was holy to those who mastered the *mantras* against poison; and
(iv) The two were later assimilated.

The identification was, probably, due to the fact that Tārkṣya is said to be the Sun-bird in the *Ṛgveda*[387] and in Garuḍa also there were traits of the Sun. It is not correct to suppose that Tārkṣya was the original form of Garuḍa or Garuḍa is an evolved form of Tārkṣya, for in that case we expect the main quality of Garuḍa — the killing of serpents — as a quality of Tārkṣya in the Vedic literature; which is rarely so. Thus we have to take it as a case of assimilation of two different deities, where Garuḍa from the aboriginal popular faith is being assimilated with the sun-bird Tārkṣya who is also said to be the king of birds.

We have noted how according to Risley's finding Kaśyapa and the nāga are supposed to be the remotest fore-fathers of many tribes in India.[389] The Kāśyapīyas are also said to be the snake-charmers or well-versed in poisons;[389] and, the giving of the poison-lore to Kāśyapa by Brahmā (*Mb*. I. 2-16) corroborates with this. The same is corroborated by the account of a brāhmaṇa named Kāśyapa nullifying the poison of the serpent Takṣaka. The account appears in the context of the death of Parīkṣit by snake-bite. Prior to the death of the king, Takṣaka meets in the way a brāhmaṇa by name Kāśyapa who also is on the way to undo the effect of the poison of Takṣaka, after the latter bit the king, and get reward for the act. Takṣaka asks him to prove his merit and bites the 'Nyagrodha' tree which instantaneously gets completely burnt to ashes due to the effect of the poison.

Now, Kāśyapa with the power of his *mantras*, causes the tree to revive. The account goes on to tell that Takṣaka himself gave reward to the brāhmaṇa and, thus taking him away from his path, accomplishes the terrible task of killing Parīksita.[390]

The association between Garuḍa and Kāśyapa seems to be an earlier one than that of Garuḍa and Tārkṣya in this particular sense as the vanquisher of snake-poison. The *Sup. Ad.* makes Garuḍa the king of birds identifying him with Tārkṣya, while the *Mb* repeating the account of *Sup. Ad.* in giving Garuḍa the kingship of the birds with the only change from Tārkṣya to Kāśyapa, adds one more point in revealing Kāśyapa as the controller of snake-poison, which is absent in the case of Tārkṣya. As a matter of fact the whole episode of the birth of the serpents is absent in the *Sup. Ad.*, while in *Mb* it is a prominent feature. When in later literature Tārkṣya is associated with the *mantras* against snake-poison[391] it has rarely anything to do with the *Sup. Ad.* — Tārkṣya (the father of Garuḍa), but only with Gāruda who is different from, and later assimilated with, Tārkṣya himself.

## Element of Deceit

The element of deceit in the legend comes in the wager where Kadrū asks her sons to blacken the horse by covering it after being hairs, black like soot.[392] This element of deceit is absent in the pre-*Mb* literature. Even in the *Sup. Ad.* where the legend first occurs in a full-fledged form, this element is totally absent. It begins only from *Mb*. The deceitful Kadrū and her sons are ultimately duped by resort to counter-deceit; for nectar is carried away by Indra as soon as it was kept on the *darbha* grass, and there we have the act described as 'counter-deceit' (*Pratimāyā*).[393] The *Sup. Ad.* also has the retaking of Soma by Indra, but the clear mention of the counter-deceit is not to be found there. The

Brāhmaṇas also describe the *Soma* juice as being taken away on the way by the Gandharva Viśvāvasu; but it is not through deceit. The *Sk. P.* has a regular didactic note inserted in the element of deceit saying that those who take anything by deceit only get humiliation at the end.[394] It is clear that the element of deceit crept up in the tale from popular belief as in tales where the party weak in prowess resorts to deceit to gain victory which is however temporary, and is nullified by counter-deceit, as Charpentier rightly points out.[395]

## Summary and Conclusion

The Vedic texts do not refer to Garuḍa. The first mention of the name Garuḍa is found in the *Tait. Ā.* but there also it is together with Śiva. Śiva and Garuḍa are invoked again together in the *Agni. P.* in the context of the poison as the deities that remove poison. The Garuḍa-legend in *Mb* depicts Garuḍa in the traditional way as the killer of snakes. The exploits of Garuḍa as mentioned in *Mb* are —

(i) The lifting and eating up of the tortoise and the elephant;
(ii) The killing and eating up of the Niṣādas, except the brāhmaṇa that was living among them;
(iii) The fetching of Soma.

Of all these exploits, the last is common with the Vedic Suparṇa. Of the two remaining, the first one boils down only to the traditional antagonism of Garuḍa with the nāgas. The tortoise (*kacchapa*) and the elephant (called also *nāga*) are really two nāgas or divisions of the nāgas that are overpowered by Garuḍa. Their being eaten up by Garuḍa[396] might have been suggested by the Garuḍa 'birds' actually lifting up big animals, but the account of *kacchapa* and the nāga in the Garuḍa legend, appears to be a real traditional account of the overpowering of the nāgas by Garuḍa. We can see this from references to the nāgas and Garuḍa in the *Rājataraṅgiṇī* and other tales from folklore. It is possible that the account of the two nāgas and Garuḍa was fashioned on the analogy of the Garuda-bird lifting up animals and eating them. Garuḍa in the Niṣāda episode appears to be only a symbol of conquest over the Niṣādas on the analogy of the Vedic tale of Māthava Videgha and the fire.

Garuḍa's main feature, as noticed from reference to him in literature and folklore, seems to be his deadly enmity with the serpents; and hence he is supposed to be the remover of snake-poison. Garuḍa thus becomes the deity of the *mantras* that are chanted to remove snake-poison. The words 'Garuḍa-vidyā' and the term 'Gārudī' associated with the idea of removing snake-poison bear testimony to this fact. The 'Gāruḍā-vidyā' is probably the same as the '*Viṣa-vidyā*' in the *Ś. B.* and other Vedic texts, *Āśval. Śr. Sū*, '*Sarpa veda*' in *Chānd. Up.* and '*Sarpa-vidyā*' in *Śaṅ. Śr. Sū*. which was taught in ancient times to the people of Arbuda Kādraveya who were the Sarpas. This lore '*Viṣa-vidyā*' is different from the lore of the birds. The '*Viṣa-vidyā*' or the '*Sarpa-vidyā*' (or *Sarpa veda*) is a lore meant to counteract snake-poison. It is not known what exactly it contained; but is seems to be very similar to — nay probably the same as — the '*Gāruḍā Vidyā*' which contains *mantras* to counter-act snake-poison. The name '*Garuḍa Śāstra*' mentioned by the *Gaṇ. P.* and the 'Garuḍa-Viddai' (as given in the Tamil lexicon) also are said to be the lores effective against snake-poison. This shows that the '*sarpa vidyā*' or the '*Viṣa-vidyā*' referred to in the Sūtras might itself have been known later as '*Gāruḍā vidyā*' or a 'vidyā', with which the name of Garuḍa was associated, from the fact of Garuḍa's being the deadly enemy of the serpents. Thus, this *Vidyā*, (later) called the '*Gārudā Vidyā*', was the special lore of the Sarpas, and also naturally of the nāgas, who came to be identified with Sarpas. The lore of the birds, whose king Tārkṣya was, was different from this '*Gāruḍā-vidya*', and was '*Vāyu-vidyā*'. If the '*Viṣa-vidyā*' (or the '*Gāruḍā-vidyā*' as it is called) is the sacred lore of the sarpas, who were later identified with the nāgas, and if the lore was called

*'Gāruḍā-vidyā'* which corresponds to the words *'Gāruḍī'* etc., Gāruḍa being involved for cure against serpent-bite, it naturally follows that those among the Sarpas (nāgas) who learnt this *'vidyā'* would have veneration for Garuḍa and might even be worshipping him in some form or the other. It would also be natural that these snake-charmers (the knowers of this *vidyā*) would style themselves as 'Garuḍaṣ' or even 'Gāruḍas' as is the case with tribal men. Thus the knowers of this 'Viṣa-vidyā' or 'Sarpa-vidyā' might be Garuḍas, though they are originally the Sarpas or the nāgas. It is for this reason that we do not find Garuḍas having a strong claim to euhemeristic interpretation, as we do in the case of the nāgas. These 'Garuḍas' (i. e. the knowers of the 'Gāruḍā-vidyā') would naturally have an air of superiority to the other nāgas (Sarpas) of whom they are a part; this superiority, most probably, might be in the sphere of magic, or charms in general and of those of the serpents in particular. The strife between the Garuḍas and the nāgas is, thus, a strife in the same tribe and not two different ones. The hereditary enmity between nāgas and the Garuḍas is a sort of a phratry-relationship in which the whole society is divided in two sub-divisions, supposed to be always at animosity towards each other, but coming together making a complete whole, uniting in some form or the other at the time of important ceremonials. The nāgas and Garuḍas are always represented as uniting through reconciliation, though they are said to have enmity between themselves.

Garuḍa, the bird, thus being the emblem for cure against snake-bite and possibly the one that was held high in reverence by certain members of the big Nāga-clans came to be represented in sculptures as killing and eating serpents. These sculptures at a certain time might have been sacred to certain sections of the nāgas who probably worshipped these. Such representations in stone where Garuḍa and the serpents are shown as part of one body probably hint at the original dual system of the social organization. Descriptions are also found in literature where the nāgas are said to be born out of the wing of Garuḍa, which again explains the principle of phratry and oneness in division.[397]

The combination of the Garuḍa-nāga (or say the Eagle-Serpent) is a motif common to other parts of the world also and the god-head representing a big eagle has the serpents either as his prey, or in association. A big bird is found in many a mythology as possessing great power. But Garuḍa has a distinct social status; and, hence, it seems probable that Garuḍa hails from a tribal and social system that was originally present in India and is much more than the mere symbol of the Sun or Light. To suppose that Suparṇa in the Ṛgvedic Brahmanic literature has given Garuḍa to *Mb.* or Sup. *Ad.* is far from being correct. Even 'Suparṇa' is originally the 'Śyena', and is only an epithet that is applicable to many a deity of the Vedas, thus having no particular connotation.

The bird that carried the immortal juice is Śyena and is *called* Suparṇa. This epithet of Śyena became current further on in the Brāhmaṇas to denote the bringer of the immortal juice or the giver of immortality; and the metres were identified with Suparṇa, and called so, because of their leading the sacrificer to immortality and freeing the gods from the clutches of death. This idea of freeing from death and giving immortality in the case of the metres was an outcome of the peculiar importance of the sacrificial system of the Brāhmaṇas giving utmost importance to the *mantras.* Hence the metres — Gāyatrī chief among them — were identified with Śyena-Suparṇa and the old episode of Somāharaṇa was cast in a new setting. Garuḍa being the deity of the Snake-charms with his power over the serpents and serpent-poison, could naturally be thought to give freedom from death due to serpent-bite in particular and due to any cause in general. Hence he also was identified with the Vedic Suparṇa and called so, *being originally a different bird* actually existing in popular faith and probably worshipped by a sect of the nāgas.

The mother of Garuḍa (Vinatā) identified with Heaven and Kadrū, identified with the Earth, were originally, probably, the Earth and the 'Śuṅgī' (Nyagrodha) tree. The Śungī tree being the haunt of the big-birds called 'Garuḍas' was thought as their mother, and the earth with serpents taking shelter in her, was thought as the mother of the latter. Hence, originally, the enmity between Garuḍa and the serpents was equal to the symbolic enmity between the Śuṅgī tree and the Earth under her. The wager with deceit is an old popular motif often found in folk-tales and was used to exemplify the competition of the Śuṅgī and the Nāgī (the earth) (as they are called in the *Sup. Ad.*). The earth was the same as Kadrū in the Brāhamaṇs. The tree with beautiful leaves also was later identified with the 'Suparṇī' of the Brāhmaṇas. Thus, the Kadrū-Suparṇī tale in the Brāhmaṇas came to be completely assimilated later with nāgī-Śuṅgī (Kadrū-Vinatā) tale at the time of the *Sup. Ad.*; and the whole popular account of the traditional enmity between Garuḍa and the serpents with the symbolic animosity between the Śuṅgī tree and the Nāgī got mixed in the ancient episode of Ṛgvedic Somāharaṇa — and the '*Sauparṇī-Kādravam*'.

Viewing closely, it appears that this bird of the original popular faith of an Indian tribe later got a place in the Brahmanical religion, not altogether without a struggle for prominence.[398] The fight between Garuḍa and Indra and the references to Garuḍa-Viṣṇu conflicts hint at this fact. He is not simply the Suparṇa of the Somāharaṇa. When Garuḍa was identified with Suparṇa in the exploit of the Somāharaṇa we see a regular challenge to Indra's supremacy and in the account of the Vālakhilyas there is a clear effort to show Garuḍa to be superior to Indra. When Viṣṇuism dominated, this bird, as the deity's Vāhana, was still predominant, being next only to Viṣṇu, and it is in this period of Viṣṇuite predominance that Garuḍa got completely assimilated into the Vedic religion, being to Viṣṇu in the same way as Viṣṇu was to Indra in the Vedic period. As the emblem of speed and strength Garuḍa inherited some of the exploits of the Vedic companion of Viṣṇu viz., Indra.

The references to Garuḍa as Tārkṣya, or as his son, need not lead us to believe that these two were one and the same. Tārkṣya is said to be the king of birds in the Vedic texts, which state the '*Vāyu purāna*' as the lore (*Vidyā*) of these people and not the Gāruḍā-vidyā. The Gāruḍā vidyā was the lore of the serpents (nāgas) and the presiding deity of this *vidyā* — the bird Garuḍa — had nothing originally to do with Tārkṣya. Tārkṣya's name in the *mantras* regarding snake-charming later seems to be because of his identification with GARUḌA.

## References

1. For Garuḍa as the emblem of the Gupta dynasty, see Banerji — *Pre-historic Ancient and Hindu India* — p. 167. It was the emblem of the kings of the Pāṇḍu Vaṁśa (moon-Vaṃśa) that ruled in Shripur (Sirpur in Raipur Dist., M.P.) in the 7th cent. AD etc. (See Majumdar and Pusalkar, *Age of Imperial Unity*, Ed., p. 145). On the tombs of many ancient Iranian kings, the emblem is to be seen as the disc of the sun with wings fluttering on both sides; for this and other examples, see Chandra Cakrawarty — *Ancient Races and Myths*, p. 20.
2. The rest of the 17th Adhyāya, the 18th and the 19th deal with the churning of the ocean, and have no direct connection with the legend in hand.
3. Crit. Ed., Adh. 18.1-11.
4. The Critical Edition omits stanzas 12 to 16a, retaining only 16b.
5. Crit. Ed. Adhyāya XIX. The rest of the verses are only a description of the sea. The whole of the Adhyāya XXII is dropped by the Crit. Ed. except the last verse (i.e. XXII. 12).
6. The Ed. of Nīlakaṇṭha has variants, but they are not very important. The Crit. Ed. drops many verses here, that

are found in Nīl.'s Ed.

7. Crit. Ed. I.20.
8. The whole of the 24th Adhyāya is dropped in the Crit. Ed.
9. The praise of Indra runs from verse 7th up to the end of the chapter. We leave it out as it has no connection with the legend.
10. Then follows a description of the showering clouds.
11. A description of the island — not needed for our legend.
12. The Citraśāla Ed. (with Nīla's com.) has two stanzas after this (cf. I.30.6 & 7) which are dropped by the Crit. Ed. These being important for our purpose, we give here, and we shall have occasion to come to them later in our discussion —

    अतिदैवं तु तत्तस्य कर्म दृष्ट्वा महर्षयः।
    विस्मयोत्कम्पहृदया नाम चक्रुर्महाखगे।।
    गुरुं भारं समासाद्योड्डीन एष विहङ्गमः।
    गरुडस्तु खगश्रेष्ठस्तस्मात् पन्नगभोजनः।।

13. Nīla. *varjitam mānuṣaiḥ deśam* (I.30.20). The Cri. Edi. has *brāhmaṇaiḥ*.
14. Then follows a short beautiful description of the Himālayas.
15. The description of the weapons etc. is dropped in our translation.
16. The Crit. Ed. omits this line — *'bhavate' pi varam dadyām vṛṇotu Bhagavān api'* — (Nīlā. on I.33.16). We have here retained the reading of Nīla. The purpose will be clear later on in our discussion.
17. Crit. Ed. has 'Kṛṣṇa' in place of Viṣṇu.
18. I.16.25. *ādāsyannātmano bhojyam annaṃ vihitam asya yat*
    *vidhātrā bhṛgu-śārdūla kṣudhitaḥ patageśvaraḥ*
19. I.34.13. *'bhaveyur bhujagāḥ śakra mama bhakṣyā mahābalāḥ'*.
    XIV.30.6. also — *nāgāste bhakṣyāḥ santu vihaṅgamendra.*
20. I.33.6; IV.50.83.
21. *Sup. Ad.* XV.30.5. *nāgān vṛṇe bhakṣyam aham śacīpate; cf. Ib.* XIV. 30.7.
    *Pad. P.V.* 44.181.
    *Sk.* P. III.38.98 ff. etc.; *Bhāg. P.* III.19.1.;

also Penzer, *Ocean of Story*, Vol. ii, p. 50 ff.
22. *Mb.* V.105; *Viṣṇu Dh.* P. III.343.26.
23. *Sk. P.* IV (Part 1) 50.25, 26.
24. *Rām.* V.153.II.
25. *K.S.S.* XII-181-201; Tawny's Tr., Vol. I, p. 182 ff. Also the well-known drama of Harṣa — *Nāgānandam*.
26. Cf. J. ph. Vogel, *Indian Serpent Lore*, London, 1926.
27. *Ibid.*, p. 278; also Crooke., *Popular Religion and Folklore in Northern India*, Vol. II, p. 122. The day is called *Garuḍa Pañcamī* in the Tamil-Nāḍu. Cf. the Tamil lexicon under 'Garuḍa'.
28. *Sk. P.* II, 4.12 ff. esp. read —

    इयं मन्नामविख्याता सर्वपापहरा शिला
    एतस्याः स्मरणात् पुंसां विषव्याधिर्न जायताम्।।३०।।

    and before that

    ततः प्रभृति त्रैलोक्ये गारुडीति शिलोच्यते।
29. *Ibid.* VIII.56.2, 3.

    वैनतेयस्तु देवेशि ज्ञात्वा क्षेत्रं तु वैष्णवम्।।
    लिङ्गं प्रतिष्ठयामास सर्वपापप्रणाशनम्
    यस्तं पूजयते भक्त्या पञ्चम्यां तु विधानतः।
    न विषं क्रमते तस्य सप्तजन्मनि सर्पजम्।।
30. Ct. *Rāj. Tar.* IV.333-1, 38; also *Raghu*, V.13 etc.
31. Vogel, *Ind. S.L.*, p. 132 ff.
32. *Ibid.*, p. 133.
33. *Ibid.*, p. 141; Jātaka, Vol. V, p. 75 ff.; also Viyogi *Jātaka-kālīna Bhāratīya Samskriti* (Hindi) — Bihār Rāṣtrabhāṣā Pariṣad, Patna, 1958.
34. Ct. '*Uraga-jātaka*', at Jātaka, Vol. II, p. 12 ff.; also Viyogi, *op. cit.*, p. 225.
35. It is interesting to note here, that the snake-charmers themselves are a caste in Mahārāṣtra and are called *Gāruḍis* (cf. *Jñānkośa*, by G.V. Ketkar; also '*Sulabha viśvakośa*', — by Karve and Date). The word '*Gāruḍī*' is from Garuḍa. Cf. also the stone called '*Gāruḍi-śilā*' (note 28-*supra.*) for Garuḍa stones; *Raghu*. XIII-53; *Kādamabarī*, III-29.
36. Viyogi, p. 225.
37. *Ibid.*, *op. cit.*, p. 237.

38. Wilkins, *Hindu Mythology Vedic and Purāṇika*, p. 376.
39. Max Müller, *History of Ancient India*, Allahabad, 1926, p. 20.
40. The *Śān. Śr. Sū.* has the same passage practically as in the *Āś. Śr. Sū.* given below under note 42. See *Sāṅk. Śr. S.* (Ed. Hillebrandt, Calcutta, 1888), XVI.2.13 and 14. The notable change is that *Śāṅ. Śr. S.* has *Sarpavidyā* in the place of *Viṣa-vidyā*. Cf. also *Ś.B.* (Mādh.) XIII.4.3.9. which is far earlier.
41. Cf. Com. of Anārtīya — *gāruḍam kākatīya vā.*
42. *ĀŚ. Śr. Sū.* IV-6.1, in *Uttara Śaṭkam.*
    *sarpāḥ sarpavidaḥ . . . tān*
    *upadiśāti, viṣavidyā vedaḥ*
    The word *sarpavidaḥ* is rendered by the commentator as *viṣatantravidaḥ.*
    For other references to *Sarpa-vidyā*, Macdonell and Keith, *Vedic Index* Vol. ii, p. 438; *Gop. Br.* (*Pūrva* — I.10) has the form *sarpa-veda*. The *Chānd. Up.* VII.2.1; 4; 4.1; 7.1 has *sarpa-vidyā*.
    Macdonell and Keith think that the word *Sarpadevajanavidyā* refers to only one *vidyā*; but Śaṅkara commenting on the passage (*Chānd. Up.* VIII.2.1) gives them as two — (i) *Sarpa-vidyā* and (ii) *devajana*. Śaṅkara renders the word *Sarpavidyā* as *Gāruḍam.*
43. *Mb.* I.20.16. *prādād viṣaharīm vidyām kaśyapāya mahātmane.*
44. Cf. Dubois and Beauchamp, *Hindu Manners, Customs and Ceremonies,* p. 250. The prayer is thiswise — 'Illustrious son of Kaśyapa and Vinatā, king of birds, with beautiful wings and sharp pointed beak — you who are the enemy of snakes, prevent me from their bite'.
45. Cf. *Gaṇ. P.* 134-28, *yathā garuḍaśāstrajñaḥ sarpam karṣati tatkṣaṇāt.*
46. *Vāyu p.* 39.39, 40.
    *vaikaṅke śailaśikhare,*
    *tatrāste gāruḍirnityam uragāri-durāsadaḥ/*
    *mahāvāyujavaścaṇḍaḥ sugrīvo nāma vīryavān//*
    It should be noted that Sugrīva is not mentioned among the sons of Garuḍa in the Mb., V.10.1, and

hence the word '*Gāruḍī*' should be taken to mean a '*Snake-charmer*'.

47. *Mb*. V. 104.
48. This identification of the sarpas and the nāgas was a confirmed fact as early as the *Sup. Ad.* and it passed on to the *Mb*. and the later literature. Kadrū, whence we have the name Kādraveya, of the Śarpa-seer, is herself said to be the mother of the nāgas in the *Sup. Ad.* I.2.1. Cf. *bhūmistu nāgyabhavat kadrunāmā*. The *Mb* has ample references to this fact. Cf. *Mb*. I.25.4; 27.1, 3; 29.10. For Kādraveya = Sarpa, see *Jai. Br.* I.345; *Vedic Index*.
49. Max Müller, *op. cit.*, p. 21; see n. 40, *supra*; for Tārkṣya, being mentioned as a person, with Ariṣṭanemi, see *Vāja-Sam.* XV.18; for Tārkṣya Vaipaścitya and his 'Birds' to be taught at the Ten-day cycle of the Pāriplava, see *Ś.B.* (*Mādh.*) XIII.4.3.13.
50. *Ś.B. (Mādh.)* XIII.4.3.13; *Śāṅ. Śr. Sū.* VII.2.17. Eggeling reads as *vāyovidyika,* which may be a misprint. The com. on *Śāṅ. Śr. Sū.* suggests *Vāyu P.*
51. *Sup. Ad.* IV.7.3. *tārkṣyasya putras tvam ariṣṭaneme*; also *Ibid., indum pītvā vīryavān tārkṣyaputraḥ*; but *Mb*. V.112.1 *naya mām tārkṣya pūrveṇa*; also *Sk*. P. I.19.28, IV.150.
52. Cf. Tamil lexicon under Garuḍa.
53. *Ibid.* written as *Karuṭa-Vittai*, due to Tamil pronunciation
54. *Agni. P.* 295-5. The *mantra,* is *Ibid* 4. *vīyater nāma mantro'yam tārkṣyaḥ śabdamayaḥ smṛtaḥ.*
55. *Ibid.* 27. The deity of the *mantra* appears to be a mixture of Garuḍa and his female aspect, cf. *Garuḍa viśikhāyai.*
56. *Ibid.* 297.1; also *ibid.*, 2. *pakṣi-rudreṇa viṣam nāśam āyāti iti mantraṇāt.*

    Further on, Rudra is called '*Pretādhipati*'; but ultimately we have — '*suvarṇa-pataṅga-Rudro*', which reminds us of the bird Garuḍa — having golden wings. '*Pretādhipati*' suggests '*Rudraśiva*', the lord of '*Pretas*'.
57. Or *Garuḍo devatā asyāḥ iti* — (*Garuḍa* + *aṇ*).

    Cf. also *Garuḍa-śāstrajñaḥ* in *Gaṇ. P.*, note 45. *Supra.*
58. Oldham, *Serpent worship in India* — *J.R.A.S.*, 1891, p. 361 ff.

59. *Ibid.*, p. 369; for Garuḍas as the dwellers of Pātāla, see *Mb.* V.101, where the names of the sons of Garuḍa are told, and they are called *Suparṇas*. For Garuḍa and Nāgas staying in one place see '*Jātaka-Tales*, Tr. by H.T. Francis & E.G. Thomas, Jaico, Bombay, 1953, p. 153, where the Garuḍa King is said to carry queen Sussondi by his supernatural power to his abode in Nāga island. Cf. also *Sussondi Jātaka, Jataka,* Vol. III, p. 187.
60. See Kennedy's letter on the article of Oldham in *J.R.A.S.*, 1891, pp. 480-81.
61. For 'Totemism' — see article of that name by Alexander Goldenweiser in *Making of man*, New York, 1931; also Andrew Lang, *Myth, Ritual and Religion;* James Hastings, *Enc. Rel. & Ethics.*
62. *Mb.* I.33.16-ff., *Sk.* P. IV.50-10 ff; *Padma P.,V.*, 44.8 r-ff.
63. See the sub-chapter on "The Wager" for fuller discussion *infra.*
64. We have already hinted at this point in the previous pages.
65. *Mb.* V.105, esp. 31.
*pādāṅguṣṭhena cikṣepa sumukham garuḍopari/*
*tataḥprabhṛti rājendra saha sarpeṇa vardhate//*
66. Cf. *Ibid.*, 101.6.
*karmaṇā kṣatriyaścaite nirghṛṇā bhogibhojinaḥ/*
*jāti-saṅkṣaya-kartṛtvād brāhmaṇatvamna labhanti vai//*
for the meaning which we took — cf. also — Hopkins — *Epic Mythology*, p. 22.
67. *Rām.* III.14.20 to 22 — The *Mb* is silent on the point of Vinatā being the mother of Kadrū and Surasā; see *Mb.* I.67.60 ff. See Hopkins, *Epic Myth.*, p. 23.
For Surasā and Kadrū as the mother of Serpents etc., cf. *Rām.* III.14.28.
68. *Mb.* I.36.10; also 67-70.
69. *Mb. loc. cit.*25. *suparṇam ca sahāyam vai bhagavān amarottamaḥ/*
*prādād anantāya tadā vainateyam pitāmahaḥ//*
70. Vogel, *Ind. Ser. L.*, p. 172. Garuḍa holding a five-hooded serpent in his beak — both theriomorphic — in the Gandhara sculpture; in the Mathurā–sculpture Garuḍa has ear rings like a human being.

71. Cf. Jean Boisselier, "Garuḍa dans l' Art Khmer", *Bulletin d l'Ecole Francaise Tome,* XXXIV, Hanoi, 1951, p. 56.
72. *Ibid.,* plates XXX & XXXI, where the upper half of the hood of the nāgas shows Garuḍa in the centre.
See also Appendix A, for Garuḍa and Nāgī in one piece, *infra.*
73. *Ibid.*, p. 76.
74. *Ibid.*, p. 70. "Nous assistarions ainsi; durant le style du Rayon, a un development constant du thème nouveau qui donnsrait une importance croissante Garuda considerē comme protecteur des nāgas."
75. *Mb.*, V. 101.8.
76. For sect-mark see *Mb.* V.101, where Garuḍa's sons are having the '*Śrīvatsa*' as a mark.
77. J. Boisselier, *op. cit.*, p. 69.
78. For nāgas as magicians cf. Saṅghamitrā bringing the branch of the Bodhi-tree in the form of Garuḍa which the *magician nāgas* wanted to win; p. 19, *supra.*
79. "Serpent worship in India", *J.R.A.S.* 1891. p. 370.
80. *Ibid.*, p. 369. We have already referred to this view of Oldham. See p. 27, *supra.*
81. *Sulabha Viśva Kośa*, Part 2, under the names in question.
82. *Mahārāṣtrīya Jntāna Kośa.*
83. It should be noted in this connection that one '*Mālaṅga*' figures in a story from the *Mb.* This *Mātaṅga* is said to have been a *cāṇḍāla* brought up by a brāhmaṇa. In order to obtain elevation to the position of a brāhmaṇa he went through such a course of austerities as alarmed the gods. Indra refused to admit him repeatedly; but ultimately, seeing the extremely arduous nature of his austerities, Indra, supporting him, *gave him powers of moving about like a bird, and changing his shape at will,* and being honoured and renowned. Cf. Dowson, *Classical Dictionary of Hindu Mythology*, London, 1953, p. 205.
Can the powers here referred to be those pertaining to magic? The changing of shape indicates it. '*Moving like a bird*' has in itself a hidden resemblance to Garuḍa the '*kāmagamaḥ pakṣī*'. When we see that Mataṅga can etymologically be the original form of Māṅga, this Mataṅga, who got the boon to move like á bird, suggests the

conception of 'Māṅga-Gāruḍi'. It is difficult to produce proof, but probably the Māṅgas were also a tribe of the nāgas, named after Mātaṅga, the well known sage, who, like Kādraveya, might be a Nāga. In the *Suparṇa Ad.* we get the 'Śuddha' and 'Padma' *nāgas* as the followers of Mataṅga (VII.14.1). We have tried to show elsewhere in this book (in the account of Tortoise and Elelphant) that these two nāgas were of the serpent class, though it is usual to understand by the word 'nāga' an elephant. In that case Mataṅga, whose followers the said nāgas are said to be, might well be an important person of the nāga clan. The word 'Mataṅga' meaning elephant might have been suggested from 'mataṅgaja' which has 'gaja' with 'matan' (maddening, ruttish— *'mādyati anena'*; see Apte's Dictionary) or it may even be taken that Mataṅga was a sage who first tamed the elephants as R.D. Karmarkar says (see notes on *Raghu*. V.53); but the sage, again, was probably of the nāga class. Rājarāma Śāstrī Bhāgavata believes that Mahāras (in the Mahārāṣṭra) are the Nāgas (*Mahā. Jn. K.*). See Appendix E. Also see *Rām.* III.73. 29, 30 where we have the sage Mataṅga living in the Mataṅgavana among the nāgas.

84. For phratry see Held, *The Mahābhārata*, London, 1935, pp. 122, 172.
85. *The Ind. Ser. L.*, p. 283.
86. We have quoted a passage to show that Kadrū — the mother of the serpents — was also the daughter (and not sister) of Vinatā, the mother of Garuḍa. See p. 27f.
87. Cf. *Sup. Ad.* I.II.1. *dyaurāsīt tatra vinatā suparṇī, bhūmistu nāgyabhavat kadrunāmā.*
    In the later Vedic texts Kadrū is identified with Pṛthvī; and Suparṇī (*not Vinatā!*) is identified with 'Vāk' and Dyauḥ.
    We shall return to it in the chapter on the 'Wager'.
87a. See Appendix B, where the view of Father Heras is given and criticised.
88. Cf. *Ś.B.* (*Mādh.*) I.2.5.1; cf. also *Jai. Br.* I.97: 99. For tribal influence on the thought and mythology of now civilized societies see A. Lang, *Myth. Ritual and Religion — Introduction*; G.L. Gomme, *Folk-Lore as an Historical*

*Science*, London, 1908.

89. For *Vṛtra* = *Soma*, cf. *Ś. B.* (Kāṇva) IV.1.3.11; (Mādhi.) 9.4.2; I.6.3.6f; *Jai. Br.* II.155; etc.
For Indra swallowing Vṛtra cf. *Mb.* XIV.11.18; Hopkins, *Epic Mythology*, p. 129. Indra asks Vṛtra to become his food, *Ś. B.* I.6.3.17 (*Mādh.*).

90. *Mait. Sam.* II.4.3; *Ś.B.* (*Kāṇva*), II.6.1.5 f.f, (*Mādh.* I.6.3.8 ff).

91. Cf. *Sup. Ad.* XIV.28.1.
esp., *madhye dvivaktrā bhujagendrarājiḥ; Ai. Br.* III.26 *tasya yad anīkam āsīt sa sarpo nirdaṁśyabhavat.*
This *'dvi-vaktrā'* (double-mouthed) line of snakes being produced from Garuḍa's feather can well be compared with the *'double hooded'* serpents enclosing Garuḍa in the *Balustrad* in the Javaṇese temple sculpture. (Cf. J. Boisselier, p. 69). Garuḍa is identified with Suparṇa who again is identified with Gāyatrī. For *Gāyatrī* = *Suparṇa*, cf. *Mait. Sam.* IV.1.1; *Kāth. Sam.* XXXIV.3.

92. It can be compared with the idea of the whole creation coming out of the Highest Principle and again going into it.

93. A. Lang, *Myth, Ritual and Religion.*

94. For a full discussion, see the chapter of that name in H.L. Hariappa, *'Ṛgvedic Legends through the Ages'*, Deccan College, Poona-6.

95. Cf. the age-old custom of sacrificing slaves as representative of kings. For this see Frazer, *Golden Bough* (on Killing of kings), London, 1890. Among the fruits, the coconut seems to be specially chosen as an offering as it resembles a human head. A clean coconut, it may be marked, resembles a head, with its two black spots in a line standing for eyes and one in the middle just below, for the nose.

96. Cf. Oldham, in *J.R.A.S.*, 1891, p. 370.

97. Cf. Review by Hewitt of Risley's *Tribes and Castes of Bengal,* in *J.R.A.S.*, 1893, p. 257.

98. *Ibid.*, p. 258.

99. It may be remarked here that Oldham does now here refer to this fact in his writings on the Nāgas.

100. Oldham, in *J.R.A.S.*, 1891, p. 364.

101. *K.S.S.*, XC; we deal with the tale in the next chapter.
102. Thus we have the tale of the 'Lion and the Hare' where every-day a victim was sent to a Lion, Pañc. Tant., Bombay, 1950, p. 65, cf. also the tale of Bhīma and Bakāsura from Mb. I. 158–163; Crit. Ed. I. 145–148.
103. In fact certain statues of Garuḍa represent him as a Dragon, cf. J. Boisselier's article, Plate XXV.
104. For worship of snake-gods, Oldham, *op. cit.*; also Vogel, *The Ind. Ser. L.*
105. For the various changes in sculpture — cf. J. Boisselier's '*G. dans and 1' Art Khmer*', *loc. cit.*
106. *Mb.* I.31; etc.
107. Cf. Crit. Ed. I.25; the verses dropped (31 to 36) are those that are not found in the Crit. Ed. Other changes are quite minor; hence not shown.
108. *Pad. P.*, I.30.30, *bhakṣayāmāsa garuḍas tāvubhau gajakacchapau*.
The *Sk. P.* follows the version of the *Mb.;* cf. *Sk. P.* III.38ff.; also *Padma P.* V.44.80 ff.
109. *Sup. Ad.* VII.13.1, 2.
110. Cf. *Mb.* I.16.25, 26.
111. *Sup. Ad.* VII.14.1.
112. '*Brunstigen*'; cf. *Die Supernasage*, p. 237. But, mark the word *bhinna* in the *Mb.* account where *bhedayanti, bhinnānām, bhedataḥ*, etc. are seen in the same account. The whole account deals with the vice of division.
113. *Sk.* P. III.38.30 ff; the *Pad. P.* refers to the tortoise and the elephant, but does not give the account of the former birth — cf. V. 44.80 ff.
114. *Viṣṇu Dh. P.* I.193; 194-18, ff; also *Bhāg. P.* VIII.5. For a study of the "Gajendra-mokṣa" see Dange, *Puranic Myth and Culture*, Ajanta Books International, pp. 67-77.
115. *Sup. Ad.* VII.14.2 a, b; also VIII.15.5.
116. *Ind. Ser. L.*, p. 57.
117. *Ibid.*, p. 283.
118. Cf. E.T.C. Werner, *Myths and legends of China,* London, 1922, p. 208.
119. Cf. Lindsay, "Makara in the Early Chinese Buddhist Sculpture" , *J.R.A.S.*, 1951, pp. 134 to 138.
120. *Ind. Ser. L.*, p. 127ff.

121. Cf. Vogel, *Ind. Ser. L.*, p. 39; we have near Mathurā seven-hooded nāga figures (p. 41); in Jāvā the head wear has five-hoods; the gate-guards of Bharhut *stūpa*, although human in shape, have a five-fold hood surmounting the head-dress, "as if to remind us of their real nature (nāgahood)!" p. 39.
122. *Ibid.*, p. 38; see also the names of serpents *Hastipada*, *Mb.* I. 35.9, *Hastipiṇḍa*, 14. Cf. also Hopkins, *Epic Myth*, p. 28.
123. *Rāja Tar.* II.28-31 referred to by Vogel, *Ind. Ser. L.*, p. 221, n. 1.
124. *Ibid.*, p. 221. It should be noted while passing that, though Vogel refers to the '*Gajendra-mokṣa*' episode on p. 57, he does not connect it with the '*Padma-nāga-saras*'.
125. It should, however, be noted here that the attribute '*padmau*' is used for two nāgas (serpents) in the *Mb.* elsewhere; cf. I. 356.10, *vṛttasamvarkaunāgau dvau ca padmāv iti smṛtau.*
126. *Bhāg.* P. VIII.3.32.
127. Vogel, *Ind. Ser. L.*, p. 39. For the *makara*-motif see Lindsay, *op. cit.*
128. How the word 'nāga' came to mean both the serpent and the 'elephant' is not quite easy to answer. Vogel touches the question and leaves it unanswered, *Ind. Ser. L.*, p. 56. Common names for serpents and elephants are noticed. One such is in the case of *Airāvata* (*Airāvata* is not, however, the nāgarāja '*Elāpatta*' as supposed by Vogel. Elāpatta has its origin in *Erākapatta* according to A. Coomaraswamy; cf. *J.R.A.S.*, 1928, p. 629). Vogel imagines that from the 'sky-dragon' to 'sky-elephant' (cf. '*Diggajas*') and from there to the ordinary elephant was a steady progress. In our opinion, the shape of the trunk of the elephant and the hooded body of the serpent might also have helped this confusion, beginning with similarity. This gets support in such words as the betel leaves being called '*Nāga-valli*' because of the shape, the stem looking like the protruding tongue. The same is true of the '*Nāgaphaṇī*' plant, which resembles the hood of the cobra. It may be of some interest to mention here that the

clouds are considered to be the nāgas according to the Chinese mythology. (Cf. Werner, *Myths and legends of China*, p. 209); *Nāga* also means cloud in Sanskrit. In all these cases the resemblance probably plays an important part.

129. It may be noted that in the *Sup. Ad.* we have only these two words used — (i) *nāga* and (ii) *hastin*. No other word meaning elephant such as '*gaja*' is used.
130. Cf. *Rām.* III.162; *Sk. P.* III.38.60; *Pad. P., V.* 44-80 ff.
131. Cf. Dictionary of Monier-Williams for such words as '*Kaccha*', '*Hasti-Kaccha*' among the names of serpents. He mentions '*Kūrma*' also as the name of a serpent.
132. *J.R.A.S.*, 1893, p. 257 ff.
133. *Cambridge History of India*, p. 548.
134. 'Kūrma' and 'nāga' appear as the names of the two breaths in Prāṇāyāma, *Agni* P., 214.14. Though these two hardly fit in here, the association is striking.
135. The *mantras* used as an antidote of snake-poison have the deity as Garuḍa. See *supra*, p. 28.
136. The two nāgas that Garuḍa devours are called *Mataṅgānucarau*. If the word 'Māṅga' is derived from 'Mataṅga' whose '*anucarau*' the nāgas are, it is clear that the 'māṅgas' are the nāgas. See note 83, *suprā*. See also Appendix E.
137. Cf. Crit. Ed. I.24 & 25. The portions not useful to the point are dropped.
138. It may incidentally be noted here that the *Sup. Ad.* puts this Niṣāda episode after the 'nāga-grāha', while the *Mb.* and the *Purāṇas* take it before the Gaja-kacchapa account.
139. Cf. *Sk.* P. III.38.44. *tān bhakṣayitvā śabarān.*
We have also the word 'Kirāta' used in place of Śabara in the same context. Cf. also *Rāmāyaṇa* III.35-33 where Garuḍa kills the Niṣādas with the branch of the Nyagrodha tree.
140. *Ibid.*, IV.50-64.
*santi tatra bahuśo niṣādā matsya-ghātinaḥ/*
*velātaṭa-nivāsāś ca tānbhakṣaya durāsadaḥ//*
141. Cf. *ṚV.* III.54.14.
*kim te kṛṇvanti kīkaṭeṣu gāvaḥ nāśīram duhre na satapanti gharmam.*

For 'Kīkaṭa' see Macdonell and Keith, *Vedic Index*, Vol. i, p. 159; see also Dr. Law's article in *Annals BORI*, XXII (1941) about Non-Aryan tribes in the *Ṛgveda*.

142. We shall return to this point again in a furher ch.
143. Cf. *Pad.* P. V.44.69 cd.
*udvamaitān saviprānścal*
*mlecchān etān samantataḥll*
144. *Ibid.* 71.
*yavanā bhojanaprītāḥ kiñcit-śmaśruyutāścaye.*
145. *Sk.* P. I.19.32, 33. Garuḍa's control over the 'Varuṇa pāśas' again speaks of his control over the nāgas, for, the 'Varuṇa pāśas' are identified with the snakes. They are called 'Nāga-pāśa' (cf. Dowson — *Classical Dict. Hindu Myth.*, London, 1953, p. 338). For Nāgas as Varuṇa-pāśa cf. also '*Siśu*, I.56, where we have '*Uraga-rāja-rajjavaḥ*'.
146. Cf. Gonda, *Aspects*, p. 191, note 34 wherein he quotes J. Boisselier.
147. Cf. *S.Br.* (*Mādh*) I.4.1.ff; (*Kāṇva*-II.3.8 ff); for Agni as the symbol of Aryan conquest in this tale, cf. Eggeling *SBE*, Vol. XII, note on p. 104, where the author quotes the view of Weber. Cf. also the devouring of the 'Khāṇḍava' forest by Agni, who asks for it in the guise of a brāhmaṇa, *Mb.* I. 221-22. The period of *Sup. Ad.* is about 1000 BC.
148. Cf. '*niṣādaḥ kasmāt niṣaṇṇam asmin pāpam iti.*' *Nirukta*, III.8; cf. *Kauṣītakī Br.* XXV.15.
149. *Indische studien*, p. 340.
150. Cf. *Manu.* X.8. *brāhmaṇāt śūdrakanyāyām yaḥ pāraśava ucyate* and *śūdrāyām nīṣādo jātaḥll*
also *Yājña. Sm.* I.91 *viprat.*
151. Cf. I.91. in *Yājña Sm.* and *Mitākṣarā* on it.
*niśādo nāma kaścin matsyaghātajīvī pratilomajaḥ; sa mābhūd iti pāraśavo'yam niṣāda iti sañjñāvikalpaḥ.*
152. *Vedic Index*, Vārānasī, Vol. II, p. 453.
153. *Ancient India*, Allahabad, 1948, p. 72.
154. *Pad.* P. V.44.50 ff.
155. Cf. *Ibid.*, 59 ff.
156. *Ka. S.S.* XC, 99-104.
157. Garuḍa had already asked Jīmūtavāhana—*K.S.S.*, XC.168,
"You are no *nāga*, great man! speak; who are you?" (*nāgo*

*naivāsi tad brūhi, mahātman ko bhavān iti*).

158. Cf. *Ibid.*, 193-95.

159. Cf. the *Nāgānandam* where the Sūtradhāra says — *vidyādhara-jātaka-pratinibaddham nāgānandanāṭakam.* In **K.S.S.** and in the *Jātaka, Jīmūtavāhana* is a Vidyādhara.

160. Cf. Oldham, "The Nāgas" — *J.R.A.S.*, 1901, p. 465.

161. Cf. *Jambhaladatta* Ed., Calcutta, 1873, tale 73.

162. *Ibid.*

163. We have already referred to Oldham on this point. At another place he notes a popular tale from Kaśmīr according to which one Jībūtavāhana saves Vāsukī from the attacks of Garuḍa. Jībūtavāhana, in this popular tale, is obviously the same Jīmūtavāhana of our tale. Jībūtavāhana is the Vazir of Vāsuki, which also shows that he was only a nāga in popular belief. For the popular tale, see Oldham — *J.R.A.S.*, 1891, p. 364; we have referred to the tale earlier; see p. 38.

164. Cf. *K.S.S. XC*. 177.
*hā katham, bodhisattvāṁśaḥ sammohād bhakṣito mayā*/

165. I.27.15-16.

166. *Ibid.*, 30.40 f.

167. *Ibid.*, 32.22-25.
In the *Harivaṁśa* (Adhyāya 122) also we have the same exploit of Garuḍa where he is said to have quenched the Āhavanīya fire in the fight against Bāṇāsura.

168. *Ibid.*, 33.2.

169. *Ibid.*, 33.6-10.

170. *Ibid.*, 33.12-16.

171. *Ibid.*, 33.18-24.
See also *Harivaṁśa* (Bhaviṣya-khaṇḍa) where the same exploit and the falling and the gaining of feathers on the part of Garuḍa occur in the context of the '*Pārijāta-haraṇa*'.

172. *Ibid.*, 34.8-20.

173. *Ibid.*, 34.22.

174. Cf. the name *Suparṇādhyāya*, also 'Suparṇākhyāna' in *Mb.* (Citraśālā Ed.) etc.

175. Cf. Sāyaṇa on the verse concerned.

176. For other references, see III.47.7; VI.20.6; IX.68.6; IX.77.2;

X.11.4; etc.; for the Aśvins saving Bhujyu, cf. *ṚV* I.112.6; 116.3-5. It is said that he was lying in sea. He was the son of Tugra and was floating in the water.

177. A.B. Keith, *The Veda of the Black Yajus School* entitled *Taittirīya Saṃhitā*, Motilal, Banarsidass, Delhi, 1976 (*HOS* 1914), p. 492 f, n. 5. *Sup. Ad.* III. 5.3.; IV.71. Keith says – not that they disputed what was the more beautiful! This comment of Keith is not correct, because the point of *rūpa* persists in other texts also as mentioned just after this by us.

177a. Compare this idea with Garuḍa having two creatures in his two claws and the branch of the Rauhiṇa tree in his beak; for the two 'pressings' in the feet and one in the mouth cf. also *Jai Br.* I.288.

178. *suparnyāḥ apatyāni*. (Pāṇ IV.1.120).

179. On this point cf. also Vogel, '*Ind. Ser. L.*', p. 54 where he quotes the views of Jarl Charpentier, Barth, etc.

180. Cf. *Gop. Br.* Uttara-ardha, V.I. (Ed. by Gaastra). *śarvarāṇi khalu ha vā asyaitāni chandāṁsi iti ha smāha. etāni vā indram rātryāstamaso mrtyor abhipatya-avārayan.*

181. *Mait. Sam.* III.4.8.
*devā asurān hatvā mṛtyor abibhayus te chandāṁsi apaśyan, tāni prāviśan.*

182. Cf. *Ibid. Mait. Sam.* III.2.3.
*chandobhireva devāḥ. svargam lokam āyan.*
cf. also IV.7.5.

183. *Jai Br.* II.381: *chandāṁsi vai svargo lokaḥ.*

184. *Ibid.*, II.381. *yad enān (devān) chandāṁsi mṛtyoḥ pāpmano'cchādayans tac chandasaḥ chandastvam; cādayanti-eva-enam mṛtyoḥ pāpmano ya evam veda.*

185. Cf. also *Jai. Br.* I.287. *somam āharāma, yajñam tanavām.* Also *Ibid* — Gāyatrī says to the Somapālas —
*aham imam ṣomam ahārṣam etam yajñam tanavā.*

186. Cf. *Tait. Sam.* VI.I.6.1 ff; also *Jai. Br.* I.288. esp.
*mukhenaikam savanam saha sarveṇa yajñenāgacchat.*

187. The same idea can be noted in the story of '*Śunaśśepa*' where Śunaśśepa was released from the fetters by uttering *mantras*. For a full discussion on 'Śunaśśepa' see Hariappa

— *Ṛgvedic legends through the Ages*, Deccan College, Poona, 1953. Also *Ai. Br.* VII.13-18.

188. The Mādhyandina has *devebhyaḥ* for '*Mṛtyoḥ*'. Cf. *Mādh. Ś.B.* III.6.2.8.

189. Even in the *Mādh. Ś.B.* this implication could be seen — V.6.2.6.
*sa yad yajate . . . mṛtyor ātmānam niṣkrīnite.*

190. Cf. Sāyaṇa on —*ṚV.* X.28.10.
It should be seen with interest how Gāyatrī it is — not Suparṇa — that is taken by Sāyaṇa to be the main actor of the Somāharaṇa exploit.

191. *Sup. Ad.* V.12.3.

192. *Ibid.* 4.
*yāni chandāṁsi caturuttārāṇi yajñam vahanti . . . tānyaham asmi vinate suparṇi.*

193. Mait. Sam. IV.I.1. *tam gāyatrī śyeno bhūtva-āharat, tasya parṇam acchidyata.*

194. *Ś.B.* I.7.1.1. *yatra vai gāyatrī somam acchā apatat tad asyā āharantyā apād astā abhyāyatya praciccheda.*

195. *Jai. Br.* I.287 ff. J. Charpentier does not refer to the *Jai. Br.* passage in his *Die Sup.*; cf. *Ś.Br.*(*Mādh.*) III.6.2.8.

196. *dhiṣṇyas* are fire-altars prepared out of earth dug for preparing earth-drums, which again are meant to produce more sound in pressing *Soma*. See Keith, *Rel. & Phil. of the Veda,* Vol. II, p. 328. The *dhiṣṇya*-s are six, and are located, in the *sadas* (sitting hall), to the west of the *havirdhāna* pandal where *Soma*-shoots and, later, the juice, are kept. These details, like those in the other Vedic ritual texts, show how the legend is used to extol ritual.

197. The same idea could be seen in the *Ś.B.* (*Mādh.*III.6.2.8; Kāṇva-V.6.2.8), "constantly closing" (falling on each other, is common to both).

198. *Kṛśānu* means fire. For *Kṛśānu* as Gandharva cf. *Taitt. Ār.* I.9.3.

199. For Āśivīṣāḥ (poisonous serpents) see Macdonell and Keith, *Vedic Index*, 1958. Mac. & Keith say that the word appears '*only*' in the *Ai. Br.* (VI.1); but it could be clear that it occurs also in the *Jai. Br.* as we have quoted (Dr. Raghuvir's Ed.). In the *Ai. Br.* the word '*āśīviṣa*' is used for the

poisonous snakes; but is in a different context than the guarding of Soma.

200. The context is of *Soma* to be fetched from heaven. '*divi vai*' etc. as from *Ś.B.* (*Mādh.*) III.2.4.1, noted earlier.

201. The *Mādh.* *Ś.B.* drops this word. This *horse* beyond the '*Suparṇya*' water is definitely the horse mentioned in *ṚV*. I.163.1 quoted in the legend of the 'churning'. He has Śyena's wings.

202. We may compare Serpents as the guards of Soma with the serpent in the garden of heaven according to the Bible. Examples from Hindu belief are quite numerous. The *K.S.S.*, *Pañcatantra* etc. are replete with such instances. Also see James Hastings, *Encl. of Rel. and Ethics* under *Serpent*. In many parts of India the serpents, especially the cobras, are supposed to be the guards of wealth underground. In Bengal, the belief is that in every house there is *Manasā Devī* as guardian of wealth. Manasā Devī is the queen-Cobra called also 'Viṣaharī Devī'; cf. Review of Risley, noted earlier. For Manasā see App. C., also note 398 *infra*.

203. *Sup. Ad.* VI.11.1 and 2.

204. *Ibid.* XI.4, 5; XII-23.1.

205. XII.23.3; for particulars of these names and others in the verse see Jarl Charpentier, *Die Superṇasage*, p. 259.

206. *Ibid.* 24.I.

207. *Sup. Adh.* XIV.27.
*eṣa chandāṁsi sahitāni śakra yajurmayaḥ sāma-tanuḥ suparṇaḥ.*

208. Cf. *Ibid.* VI.12.3, 4.

209. *Ibid.*, 12, *bhūtāni cānyāni mahānti tatrā.*

210. *Ibid.* Garuḍa saying to his mother *nihatya rakṣas tarasā.*

211. Cf. De and Dasgupta, '*Hist. of Skt. Lit.*', Calcutta, 1947, p. 631.

212. 'Garuḍa' first appears as a name in the *Tait. Ār.* X.1, 5, but there also he is not associated with Somāharaṇa, see note 218 below for the exact quotation.

213. *Sup. Ad.* XIV.30.6; also *Mb.* I.34.13.

214. Translation in Bloomfield's *Atharvaveda*, p. 25. See also Whitney's Translation *of Atharva-Veda Saṁhitā*, Cambridge, 1905, p. 153.

215. Cf. *suparṇaḥ śobhana-pakṣopeto garutmān.*

216. On *AV.* II.27.2. *suparṇastvā anvavindat.*
Śāyaṇa, *suparṇaḥ śobhana-pakṣopeta vainateyaḥ.*

217. For other references to Suparṇa in the AV. see VI.8.2, 83.1; VII.42.1; IX.15.28; XII.3.38; XIII.2.9; 32; 33; 36 etc.

218. Cf. *tatpuruṣāya vīdmahe suvarṇa pakṣāya dhīmahi tanno garuḍaḥ pracodayiāt.*

219. *purāṇādiṣu prasiddha-pakṣirāja-mūrtidharam devam.*

220. Cf. *AV.* II.27.2, *sūkarastvā-anvavindannsā.*

221. '*Suprana*' probably comes in this context as the epithet turned into a separate appellation to denote a 'divine being' in the same way as it is applied to various Ṛgvedic gods. We shall deal with it shortly in our discussion.

222. Cf. Chapter on 'Garuḍa and the nāgas', see notes 54 and 55 *supra.*

223. Cf. Agni P. 297.5 and its variant.
The whole mantra is —
"ॐ नमो भवगते रुद्राय प्रेताधिपतये। शृणु शृणु गर्ज गर्ज भ्रामय-भ्रामय मुञ्च-मुञ्च मुह्य-मुह्य कट्ट आविश आविश सुवर्णपतङ्गरुद्रो ज्ञापयति।"

224. Markable is that Śiva is always represented as having serpents coiling round his body. Rudra is also called 'Pakṣi-Rudra' in *Agni* P. 297.1, and 2. See Appendix B, last paragarph.

225. *Sup. Ad.* 1.1.2. *sauvarṇaparṇam . . . vainateyam.*

226. *Ibid.* 5.

227. *Ibid.* 4.

228. *Mb.* I.33.22 to 24. The *Sup. Ad.* has this account of the falling of the wing of Garuḍa, but does not have the gaining of the name 'Suparṇa'.

229. *Sk. P.*, Nāgarakhaṇḍa, VI.80.13 ff.

230. *Ibid.* 82.26.

231. It should be noted that in the account of Śāṇḍilī as it occurs in the *Mb.* V.113 Garuḍa's becoming 'Suparṇa' is not found as elaborately as is given in the *Sk. P.*, though the note of punishment inflicted on those who indulge in criticism of pious ladies, is present there. There Śāṇḍilī is on the mountain Ṛṣabha and in her hermitage Garuḍa takes shelter with Gālava. The words of Śāṇḍilī are,

*na bhetavyam, suparṇo'si*; *Ibid.* 3.

232. *Sk. P.* III (Brhama-khaṇḍa), 38.96.

233. Cf. *Viṣṇu Dh. P.* III. 343.25, 26.
Cf. also *Mb.* V.105 for the same account; but in the *Mb*, Garuḍa's becoming Suparṇa does not occur in this context prominently.
The falling of the wing of Śuparṇa-Śyena is first mentioned in the *ṚV*, as we have already noted; but there, nowhere is to be found the explanation of the term *suparṇa* nor does the bird get new wings. Though it is probable that this was taken by the *Mb.* and the later accounts, the clear efforts to show how *Garuḍa came to be Suparṇa* is to be marked.

234. This verse is dropped in the Crit. Ed., yet we have noted it here as an instance of an effort to give etymology of the word 'Garuḍa'. It should be marked that here we do not have that "Suparṇa becomes Garuḍa because he carried the heavy weight", etc. The carrier of the heavy-weight is the 'Great-bird' who is *'the eater of snakes'*; clearly, *not Suparṇa.*

235. See, *Religious Thought and Life in India* or *Brahmanism and Hinduism*, p. 231. Cf. also *Mb.* where Garuḍa is mistaken for fire (I.23.10).

236. For the sun-fire see *Vāj. Sam.* VIII.50, *Jai. Br.* I.7, etc. AV.XIII.4.4.6; also that the sun is one of the five fires in the *Pañcāgni*-vrata. The identification of the sun and Agni can be seen even from such later passages also as *Raghu* IV.2 with the belief that the setting sun deposits his lustre in the fire.

237. Hopkins, *Epic Mythology*, p. 22.
For other references see :—
(a) Zimmer, *Myths and Symbols in Indian Art and Civilization*, p. 75 where he derives Garuḍa from √*gṛ* 'to swallow'.
(b) Lenceis, *Miscellanea Etymologica Series* 7, where he compares it with Tvaṣṭṛ. and gives *Garutmat* from *Tarugmat* by metathesis. Well, interesting!

238. It may be of interest to note in this context that there is another bird that is called the 'eater of snakes' (*bhujagāśanaḥ*) and has beautiful wings (*citrāṇi barhāṇi.*)

(*Mb.* XII.120). Nīlakaṇṭha renders it as the peacock. Remarkable again is the fact that the peacock himself is the gift of Garuḍa to Skanda (*Mb.* IX.46.51). This goes well with the fact that the peacock was produced from the tip of Garuḍa's fallen wing; *Sup. Ad.* XIV.28.1 *tasyāgra bhāgād abhavan mayūraḥ* thus connecting *mayūra* (peacock) and *Garuḍa* in the context of *control over snakes* (i.e. their poison).

239. *Mb.* I.33.6; V. 105.19.
240. See subtitle 'Garuḍa and the Sarpa-vidyā'.
241. See Dubois (and Beauchamp), *Hindu Manners, Customs and Ceremonies*, p. 640. The bird is identified as the 'Malabār Eagle'.
242. *Ibid.,* p. 133.
243. Probably this sect of the Garuḍa worshippers was long ago converted to Viṣṇuism. Whether Viṣṇu was a non-Āryan deity or an Āryaṇ is not in the scope of this discussion. For it, however, see Gonda, *Aspects of Early Viṣṇuism*, p. 4, where Gonda quotes Pryzluski.
244. Had Śyena not been different from Garuḍa, Abbe Dubois might have called him only the hawk. Garuḍa is thus a special type of eagle, different from the hawk or other species of eagles!
245. Cf. *Vedic Index of names and subjects*, Varaṇasi, 1958.
246. Cf. S.K. Chatterji in *Vedic Age*, London, 1952, p. 163. The Tamil lexicon, surprisingly, does not give the word 'Kazu' or 'Kazuh', but only has the Sanskrit name written in Tamil, i.e., which, exactly pronounced, will be both '*Karuṭan*' and '*Garuḍan*'.
247. 'Zh' cannot properly represent the pronunciation. In the Tamil pronunciation the tip of the tongue takes the back position as for 'ழ' but never touches the palate, the breath passing forcefully out. Cf. *pazham* in Tamil = *phalam* in Skt.
248. Cf. Keith, *Rel. & Phil. of the Veda* (*HOS*, Vol. 32), p. 633. He refers to P. Schmidt, according to whom the word is Kalāṅ.
249. Cf. *Gop. Br.* Pūrvārdha, IV.8. Cf. also *Vāja. Sam.* XXIV.25, *samvatsarāya mahataḥ suparṇāya.*

250. Cf. *Sāma V.* Uttara, XX.7.1; also *Mait. Sam.* II.12.3, III.3.9 etc.
251. *Sāma V.* Pūrva, IV.7.9; *ṚV.* I.105.1.
252. *Gop. Br.* Pūrva. III.10.
253. Cf. *Jai. Br.* I.292; II.246.
254. *Ibid.* III.158; also *Mait. Sam. I,12.2; Tāṇ. M. Br.* XIV.3.10.
255. *Mait. Sam.* III.4.7; Śyena himself is Suparṇa.
256. *Sam. V.* Uttar. XX.22 and Sāyaṇa thereon.
257. *Vāja. Sam.* VII.60.
258. Cf. Yāska, *'Nirukta'*, III.12 *supatanaśīlāḥ*.
259. See A.R. Hope and Monrieff, *Classical Myth and Legend*, p. 29. The boy is said to be a Trojan prince.
260. A. Lang, *Custom and Myth*, London, 1884, Vol. II, p. 54. Also see Penzer, *Ocean of Story*, p. 105 where mention is made of the bird Griffin having half man's body and half that of a bird. The bird (like Garuḍa!) is connected with the Sun.
261. A Lang, *Custom and Myth*, vol. II, p. 95.
262. A Lang, *Myth, Ritual and Religion*, Vol. I, London, 1913, p.133. Compare with this bird our Garuḍa who thunders and causes the mountains to shake. The causing of rain by Garuḍa can be seen in his carrying the nāgas and Indra sending rain.
263. *Ibid.*, pp. 164-65.
264. Borrow-Smith, *Natives of Victoria*, quoted by A. Lang, *op. cit.*, p. 423.
265. *Ibid.*, p. 187.
266. See Chandra Chakrawarty, *Ancient Races and Myths*, p. 132; see also Frances Berden, *The Aztecs*, p. 27 ff.
267. A. Lang, *Custom and Myth*, p. 95.
268. See for a full view on this subject, Lang, Introduction — *Myth, Ritual and Religion*. Mackenzie believes in "cultural transmission." For a short discussion on these views See Dange, *Pastoral Symbolism from the Ṛg-Veda*, Poona Uni. Publication, 1968, Lecture I; also Dange, *Towards Understanding Hindu Myths*, New Delhi, 1996, p. 14f.
269. Chakrawarty, *'Ancient Races and Myths'*, p. 131.
270. *Ibid.*, p. 128.
271. Note 71, *supra;* also Note 119.
272. *Myth, Ritual & Religion*, Vol. I, p. 224.

273. *Mb.* I.31 (Crit. Ed. I.27. Practically the same with slight difference in words in only a very few cases).
274. The full account in translation is given in Chapter I.
275. I. 31.30. The words *tvatsahāyau . . . bhrātarau te bhaviṣyataḥ* are to be particularly marked.
276. Cf. *Sk. P.*III.38.70 ff; for Garuḍa's penance and propitiating Śiva for being Indra among birds, cf. *Ibid.* V.186.10; cf. also VI.79.3; also *Ibid.* 36.
277. *Jai. Br.* I.287.
278. *Jai. Br.* II.440, (Ed.), Dr. Raghuvīra, Nagpur, 1954.
279. For a full study of Saramā, see Dr. Hariappa, *Ṛgvedic Legends Though the Ages*, Poona, 1953.
280. Probably Suparṇa was given the task of finding the cows later because of his swift flight across the sky; but why he was humiliated is difficult to answer. Most probably it accounts for the actual eating of rubbish on the part of a bird, identified later with Suparṇa.
281. Cf. *Mb.*, I.33.25, where Indra says to Garuḍa, "I desire to know your strength and solicit your friendship".
282. *Sup. Ad.*, XV.29.4. Also cf. he is called 'friend' of Indra, *Sup. Ad.* XI.9.5.
283. Cf. *ṚV.* III.48.24; also *Ś.B.* (Kāṇ) II.6.1.5; *Jai. Br.* II.156, etc.
284. Cf. *Ś.B.* I.1.6.4; see passages quoted in "The Legend of Kaca", *infra.*
285. *Mb.* has Garuḍa not *drinking amṛta;* cf. *Mb.* I.33. ff, *apītvaivāmṛtam pakṣī* though the *Sup. Ad.* has him drink it, XIV.27.1, *indum pītvā.*
286. See Wilkins, *Hindu Mythology, Vedic and Purāṇic*, p. 341.
287. *Mb.* I.63, esp. 17, *yaṣṭim ca vaisṇavīm tasmai dadau vṛtraniṣūdanaḥ.*
288. *Ibid.*, XII.333.32 ff; see also *Viṣṇu Dh. P.* III.346.3.
289. Cf. *ṚV.* II.42.1.
290. Cf. *ṚV.* IV.27.1.

The poet is Vāmadeva here who speaks about himself; but Vāmadeva himself is identified with Indra in IV.26.3 where he is said to have destroyed nine times ninety fortresses of Śambara, which is an exploit of Indra in II.12.11; II.14.6. See also Sāyaṇa on IV.27.1.

It is not in the scope of this book to see whether Indra is *Suparṇa*; for it, see Bloomfield, "The legend of Soma and Eagle", *J.A.O.S.*, XVI. Whatever might Bloomfield say, at least in one more place Suparṇa and Indra are said to be the same; cf. *Kāṭhaka Sam.* XXXVII.14. We have noted the ref. in another context, "Legend of Kaca", *infra*.

291. Cf. *Mb.* I.30.13 *bhettāram giriśṛṅgāṇām.* For Indra cutting the wings of the mountains, cf. *ṚV.* II.12.2. Cf. *Mait. Sam.* I.10.13.

292. Cf., *Ibid.*, *Mb. loc. cit.*, 8 *pakṣaiḥ śailān prakampayan*; also 26.

293. *Sup. Ad.*, XI.20.2. *nava navatīr vedyāḥ śatāni;* and just before *ṣaṣṭim sahasrāṇi.* Both are typological expressions in *ṚV.*

294. Hopkins, *Epic Mythology*, Strassburg, 1915, p. 26.

295. In this connection, it is good to recall A. Lang's remark, "Probably the deities had in the majority of cases, superseded the animal and succeeded to his honour. But the conservative religious sentiment retained the beast", *Custom and Myth*, p. 118. Garuḍa thus represents the survival of the older conservative faith that could not be completely dominated by the new one!

296. *Sup. Ad.* XV. 30.5 *vaheyam yajñam, praviśema vedān.*

297. Gonda, *Aspects of Early Viṣṇuism*, pp. 255-56, remarks, "The general import of the myth appears to be that the sun, the source of light (Viṣṇu) bestows on Indra his own '*Ketu*' (i.e. the ensign and the first glimpse of the day) before which the spirits of darkness must vanish." This cannot, however, be accepted, as it seems to be an unnecessarily laboured interpretation. The more natural explanation seems to be an improvement of the idea of the giving of the staff to Vasu by Indra (*Mb.* I.63.17 ff), which indicates that Indra vacated in honour of Viṣṇu mythologically. Instances of this type can be multiplied. This particular account seems also to be a reflection of the Vedic idea of Viṣṇu helping Indra often to conquer the enemies. For Indra helped by Viṣṇu, cf. Macdonell, *Ved. Myth.*, p. 39. The point is, Gonda has based his interpretation on a myth told in the *Bṛhatsaṁhitā* (ch. 43), which is a later work, i.e. of the fifth century A.D.

298. *Tait. Br.* III.7.11. The *mantra* is *svastidā viśaspatir vṛtrahā* etc., originally fr. *ṚV*, X.152.2.
299. Gonda, *op. cit.*, p. 246.
300. *Viṣṇu Dh. P.* II.160.
शक्रक्रतो महावीर सुपर्णस्तत्सुताश्रितः। (सुपर्णस्तु त्वदाश्रितः)
पतत्रिराड् वैनतेयस्तथा नारायणध्वजः ॥१०॥
काश्यपेयोऽमृतहर्ता नागारिर्विष्णुवाहनः।
अप्रमेयो दुराधर्षो रणे चैवारिसूदनः॥११॥
गरुत्मान् मारुतगतिस्त्वयि सन्निहितः स्थितः।
साश्ववर्मायुधान् योधान् रक्षास्माकं महद्रिपून्॥"
301. For king as an incarnation of Viṣṇu, see Hopkins, *Epic Myth*, p. 166. Cf. also Gonda, *Aspects*, p. 101; note 34, where he quotes J. Boisselier.
See also Dange, *Images from Vedic Myths and Rituals*, New Delhi, Ch. "Aspects of War".
302. *Sk. P.* IV.50.105 ff. It should also be noted that it is Viṣṇu in this account that takes back nectar to the gods. For other accounts, see *Ibid.* III.38.
303. Cf. *Padma P.* V. 44.81ff.
304. Cf. *Ibid.* 93 ff. *asmadbāhum samāruhya bhakṣemau gaja-kacchapau.*
305. *Ibid.*, 101 cf.
*bhujasya mama māṁsam tu bhakṣayitvā sukhī bhava* and, *khāditam kṣudhayā putra vraṇam tasya na vidyate//*
The eating of Viṣṇu's arm by Garuḍa is similar to the eating of Jīmūtavāhana by Garuḍa. In both cases there is lack of pain. See Dange, "The Genesis of the Story of Jīmūtavāhana", *J. Asiatic Society of Bombay*, Vols. 34-35, (for 1958-60), Bombay, 1962, pp. 68-74; also his, *Critiques on Sanskrit Dramas,* 2nd Ed., New Delhi, 1994, pp. 95-112.
306. Cf. *Mb.* I.33.16a.
*bhavate' pi varam dadyām vṛṇotu bhagavā api.*
(This line is, however, dropped in the *Crit. Ed.*, but the next is common to both) —
*tam vavre vāhanam viṣṇur garutmantam mahābalam.*
307. Cf. *Sk. P.* IV.50.109.

*hasitvā garuḍaḥ prāha . . . aham eva prasanno'smi tvam prārthaya vara-dvayam.*

308. For the whole account, see *Mb.* V.105. Mark especially what Garuḍa says to Indra, *Ibid.*, 11.
*asahyam ṣarvabhūtānām mamāpi vipulam balam.* He says to Indra (V.12) that he was also in his (Indra's) banner (*dhvajastamabha-gataḥ*).
This suggests that Garuḍa was in the banner of Indra. It tallies with the idea of the identification of the Indra-dhvaja and the Garuḍa-dhvaja, as we have noted in the section of that name.
Cf. also Viṣṇu *Dh. P.* III.343.

309. Cf. I.33.13 and Nīlakaṇṭha on it; the words are, *sa vavre tiṣṭheyam upari.*
Cf. also *Sk. P.* III.3.91, *tavopari sthitir me syāt.*

310. Cf. Gonda, *Aspects*, p. 103, note 48.

311. Cf. *Sk.* P. IV.50.107 *kṛtvā yuddham sumahat. . .*

312. Cf. *Rāma.*, VII.8.19 ff. where Garuḍa is said to help Viṣṇu in fighting for him. Also *Sk.* P. I.19. 21-31 where Garuḍa helps Vāmana (Viṣṇu) in subduing Bali. For Viṣṇu helping Indra in the Vedic literature, cf. *ṚV* VIII.100.12. *sakhe viṣṇo vitarm kramasva . . . hanāva vṛtram . . .* This thought occurs even at other places.

313. Cf. Gonda, *Aspects. . . .*, p. 103.

313a. Cf. J. Charpentier, *Die Sup.*, pp. 328 and 330 and his remark thereon.

314. Cf. *Mb.* I.33.2 *sa cakram kṣuraparyantam apaśyad amṛtāntike.* Cf. also *Sk.* P. III.38.87 *sitadhāram bhramaccakram.*

315. *Sup. Ad.* XIII.25.3— *yanme cakram nimiṣato javīyaḥ.*

316. *Cf. Ś.Br.* V.6.2.8; *Jai. Br.* I.287.

317. *Kaṭh. Up.* I.3.9.

318. *Mait. Up.* VI.30.

319. Cf. *Mb.* I.23.26.

320. Cf. Yāska, '*Nirukta* III.12, *Suparṇāḥ-śobhanapatanāḥ āditya-raśmayaḥ.*'

321. See Gonda, *Aspects*, p. 83, note 13; cf. also *Mb.* XIII.16.14.

322. *Bṛhad Ā. Up.*V.10.1; see also *Chānd. Up.* VIII.6.2; *Muṇd. Up.* I.2.5 etc.

323. Cf. also *Jai. Up. Br.* I.3.5. for ref. to virtuous souls escaping

through the opening of the sun.
It may, by the way, be marked that according to the Ṛgveda the sun is the abode of the virtuous; cf. *ṚV*.42.8. The moon also is the door of the heavens, cf. *Kau. Up.* I.2.

324. *Crit. Ed.* I.20.10 ff.
325. Cf. com. on the verse.
326. Cf. *Jai. Br.* I.131; II.89; II.131; *Go. Br.* I.33.
327. Cf. *Mait. Sam.* III.1-3; III.2-3; III.6-3, etc.
328. *Mb.* I.31.
329. *Ibid.* 30.2. For their size as the thumb, I.31.8 *riṣīn hrasvān aṅguṣṭhodaravarṣmaṇaḥ.*
330. *Ibid.* I.30. See Nīlakaṇṭha- *marīcim sūryamaṇḍalam pānti iti.* Also *Rām.* III.35.30.
331. Cf. *Tait. Ār.* I.23.41 —
*(tasya) ye vālas te vālakhilyāḥ.*
332. Cf. *Sk. P.* I.26.16 ff. The context is of the marriage of Śiva and Pārvatī; also VII.19.66, 67. For more information see Dange, *Encyclopaedia of Puraṇic Beliefs and Practices*, Vols. IV and V, New Delhi, pp. 1162 and 1491f, respectively.
333. *Die Suparṇasage*, p. 333.
334. Cf. Barnett, "Study in Indo-European Psychology", *J.R.A.S.* — (1929), p. 748, note.
335. *Ibid.;* also *Mait. Up.* II, 3 ff.
336. For soul equal to the thumb, cf. *Chānd. Up.* III.14.
337. Gonda, *Aspects* . . ., p. 91ff. where he criticises the view of Geldner that the thumb represents phallus.
338. Noteworthy here is that Yama takes from the body of Satyavat the soul of the size of the thumb, *Mb.* III.293. See also *Śvet. Up.* III.13; V.8.
339. *Mb.* XII.59; see also Hopkins, *Epic Myth*, p. 166.
340. *Śvet. Up.* IV.6. Earlier, *ṚV.* I.164.20.
341. Hopkins, *Epic Myth*, p. 208, also p. 7; *Mb.* XIII.126-5; 149.101.
342. 'Nyagrodha', it may be incidentally remarked, is one of the epithets of Viṣṇu. If 'Nyagrodha' is the same as the 'Rauhiṇa' the idea supports our interpretation above. The idea is that the 'Nyagrodha' is the tree of life (Viṣṇu) and the Vālakhilyas as the minute *principles of life* rest on it. Nyagrodha also comes in the story of Sāvitrī later

as a symbol of life. For this see A.H. Allen, "Vaṭasāvitrī-Vrata", *J.A.O.S.* XXI-2, p. 581. It may, incidentally, be remarked here, that the Nyagrodha tree and Garuḍa are associated with each other even in Indonesia. The Indonesian national flag has the tree and Garuḍa on it. See also Dange, "Savitri and the Bunyan," *Purāṇa*, Vol. V-2 (Jan. 1963), later included in his book, *Puranic Myth and Culture*, pp. 59-66.

343. Cf. Gonda, *Aspects*. . ., p. 103, "Though comparatively early he is represented as a bird, he is in all probability, correctly to be considered an equine bird, *representative of the powerful light.*"
Cf. also Charles Coleman, *Mythology* of the *Hindus*, London, 1832, p. 55. Johansson and Jarl Charpentier take Garuḍa to be another form of Viṣṇu, *Die Sup.*, pp. 328, 330.

344. *Cf. Mb.* I.24.5; 17. The whole Adhyāya is dropped in the *Crit. Ed.*

345. *Ibid.* I.23.16.

346. *Sk.* P. IV.50.33 ab, *svarūpeṇa pataṅgī tvam pataṅgo'sau sahasraguḥ.*

347. *Mb.* I.32.24; *Sup. Ad.* XIII.26.4.

348. For Indra as the god of rain, see Hopkins, 'Indra as a god of fertility', *J.A.O.S.*, XXXVI, p. 242 ff. Also Review on Risley, *J.R.A.S.* (1893), p. 281. The *Sup. Ad.* compares Garuḍa to the *mahāmegha* in this act of taking the waters up, which is far from being the sun. XIII.26.5.

349. Cf. *Sup. Ad.* IV.8.1, 2; *Mb.* I.25.6; *Sk.* P. IV.50.33 ff.

350. Chandra Chakrawarty, *Ancient Races and Myths*, pp. 20, 39.

351. Note 260, *supra*.

352. Cf. J. Boisselier, "Garuḍa dans l'Art Khmer," plate XXIII.

353. Oldham, "Serpent Worship in India", *J.R.A.S.* (1891), p. 371. We have already expressed our difference from Oldham's view that Garuḍa and the Nāgas were different tribes. We believe that Garuḍas were only a sect of the Nāga totality.

354. Cf. W.J. Perry' "The coming of the Warriors" in *Making of Man*, New York, 1931, p. 306.

355. *pataṅga* — *Sk.* P. IV.50.33; Māgha, '*Śiśu*-I.5; even earlier

*ṚV*. X.177.2 and Sāyaṇa on it.

356. Perry, *Making of Man*, p. 310.
357. See Chapter 4 for detailed account.
358. It should be noted that Vinatā is never called *Vāk*. in *Mb* and later.
359. Cf. *Vāj. Sam*. III.5 and Sāyaṇa thereon; also *Tait. Sam*. I.5.4.
360. Hopkins, *Epic Myth*, p. 23; cf. also the Nāgas called 'Sauraseyāḥ' — *Sup. Ad*. V.9.2; also *Crit. Ed*. (*Mb*) XII.348.3.
361. I.2.1. *dyāvāpṛthivyau bhavato bhaginyau* and *dyaur āsīttatra vinatā suparṇī bhūmistu nāgyabhavat Kadrunāmā*.
362. Vogel, *Indian Serpent Lore*, p. 54.
363. Barth, *The Religions of India*, p. 265.
364. *Sup. Ad*., 4 III.5.4; 6.2.
365. *Ibid*., I.2.2.
366. *Ibid*., IV.8.2. *yad āha śuṅgī*.
367. Cf. *Tait. Sam*., *ātmarūpayoḥ*'; *Kāṭh. Sam*. XXX.10; Cf. also *Sup. Ad*. III.5.3 '*svarūpayoḥ*.
368. Cf. *Ś.B*. (Kāṇva) V.6.5; *Sup. Ad*. III.5.5; III, 6.3; *Mb*. I.20.2 ff.
369. '*kad*' *kutsita* in '*Kadannam*'; '*Kadartha*' etc.
370. *Die Sup*., p. 306; Vogel, *Indian Serpent Lore*, p. 54.
371. Any number of such tales are found in folklore. Cf. the Bālanāgammā-tale current in Andhra. The tale of a *Rākṣasī* who becomes the queen and ousts others, Parker, *Village folk-tales of Ceylon*, London, 1910; Story 'The white turtle", page 113, "Gule Bakāwalī" etc. in Vol. I. Cf. also Grimm, *Household tales*, Vol. II, London, 1884, the story of 'The Goose-girl" where the maid servent dons the princess's dress and marries the prince and is ultimately punished.
372. Cf. *Rām*. III.35.36. *suparṇakṛtalakṣaṇam nāmnā śubhadam nyagrodham*.
373. *Ibid*., 30, i.e. 'full with Leaves'.
374. *Die. Sup*., p. 369.
375. For Nyagrodha as the haunt of these birds, cf. *K.S.S*. — passage quoted by J. Charpentier — *Die. Sup*., p. 353, also Tawney-I.220 ff. (The episode of Śaktideva); for huge

trees as haunts of huge birds, cf. reference by Charpentier — *Die-Sup.*, p. 356; ff.; for Garuḍa birds residing on a tree called 'Campangaughi' (which means *'The place of the wind'*, see *Die. Sup.*, p. 359.

376. *vitnātā vibhir natā*; and *vi* + *natā* = *viśeṣeṇa natā.*

377. The branches of the Vaṭa tree go down deep in the ground and hence the tree can be said to be 'Vinatā' in other sense — (bent). *Nyagrodha* also means *'shooting downwards'* from nyak + rudh (< *ruh*) (to grow) with the Kṛt affix, the meaning coming nearer to the words 'Vinatā'. The name Nyagrodha is explained with the same etymology at *Ai. Br.* VII.30 = 35.4, *Yau nyañco'rohans tasmān nyaṅgrohati nyagroho . . . tam nyagroham santam nyagrodha ityācakṣate.*

378. Cf. *Mb.* I.23.3; also, I.30.41 *nāgakṣayakaras' caiva kāśyapeyo mahābalaḥ.*

379. Cf. *Sup. Ad.* IV.7.3; *Mb.* I-30.31; V.105-18; *Viṣṇu. Dh.*, P. III.34.

380. For a detailed treatment of Kaśyapa, see *Die. Sup.*, p. 315 ff; Charpentier seems to see in the name totemistic origin. Compare with Charpentier, Risley's observation that the tortoise (Kaśyapa) and the nāga were the ancient parents according to many castes of India, *J.R.A.S.*, 1893, p. 285 ff.

381. Cf. *Die. Sup.*, p. 326.

382. *Tait. Ā.* X.I.6.; n. 218, *supra.*

383. Cf. *Die. Sup.*, p. 328.

384. For similarity between Rudra Śiva and Garuḍa in this respect, see note 223 *supra.*

385. *Agni* P. 295.5; see n. 54, *supra.*

386. Cf. *Aś. Śr. Sū*; (Uttar, IV.7). *navame'hani tārkṣyo vaipaścitaḥ, tasya vayāṁsi viśaḥ; Ś.B.* XIII.4.3.13 *tārkṣyo vaipaścito rājā*; rest the same; cf. also *Śāṅ Śr. Su.* XVI.2 (Ed. Hillebrandt, Calcutta, 1888).

387. Cf. Macdonell — *Vedic Myth.*, p. 149; also Macdonell & Keith *Vedic Index*, Vol. I, p. 308.

388. Cf. also *Tait. Ār.* I.23.1 where the creature kūrma (tortoise) is said to be even earlier than Prajāpati.

389. See note 42, *supra*. The word *sarpavidaḥ* is rendered by the commentator as *Kāśyapīyādi-viṣatantravidaḥ.*

390. Cf. *Mb.* I.43.
391. Cf. *Agni* P. 295.5.
392. Cf. *Mb.* I.16.6; *bālā bhūtvā-añjanaprabhāḥ*;
Cf. *Sk.* P. III.38.12; IV.50.18, where the Sarpas are asked to shower venomous breath on the hair of the horse. Cf. also *Pad.* P. V.44.135 "by venomous breath".
Cf. *K.S.S.* the serpents are asked to spit venom.
393. Cf. I.34.22.
394. Cf. *Sk.* P. IV.50.124-25.
395. Cf. Charpentier quoted by Vogel, *Ind. Ser. lore*, p. 54.
396. For reference to Garuḍa or such big birds really eating elephants, buffaloes or the like, cf. *Die. Sup.*, p. 330 ff. where Charpentier quotes all relevant authorities with passages. Cf. also *Encycl. Britt.* (1910), Vol. VII, p. 822, where we read that golden eagles were used in India to capture beasts of prey. Tarturs used the bird for capturing antelopes, also foxes etc.
Donald Mackenzie, however, believes that the myth of the Serpent killing birds first originated in Egypt, with the secretary-bird killing the serpents. See, *Myths of Pre-Columbian America*, p. 45 ff.
397. See Appendix A — *Garuḍa and the Nāgī.*
398. We have a parallel in the story of Manasā (The snake-goddess) which Thomas relates in detail:—
(Cf. '*Epics, Myths,* etc.', p. 37 ff.) According to the story a Brāhmaṇa is averse to the worship of Manaṣā, the serpent deity. She troubles him but still he does not accept her as fit to be worshipped. Ultimately the death of his son by snake-bite, and restoration of life by Manasā changes him and he accepts Manasā as fit to be worshipped; but even then he accepts to offer her flowers only by his left hand with his face turned away from her idol, to which Manasā has no objection. This shows Manasā being accepted in the fold of the worshipped gods at a loss to her prestige, and resembles the case of Garuḍa, fighting with Indra and Viṣṇu and ultimately becoming the latter's vehicle, thus getting a place in the Vedic fold, but definitely a lower one.

# II
## Kaca and Śukra

*The important motif in the legend of Kaca is the swallowing and the disgorging of the initiate by the preceptor, with the gain of new life on the part of the initiate.*

*This motif in the legend represents a fine blending of the sacrificial rite of consecration described in the Brāhmaṇa-texts and the initiation rites of the tribals.*

# 1
# THE LEGEND

Unlike the legend of Garuḍa, the Kaca legend is not seen to have a footing in the past, i.e., Kaca as the hero of the legend is rarely to be found in the literature anterior to *Mb.* This is not to say that the motif of the legend is unique to *Mb*; but the legend with Kaca as the hero as such has the first full occurrence in *Mb.* We shall take up the whole legend, as it is in *Mb.* and pursue the motif elsewhere. This legend occurs in the Yayāti-Upākhyāna and tries to explain the 'why' of the *'Pratiloma'* type of marriage between Yayāti and Devayānī (*Mb.* I.76-77).

There happened to be a mutual contest between the gods and the Asuras for prosperity in the three worlds. The gods, with the desire of victory selected the sage Aṅgiras, while the others (Asuras) appointed Kāvya Uśanas as their preceptor. Those two brahmins were keenly competing with each other for ever. But whosoever of the gods the Asuras killed in the battle, Bṛhaspati could not bring back to life though endowed with the height of intellect. He did not know that lore which the mighty (*'vīryavān'*) Kāvya knew — the *Sañjīvanī Vidyā* ; and hence the gods were driven to deep despair. The gods, being afraid of Kāvya Uśanas, went to Kaca, the eldest son of Bṛhaspati and said to him — "Be thou mindful (*'bhajasva'*) of us, who are praising thee and give us thy excellent help. Do thou take away hither that lore which rests with that Brāhmaṇa Śukra, of limitless prowess. Thou shalt have a share with us (in the sacrifice). Thou canst, possibly, see that Brāhmaṇa with Vṛṣaparvan (the king). He protects the demons there, and does not protect those who are not Dānavas. Thou, young as thou art, art capable of propitiating the learned one and also Devayānī — the beloved daughter of that great man. Thou (alone) art capable — there is nobody else — by virtue of thy character, benevolence and thy charming behaviour with thy control (over senses). When Devayānī is pleased, doubtless thou wilt obtain the lore."

"Be it so", said Kaca, the son of Bṛhaspati; and, being honoured by the gods, went where Vṛṣaparvan was. Without loss of time Kaca, going to the city of the Asuras, saw Śukra and said to him, "I am Kaca the grandson of Aṅgiras and the son of the very Bṛhaspati. Do thou accept me as thy disciple. I shall practise the vow of a student (*brahmacarya*). Allow me, O Brāhmaṇa a period of thousand years near thee."

Śukra said, "Welcome, Kaca I accept what thou hast said. I shall worship thee fit to be worshipped. Let Bṛhaspati be worshipped (thus)."

Kaca accepted what Śukra said; and agreed to the period for the vow (of *brahmacarya*), (thence) propitiating the preceptor as well as Devayānī. Young Kaca thus propitiating her — now dancing, now singing and now playing on musical instruments for her — pleased the young Devayānī with the gifts of fruits and flowers etc. always having her in mind (*samśīlayan*). Devayānī also sportingly (dallying), moved with him — the devout brāhmaṇa, in seclusion ('*rahaḥ*'), singing after him. Thus five hundred years elapsed, since the time when Kaca began practising the vow of *brahmacarya*. Then the Dānavas, knowing (who) Kaca (was), seeing him protecting the cows in the forest, came together in a conference, and they killed him due to their spite against Bṛhaspati and also for the protection of the lore. Killing him they gave him to the *Śālavṛkas* (wolves), cutting him into pieces like sesamum-seeds. Then the cows returned to the haunt without their protector. Seeing the cows thus returned without Kaca, Devayānī said thus, "O Father! you have not (*ahūtam*) offered oblation to the Agni and the Sun has set; the cows have returned without their head (but) Kaca is not to be seen. Clear it is that Kaca is killed or dead. I shall not remain alive without Kaca, O Father! This I tell unto thee the truth." Śukra said, " I shall bring him back to life by the words, 'Come hither,'."

Then he called Kaca, by applying the '*Sañjīvanī-Vidyā*'. Thus being called, Kaca came forth without any injury. When asked, he said that he had been killed.

Again he (Kaca) went to the forest to fetch flowers as directed by Devayānī, and there (again) the Dānavas saw him. They killed him the second time, and burnt him and changing him into powder, they gave it to the Brāhmaṇa (Śukra) himself in Surā (liquor). Devayānī again approached her father. Śukra said, "The son of Bṛhaspati, O daughter, is dead. Even after being brought to life he is killed — what should I do? Grieve not, O Devayānī; shed no tears. (A girl) like thee should not grieve for a mortal. All the gods, (nay) the whole universe, doth bow before the ravage that cometh." Devayānī said, "He whose grand-father is the old Aṅgiras, Bṛhaspati — the sage — is father, how shall I not grieve for him, who is the grandson of such a sage? He is a Brahmacārin and always upright in penance and efficient in his duties. I shall follow the path of Kaca and shall not eat. The handsome Kaca is dear to me." Śukra said, "Surely the Asuras are against me as they kill my disciple, who is devoid of any sin. Those cruel ones desire to make me an *a-brāhmaṇa*, as they — the Asuras — have started thus. Might this sin have an expiation? For, whom might not the 'killing of Brāhmaṇa' burn, may he be even Indra!" Being urged by Devayānī, the great sage again called with a great effort Kaca, the son of Bṛhaspati ('*Bṛhaspatisutam*'). Being afraid of the preceptor and being called by virtue of the lore (Kaca) slowly answered from the stomach (of the preceptor). Him did Śukra ask by what way he entered his stomach. He replied, "I still remember due to thy favour; and I can recollect all that happened and how I am given to thee, O Kāvya, in thy *surā* (wine) by the Asuras, after being killed, burnt and powdered. How can the guile of the Asuras surpass that of the Brāhmaṇas even as thou dost stand?" Said Śukra, "What good shall I do to thee, O daughter? By my death shall Kaca gain life, O Devayānī! Kaca can never be seen except for the breaking of my side." Devayānī, spoke, "Both these sorrows burn me like fire — viz., the ruin of Kaca and thy death. In the ruin of Kaca my weal is at naught, in (the event of) thy death I cannot be alive."

Śukra said, "Well formed, O son of Bṛhaspati, art thou; to thee, the devoted, is Devayānī attached. Obtain this lore and also (thy) life to-day, if thou be not Indra in the form of Kaca. None except a Brāhmaṇa shall return alive from my stomach; hence, obtain thou the lore. Being my son, produced (full of life) by me, do thou cause me to be alive again coming out of this place (stomach). Do thou abide by the agreement of Dharma (*dharmavatīm avekṣām*) on obtaining the lore from the preceptor."

Having obtained the lore from the preceptor, the brāhmaṇa Kaca came out breaking the right side of the brāhmaṇa (Śukra) even as doth the moon on the full moon night, at the completion of the bright (half of the month).*

On seeing the 'heap of knowledge' (*brahmarāśim*) (in the form of the) dead (preceptor), Kaca also brought him back to life. Having obtained the perfect lore; and, bowing to his preceptor, Kaca said thus to him, "Those who respect not the preceptor, the giver of the peerless divine truth (Ṛta), the receptacle of the four kinds of wealth (*nidhim nidhīnām caturanvayānām*) of learning, go to the bottomless abodes of the sinful."

Seeing the handsome Kaca whom (erstwhile) he drank up in ignorance under the power of wine, being deceived in the act of drinking it (leading to) the terrible oblivion of

---

**Mb.* I.76.61 *śuklātyaye purṇamāsyām.* The 'full-moon' is the last day of the bright half of a month.

senses, the mighty Kāvya Uśanas, getting up in rage, said thus, full of hatred for wine and with the desire of the good of the brāhmaṇas, "An ignorant Brāhmaṇa, who from this day, shall drink wine, shall be devoid of virtue (or shall fall from his duties), shall be (guilty of the sin of) the killer of a brahmin; and shall be criticised in this world and also the other. I have set a limit in this world in this speech for the brāhmaṇas. May the brāhmaṇas be ready to hear what their preceptors say. Harken you, all the gods and all people!" Saying thiswise he, of great prowess and the limitless receptacle of the wealth of penance, calling forth all the foolish dānavas, said thus unto them, "This do I tell unto ye, O Dānavas! You are all childish. Kaca, having fulfilled his desire, shall stay with me. Kaca, who, obtaining the invaluable 'life-giving' lore, has become of equal power with Brahmā — (nay) — has become the very Brahmā."

Remaining with the preceptor for a thousand years, Kaca, getting his permission, desired to go to the abode of gods.

To him (Kaca), who had started for the abode of gods after the fulfilment of his vow and being permitted by the preceptor, Devayānī said thus, "O Thou, the grandson of Aṅgiras! Thou dost shine with thy behaviour, thy noble birth, by thy learning, thy penance and by thy self-restraint. As the renowned sage Aṅgiras is worthy of respect for my father, so is Bṛhaspati for me honoured and revered. Knowing thus, consider what I speak, O Tapodhana (penance is whose wealth)! As I behaved with thee in thy vow of austerity and self-restraint, likewise thou, now having accomplished the lore, shouldst behave with me, who am devoted to thee. Do thou accept my hand (in marriage) according to the rites and with the mantras." Kaca said, "As thy father is honoured and revered to thee, so is he to me. Likewise thou, O perfect limbed one, art to me more revered. Thou art more beloved to the great scion of the Bhṛgus (Śukra) than even his life. Thou art always revered to me according to Dharma, being the daughter of my preceptor. As for me, thy father Śukra is always honoured; likewise, O Devayānī art thou. It doth not behove thee to speak thus to me." Devayānī spoke, "Thou art the son of my father's preceptor's son, and not my father's son. Herefore art thou honoured and revered to me, O the best of the twice-born! But remember my love to thee, when thou wert again and again killed by the Asuras. Know my devotion to be the excellent in friendship and also in the matter of love. It doth not behove thee, O Knower of the right (Dharma)!, to discard me — the guileless devotee of thine." Said Kaca, "Thou art engaging me to something, O thou of virtuous vow!, which is not fit for me. Be pleased with me, O thou of beautiful eyebrows; thou art (to me) even greater than my preceptor. Wherein thou didst dwell, O moonfaced one endowed with beautiful eyes!, even there I did reside — in the stomach of Kāvya, O thou brilliant one! Thou art my sister by Dharma; do not speak thus, O thou of auspicious face! I dwelt (here) with pleasure (and) shall go; speak thou of the auspicious, on my way. May I be remembered, not contrary to righteousness, in thy talks. Being always alert, do thou serve my preceptor."

Devayānī said, "If thou dost avoid me, being urged by me in righteous love, thee O Kaca, I curse thiswise! Thy lore will not see fulfilment!"

Kaca said, "I speak in reply, thinking thee to be my preceptor's daughter and not with any (fault of) spite. I am permitted by the preceptor; curse me if thou dost like, O Devayānī! Cursed am I by thee, even when I speak according to the ancient Dharma; I do not deserve this (curse of thine). I am cursed by thee through Kāma (sexual desire) and not righteousness. Therefore thy desire shall not be fulfilled. No ascetic's son will accept thy hand in marriage. Thou didst say that my lore will not be fruitful. Be it so. Him will it be fruitful to, whom I shall teach the same!"

Saying thus to Devayānī, Kaca, the foremost of the

twice-born, went quickly to the abode of the gods. Seeing him return, all the gods with Indra as their leader, honouring Bṛhaspati, said thus to Kaca, "As thou hast performed an act beneficial to us, thy glory shall be unabated; and thou shalt have a share with us" (I. 77).

# 2
# GODS, ASURAS AND 'SWALLOWING'

The constant fight between the gods on the one side and Asuras on the other and the ultimate victory of the gods is an important pattern in mythology. On the Hindu side this is noted from ancient works in various passages.[1] It is also to be found that the gods were devoid of things necessary for the sacrifice or life and these things were with the Asuras. Thus Vṛtra was endowed with all that was necessary for the sacrifice and it is only by killing him that Indra got these things.[2] Often the gods resort to deceit and win. The legend of Kaca reflects this motif which can also be seen in the Brāhmaṇa texts. In the Jaiminīya Brāhmaṇa,[3] we have the following story about the conflict of the gods and Asuras and the ultimate success of the gods.

"The gods and the Asuras were at war for a long time. Either could not win. Bṛhaspati was the preceptor of the gods, Uśanā Kāvya of the Asuras. Whatever intellectual deed (*Brahma*) was done this side was (also) performed that side. That intellect (*brahma*) did not win its equal. The gandharva Triśīrṣā knew about their victory. His, indeed, was the floating city (made of) boats in the water. Indra knew that Triśīrṣā was in the know of victory. He approached his (the latter's) wife for the purpose of this victory. He said to her, 'Ask (thy) husband' (as to) these gods and the Asuras that are fighting (among themselves) for a long time — who of these will win.' He (Indra) then came when those two were conversing. He, indeed, hung on (stuck up) in the boat-pavilion becoming a water-louse or a little straw (*tṛṇakam*). She asked (her) husband, "These gods and Asuras that are fighting — who of these will be victorious?"

"Do not (speak) loudly; the earth, indeed, has ears. Hence they say it, that the earth has ears."[4] "No," said he. "Do thou tell" (said) she. He said, "These two Brāhmaṇas have equal knowledge—Bṛhaspati among the gods, Uśanā among the Asuras. Whatever these two do, comes to be equal; which-ever offerings doth one offer (in the fire) the other (also) the same. Those (offerings), meeting together, turn back; both alike. Out of these two (gods and Asuras), whosoever shall approach the others, those (of his side) will be victorious." Indra, knowing that, flew up in the form of a parrot (*suka*).[5] On seeing him fly, (the Gandharva) said, "Of whom this green and golden-coloured (*harita-varṇakaḥ*) (bird) flies, those will win." He (Indra) came to Uśanas Kāvya among the Asuras and said to him thus, "Whom these people dost thou increase? Thou indeed art ours and we thine. Do thou return (to us)." "How" said he, "what with dost thou invite me?" "These cows of Virocana — the son of Prahlāda, with these. Do thou return (to us)." They (together) ran forth. The Asuras ran after those two. They followed these two. He (Indra) said, "O sage, behind us, indeed, these Asuras are coming." He (again) said, "Do such (a thing) that these may not follow us." Those two found this verse.

'Endowed with brilliant weapons doth the god Indu (*Soma*) stream forth— the killer of enemies and the protector from the wicked (sin); protector of the gods, the restorer and the good benefactor, the supporter of heaven and the prop of the earth.' They got shelter of the pillar, which went up the heavens.[6] The Asuras did not cross that. With these verses— the desire-yielding ones-they went to the gods. The verses belong to Uśanā. Uśanā, the Kāvya, desired the immortal world of the Gandharvas among the gods. He saw this laudatory verse (Sāma). Praised with this."[7]

On studying the above story we get the following points in common with the legend in the *Mb.* and also certain other important points.

1. Indra who goes to Uśanā on whom depends the victory of gods, resembles Kaca;
2. But, here the preceptor himself comes to the side of the gods which easily suggests the *Mb* idea of giving protection to Kaca especially against the Asuras — when we have Uśanā warding off the Asuras;
3. The wife of Triśīrṣa-gandharva, acting as an instrument for the gain of the secret, faintly suggests the later Devayānī who helps Kaca gain his life, ultimately leading him to the secret knowledge of immortality;
4. Indra taking the form of a straw or a louse in the abode of the gandharva comes quite close to Kaca staying with Śukra with the vow of Brahmacarya. The minuteness that is reflected in the straw and the louse can be well compared with the minutest form of Kaca residing in the stomach of Śukra — the preceptor. In both these, can be marked the point of disguise;
5. There is no clear parallel to the gain of *Sañjīvanī*; but the secret of victory can well be compared with *Sañjīvanī*, which ultimately gives victory to the possessor of it;
6. Swallowing is completely absent here;
7. It is not Indra that gets the 'Immortal world', but it is Uśanā Kāvya, who gets it, coming to the side of the gods;
8. The winning of *Sañjīvanī* is suggested by the winning of the possessor (i.e. Śukra) of the lore himself;
9. Uśanā and Bṛhaspati were equal;
10. No name is seen as Śukra.

There is another tale that from the *Kāṭhaka Saṃhitā*,[8] which comes near to that of Kaca.

"The gods and the Asuras were at war. Nectar (*amṛta*) was with the Asuras (and) among them with the *dānava* (demon) Śuṣṇa. Śuṣṇa carried it away in his mouth. Those of the gods who died remained (just) so. Of the Asuras (who died), Śuṣṇa breathed upon with *amṛta*. They revived. Indra perceived — with the Asuras, with the *dānava*-Śuṣṇa, is *amṛta*. He, having changed himself into a lump of honey, lay upon the way. This Śuṣṇa swallowed; and Indra, changing himself into an eagle-hawk (*śyena*) snatched *amṛta* from his mouth. Indra came out. Hence this one is the strongest of the birds, for he is one form of Indra. *Amṛta* doth he hold who knows thus; whomsover one desireth to live without disease, *him should he breathe out after having taken in* (swallowed). With *amṛta* (immortality) indeed doth he breathe him out. He gaineth full life; not before his (full attainment of) life doth he die."

Here we get the main point of the *Mb* tale of Kaca, i.e. the bringing of *amṛta* or immortality. *Mb* tells clearly that Bṛhaspati was unable to give life to the gods while Śukra Kāvya had that lore by which he could bring the Asuras to life. Viewing the above tale from the *Kāṭha. Sam.* we have these points:—

(i) We have here *amṛta* with the Asuras; and Indra goes to fetch it; and hence is the divine messenger;

(ii) Śuṣṇa, who was in possession of it, had the nectar in his mouth and he would breathe upon the dead Asuras so as to make them alive. This breathing of *amṛta* to revive the demons is exactly the same as the chantīng of Sañjivanī by the mouth so as to infuse the breath with immortality. Śuṣṇa's having nectar in his mouth can also be well compared with Śukra's having the Sañjīvanī lore in his mouth;

(iii) Indra's getting into the mouth of Śuṣṇa marks a similarity with Kaca, both doing so without the least knowledge of the swallower;

(iv) The most striking point however in this account is *swallowing and again getting out*, which exactly corroborates with the Kaca account. Indra being swallowed comes with *amṛta* and we do not know about the fate of Śuṣṇa; the Kaca-account is a more refined one in that Śukra gets killed and is the first for Kaca — the disciple — to use the lore upon;

(v) The idea of Indra changing himself into an eagle-hawk is worthy of note and is similar to his changing himself into a bird in *Jai. Br.*;

(vi) There is, of course, no reference to the names of Śukra or Uśanā, to Sañjīvanī and Devayānī.

The conflict between Indra and Śuṣṇa is found in the *Ṛgveda* also when Indra kills this demon of drought.[9] Śuṣṇa has his movable city,[10] which brings to our mind the 'Naval-city' of the gandharvas Triśīrṣā (in the passage of the *Jai. Br.*) which is floating.[11] Thus Śuṣṇa of the Kāṭhaka and Triśīrṣā of the *Jai. Br.* present a similar case.

We saw that in both these accounts it is Indra that acts as the messenger; but elsewhere Agni is also said to be the messenger of gods. He once goes to the sage Uśanā, not being loved by the gods; the latter loves him and accepts him as a friend,[12] which resembles Śukra accepting Kaca. Agni is asked by the gods to invite the seasons that had gone away to the Asuras.[13] Agni is identified with Aṅgiras,[14] whose son is Bṛhaspati, the preceptor of the gods. It is Bṛhaspati, who acts with Agni to help the gods.[15] Bṛhaspati, as the preceptor of the gods, sends Agni as a messenger to the Maruts.[16] In *ṚV.* Bṛhaspati is identified with Agni (ṚV. II.1.3)[17] and this identification goes well when Bṛhaspati is the preceptor of the gods and Agni is also called the Purohita of the gods.[18] Bṛhaspati thus comes to be the one who guides the gods by sending proper emissaries to effect functions. In the epic elsewhere we have Bṛhaspati sending Agni to find out where Indra was, being afraid of his sin of killing a brāhmaṇa (Brahmahatyā). It is again Bṛhaspati, who advises Indra to go to Śukra Uśanas, who advises him to go to Prahlāda, the Asura king to beg for his *śīla*[19] (character). The above instances are enough to show how Indra and Agni, aided by Bṛhaspati, who himself is another form of Agni, come together to avert the disasters that threaten the gods.[20] As Indra and Agni are of foremost importance in sacrifice, it is easy to understand how Indra appears to protect the sacrifice by going himself or by sending one of his associates. The episode of Dīrgha-jihvī can be remembered in this connection. According to it Indra sent Kautsa to the Āsurī Dīrghajihvī who constantly licked the sacrificial Soma, and ultimately subdued her with deceit.[21] Indra is, elsewhere, actually said to have resided among the Asuras, being enamoured of the Āsurī Vilesteṅgā, assuming the form of a female among females and of a male among males.[22] We also hear of another Asura female drawing Indra away from the gods.[23]

From the above instances the following points come forth:—

(i) Indra and Agni figure prominently as messengers; and Kaca, as the messenger of gods, resembles these and might have been suggested as an understudy of these divine messengers;[24]

(ii) In certain cases Indra or the messenger sent by him (on behalf of the gods) resorts to deceit which is similar to the deceit of Śukra by Kaca; though it is not prominent but implied;

(iii) The alluring by the Asura girls is the same in the case of Indra and Kaca.

It could thus be seen, that Kaca as the messenger of the gods falls in line with the other divine messengers who, with a definite aim, go to the side of the Asuras and fulfil the aim for the good of the gods. This pattern is seen at the background of the conflict between gods and Asuras.

## Swallowing and Letting Out

We have already seen from the passage of the *Kāṭh. Sam.* quoted above that the motif of swallowing and letting out is quite an ancient one, and how it is connected with some definite gain on the part of the gods. In the passage quoted, it is Indra (in the form of the lump of honey) that is swallowed by Śuṣṇa, the Asura. Some other examples may be noted.

### (A) Indra and Vṛtra

The motif of swallowing and letting out can be seen, with slight variations, where Agni and Soma are said to reside in the stomach of Vṛtra, the Asura, and come out, killing him. In the account of the creation of Vṛtra by Tvaṣṭṛ to take revenge on Indra, this motif is present. Thus we have in the *Ś. Br.;*[25]

"He, indeed, Tvaṣṭṛ, got angry (saying), '(Indra) alack, uninvited ate my Soma'; he himself deformed the sacrifice. Whatever Soma was left in the 'droṇakalaśa' (the vessel of Soma) he caused to turn (roll) saying, 'Grow thou, the destroyer of Indra.' 'He came forth uniting with Agni', say some; 'without (Agni) did he come forth' others (say). He (united) with Agni and Soma, with the whole lore, all success, all the food, all glory . . . . He — Indra — in the same way being pursued (by Vṛtra), running addressed Agni and Soma, 'You, indeed, are mine; I yours. He, indeed, is not yours; whom do you increase (by power) — this miscreant: Do return to me.' . . . 'Be it so' (said they).

"Then, indeed, Vṛtra was killed. Him did (Indra) lengthwise dissect in twain. What part of him (Vṛtra) was Soma, he made it the moon; what was 'Asurya' (belonging to the Asura) with that the progeny. Of Agni and Soma, indeed, is this whole progeny — the creatures. The sun is that which belonged to fire, (and) the moon that belonged to Soma. The day is that of fire. The night is of Soma. The half-month that waxes belongs to Agni, that which wanes to Soma."[25]

The following points can be seen from the above passage:—

(i) Agni and Soma were both in the body of Vṛtra.
(ii) They came out for the good of Indra, killing Vṛtra, Indra's enemy.

It is true that Agni and Soma are not clearly said to have been swallowed by Vṛtra; but the idea is implied. It can also be noted that it is not only Agni and Soma that are inside the body of Vṛtra. Everything that is worth having is in his body — the lore, success and even the glory. Agni and Soma are the most necessary ingredients of sacrifice. When Vṛtra comes out with these in his body it amounts to his 'swallowing' them and when Indra releases them, they kill their old resort and come out alive.[26]

We now take up the example of the '*Sautrāmaṇī iṣṭi*'[27] which is said to be the rite that rejuvenated Indra who died due to the heavy drinking of Soma. When Indra drank too much of Soma it ran through all the openings of his body and not only through his mouth. We shall take the account as given in the *Jai. Br.*

"Him — Indra — did the unoffered king Soma trouble' being drunk. Through all his openings did he (Soma) rush (out), not alone from the mouth. Hence was he (Indra) apt to be treated by medicine (became ill). Whatever came out of his (*tasyeda-vāyoga*) that became the *surā vāriṭakā*; what from his generative organ became the *parisruk*. Thrice did he spit out. That which he spat out first became *karkandhu*-fruit. What the second time, became the *badara* (fruit). What the third time became *klava*. Then, of all these the eaten (*annam*) and the juices, came out for the fourth time with a *khāṭ* sound (in clearing the throat). That itself became the mango. Him in that condition did the gods approach and sat in front (saying), 'He was our only hero. He went this way. Where shall we be!' He, too, said, 'We know not what to do.' 'What?' (said they). (He said) — 'Or else I desire to have a cough'. Hence, indeed, they die having coughed before. To him did they say, 'Thou cough'. Do thou live'. He, indeed did cough. Him did they say, 'Do thou come to life". He indeed came to life."[28]

The following points are to be noted from this passage: —

(i) Indra swallowed Soma;
(ii) It came out of Indra's body;
(iii) Indra almost died but was brought back to life;
(iv) The whole creation as it were — various animals and fruits etc. came out of Indra's body along with Soma, that sprang forth from the various parts of his body (*Ibid.*).

Tallying the two accounts, viz.

(i) Vṛtra's letting out Agni and *Soma* intaken by him; and
(ii) Indra's letting out of *Soma* swallowed by him,

we find a close similarity in the final result, namely:—

(i) They both 'intake' *Soma* and die;
(ii) The swallowed Soma again comes out;
(iii) The swallower again comes to life.[29]

Though the point of Agni being the messenger of gods does not strike well in these two present accounts, the most important factor of the sacrifice Agni, the very *purohita* of gods (RV. I.1.1) lies in the body of Vṛtra (with Soma) and again comes out with the very sacrifice and other ingredients for sacrifice.[30] There is a twofold pattern of identification, based on complementary rivalry. The first fold is as follows:—

(i) Soma is intaken by Indra and Vrtra; they died and came to life;
(ii) They are equal in this exploit.

Now, Soma is himself (itself!) identified with Vṛtra[31] who is the food of Indra, as we have seen. The very fact that it was *Soma* that was thrown in the fire and that, because it rolled on, it was called Vṛtra, goes to suggest the identification of Soma and Vṛtra.[32] Vṛtra's head is itself the Soma-vessel.[33] When Indra drinks Soma, his favourite drink, which is identified with Vṛtra (who himself is Indra's food), it is a natural step to take that Indra eats (swallows) Vṛtra

(Soma) who comes out of the former's body leaving him dead. The second fold of the pattern is:—

(i) Indra swallows Vṛtra who dies;
(ii) Vṛtra comes out of Indra's body which also becomes lifeless;
(iii) Both the swallower and the swallowed die and again come to life;
(iv) There is equality between them.

There are references where the equality between Indra and Vṛtra is suggested in other ways. Thus, in the *Tait. Sam.* it is stated that Indra killed Vṛtra and immediately lost his strength,[34] which shows that both are equal, one dying and the other being powerless at the same time. It is not that, only Indra swallows Vṛtra.[35] Later we have references where Vṛtra also swallows Indra, who again comes out of the former's gaped mouth exactly as do Agni and Soma.[36] All these references go to establish the predominance of a perennial thought that the *eater and the eaten both are equal* in prowess. The same suggestion is made variously in various contexts. Sometimes, the powerlessness of Indra is suggested only by being enveloped by darkness (that swallows him).[37] Indra and Vṛtra swallowing and being swallowed, dying and again coming to life present another important point which is particularly interesting in this connection. The one is the god and the other is the Asura. Looking from another angle, it is the god who swallows the Asura and kills him. He again comes to life. The Asura being swallowed, kills the god who dies and again comes to life, or *vice versa*.

This particular motif is the same as in the legend of Kaca. Kaca — a god himself (being the god's preceptor's son) — is swallowed by Śukrācārya — the Asura-priest, and is again brought to life. Śukrācārya dies but is again brought to life by Kaca. The death of Śukra, after Kaca comes out of his belly, and not immediately after he swallows Kaca, only proves the modification of the old motif not altogether changing it. It should be noted that, even in the legend of Kaca, the swallowing of the divine hero by the enemy-priest immediately *renders the latter helpless*; for he either incurs Brahma-hatyā by keeping Kaca in the stomach or kills himself by getting him out. This goes well with such passages as we have just seen where Indra, though not killed, gets instantaneously powerless as soon as he kills Vṛtra, or swallows him.

## (B) The Sun and the Moon

From Vṛtra to take a step further to Soma, it is Soma that is always swallowed.[38] Soma is identified in the Brāhmaṇas with the moon,[39] who is again said to be Vṛtra on the same analogy of Vṛtra = Soma. The swallowing and letting out bring us to another step which is 'Temporary Death' leading to ultimate gain of life. This idea is common like the one stated above, and, what is true in the case of Kaca-Śukra, is a principle expressed in various ways, in the case of Indra and Vṛtra (*Soma*) who are constantly referred to as the sun and the moon respectively. Thus in the *Ś.B.* we have :—

"Indra, indeed is the one that burns (i.e. the sun), Vṛtra the moon. He (Indra = sun) born for the enmity of him (i.e. Vṛtra's = the moon's) devours him (the moon); hence, though previously at a distance, he (the moon) moves near him this night (i.e. on the new-moon-night). He (the sun = Indra) takes hold of him; devouring him does he rise. Having sucked him completely empty he (the sun) throws him out; and he (the moon), thus pushed out, is seen in the western sky and again increases, (only) to serve as food for him (the sun)."[40]

The passage shows two things :—

(i) The moon is always eaten, being the food, by the sun;
(ii) The moon, though eaten (sucked or swallowed

completely) comes back.

It is not that the moon alone suffers this temporary extinction amounting to death. The sun also undergoes the same fate — i.e. dies — and again comes to life, the idea being suggested from the daily setting and rising. He is said to be brought back to life in several ways, from the plants, from the milk etc. He enters the night as the embryo and is reborn in the morning due to the offerings.[41]

It could be noted how this temporary death of the sun and the moon corresponds to the temporary death of Kaca and Śukra. In this context the sun is identified with Indra both being the eaters and the moon the eated. Now, the sun himself is said to be 'Śukra', thus identifying all these three — the sun, Indra and Śukra. And even Śuṣṇa.

### (C) 'Śūkra' and 'Manthin' Cups

In the context of the Śukra and Manthin cups of Soma we have the following in the *Ś.B.*:

"He indeed is Śukra — he that burns. Thus, as he doth burn this, hence is the Śukra. The moon alone is the Manthī."

And further, Śukra is said to be the eater.

"One of these (two) is the 'Eater', the other the 'Eaten'; The 'Eater' is verily the 'Śukra', the 'Eaten' the '*Manthī*' ".[42]

In the same passage, Śukra (the cup) is addressed as — 'brilliance-enveloped', burning and wandering across the sky.[43]

The *Mait. Sam.* clearly identifies the *Śukra* (cup) with the sun.[44] On the sixth day of the 'Twelve-day'-sacrifice, the *Śukra* cup is drawn first, the cause being that the day belongs to Indra. This also goes to prove the identification of Śukra and Indra.[45]

It will be seen that, as far as the motif of swallowing is concerned (i) *Soma* has stayed to be the one that is to be eaten or swallowed, may be in the form of the liquid juice or in the form of the moon that shines in the sky; and the moon itself is identified with the *Manthī*; and (ii) Indra, the Sun and Śukra are the ones that are said to be the eaters.

The eater 'Śukra' of these passages corresponds to the swallower Śukra of our legend. To take a glimpse back to the 'Indra-Śuṣṇa tale' of the *Kāṭh. Saṃ.* There Indra takes the form of a 'lump of honey' — (*madhvaṣṭhīḷā*). The name of the eater there is 'Suṣṇa' which suggests 'brilliance' which also is the quality of the Sun, and the name 'Śukra' also, suggests the same.[46] The eaten on the other hand, though said to be Indra himself, is the 'lump of honey' and comes nearer to the moon or Soma. It could thus be seen that the swallowing of the *madhvaṣṭhīlā* by Śuṣṇa resembles the swallowing of Soma (or the moon) by the sun who is identified with Śukra. As Indra, as the lump of honey, gives a glimpse of this being identified (at least in the said passage) with the moon (Soma), so is *Śukra* (identified though with Indra) the name of Soma,[47] thus hinting at complete oneness or equality of the eaten and the eater.

The 'Śukra'-*graha* identified with the Sun and Indra contains white *Soma* thus giving an idea of the bright sun, and the Manthin, identified with the moon, contains *Soma* mixed with barley-malt (or *saktu*) thus giving it the colour of the moon. In the context of the 'Śukra' and 'Manthin' cups, we have also the ritual of the residue of the 'Manthin' cup being poured into the 'Śukra' cup.[48] This is done so as to make the food, i.e., 'Manthin', (the *Soma* in it) which is the 'eaten', pay tribute to its 'eater'.[49] The whole idea comes very close to the symbolic *swallowing* of the Manthin by the Śukra. The rite further lays down that, after the residue from the cup of the 'Pratiṣṭhātṛ' ('Pratiprasthātṛ, in the *Kāṇ.*) — who holds the 'Manthin' cup — is poured into that of the 'Adhvaryu', who holds Śukra cup; the same is *again poured* into the cup of the Hotṛ thus making the idea complete in *disgorging Soma* from the Śukra cup. Thus, *Soma* mixed with barley malt symbolically gets to be eaten by (pays homage to the eater) the Śukra (*graha*) and again gets out of it and corresponds to the moon that is eaten by the sun and again disgorged.

The same is the case with the sun and moon, who are identified, respectively, with Indra and Soma. We now take up another pair — that of Agni and *Soma.* Agni and *Soma* were both in the body of Vṛtra and they came out of it. Often they are invoked together and are said to be complementary to each other. Agni is said to be the day and Soma the night.[50] Soma is the lordly power and Agni the holy power.[51] The consecrated enters the mouth of Agni and Soma and frees himself by offering to these two.[52] He who is long ill should offer to Agni a beast with black neck, and to Soma a brown one. The body of him who is long ill goes to Agni, and the sap to Soma, and he ransoms his body from Agni and the Sap from Soma.[53] Agni and Soma are variously invoked together.[54] A man desiring splendour should offer to Agni and Soma.[55] Soma went to the hill and Agni followed him and thus they both got united.[56] These passages would be sufficient to give the idea of the equality of Agni and Soma. Now there are a number of passages, again, to show that Agni himself is identified with the sun,[57] who is identified with Indra and Śukra, who corresponds to the eater. The sacrificial fire is called Śukra;[58] and when oblations of Soma are offered to this same Agni, the idea is similar to saying that Agni swallows Soma and hence is the eater. Thus Agni is the eater and Soma the eaten.

From all these instances two points suggest themselves to us :—

(i) The one that is swallowed or the eaten is Soma (or the moon), and the eaters are Indra, Śukra, the sun, and Agni;

(ii) The swallowed and the swallower are suggested to be equal to one another. They are two phases of the one whole.

### (D) The Killing of Soma and Again Bringing to Life in Sacrifice

Having seen that the favourite food of the gods is *Soma*, the king, we now turn to such passages where Soma as a god is often said to be killed and rejuvenated. This is seen in the context of sacrificial pressings, where we read:—

*ghnanti vā etat somam yad abhiṣuṇvanti*[59]
"They, indeed, kill *Soma*, in that they press him".

It is said to be a cruel act that Soma is killed while pressing.[60] But, the killed *Soma* is always said to be reborn.[61] The stone '*Upāṁśu*', whereupon Soma is pressed, is said to be Soma's own body. The stone is also called '*Āditya*'.[62] Thus the idea is clearly the same old one in a new form, viz. the eating and disgorging of *Soma* (the moon) by the sun. When Soma's body is denoted by the 'Āditya' (the Upāṁśu) stone as the former goes under it, it clearly signifies complete enveloping of Soma on the part of Āditya; and this is the symbolic 'swallowing' of Soma by Āditya — the sun; and when the *Soma* shoots are thrown out, it suggests the idea of Soma (the moon) thrown out after completely being sucked only to be rejuvenated in the Nigrābhya waters, which again is completely similar to the idea of the moon waxing; and as the moon waxes again to be sucked, so are the Soma-shoots swelled in the waters only to be pressed again by the stone meaning thereby, being symbolically sucked by the Āditya in the form of the Upāṁśu stone. Utmost sympathy seems to be shown to *Soma* when the shoots are pressed, for he is a god; and it is enjoined that, while the shoots are pressed, the name of a person that is hated, should be thought of (and not the name '*Soma*') as we should do when killing a human brāhmaṇa.[63] This also faintly suggests that Soma is a brāhmaṇa, though divine.

## (E) Kaca, Consecration and Studentship

Kaca is the son of Bṛhaspati, a brāhmaṇa. He goes to Śukra, the preceptor, as a student consecrated for studentship.[64] The consecration for studentship and for sacrifice having the same idea, we shall first see consecration for sacrifice. We have seen up to this time that it is Soma that is always swallowed by the gods—Agni, the Sun, and Indra, who are also identified with Śukra. Though it be argued that the preceptor of the Asuras is different from the Śukra that occurs in this connection, it cannot only be a happy coincidence, that the Śukra of our legend and the 'Śukra' (that is said to be Indra and the sun) are both the swallowers. The principle is the same; and we go further to see whether *Soma* that is said to be always swallowed in the form of the moon, or pressed in the form of the plant — thus getting a temporary death — stands symbolically for the consecrated; and whether we have an equation as to the sacrificial material = consecrated.

We have already seen that the consecrated (or the man who consecrates for sacrificial performance) enters the jaws of Soma and Agni, thus suggesting his temporary death, and also that he redeems himself of death by offering to these two deities.[65] The killing (pressing) of Soma, the sacrifice itself is killed and with the sacrifice the sacrificer (i.e., one who has consecrated for the sacrifice).[66] This brings out —

(i) Soma = The sacrificer (consecrated);
(ii) The sacrificer — The sacrifice,

thus establishing also the oneness of the sacrifice and the sacrificer. Not only this, but the sacrifice, the sacrificial material and the consecrated are all suggested to be one.[67] When the sacrificer offers to Agni and Soma, he offers himself in the form of the beast.[68] This offering and killing of the beast, or the pressing of the Soma which means, symbolically, the offering of the sacrificer himself is not a suicide; but only a complete union with the sacrificer or the divine essence.[69] This tallies exactly with the oneness that is suggested in swallowing and disgorging. *Soma* being the worthiest of the materials for the sacrifice, it is understandable how the sacrificer (the consecrated) and *Soma* are spoken of as one, the sacrificer getting symbolically killed and rejuvenated with the killing (pressing) of the Soma plant and its getting swelled again. The same is seen in the sacrificial bath, the *avabhṛtha* with which both Soma and the sacrificer are supposed to get new life. To quote from Eggeling's translation of the *Ś.B.*

"He (the consecrated) now, betakes himself to the expiatory bath. The reason why he betakes himself to the expiatory bath is this. What vital sap there has been in him (Soma and the sacrificer), that (sap) of his he (the priest) has produced (extracted) for the offerings. Now that body (of Soma, i.e., Soma husk), there is no sap in it; yet it is not to be cast away. They take it down to the water — and, water being sap — he puts that sap in it. Thus he unites him with the sap and thus he produces him from it. He, (*the Soma*) *(even when produced) produces him (the sacrificer);* and, because they take it down (*ava* + √*hṛ*) to the water, therefore, the bath is called the '*Avabhṛtha*'.[70]

According to the Mānava Sūtra quoted by *Kāt. Śr. S.* the sacrificer wraps himself up in the cloth in which the Soma stalks are tied, which also go to point out the complete oneness of Soma and the sacrificer.[71]

Closely associated with the idea of oneness of Soma and the sacrificer is the ritual of purchasing Soma, where Soma and the sacrificer are both said to be the embryos.[72] The sacrificer is said to rise after the immortals after he has purchased the immortal *Soma*.[73] The oneness of the sacrificer and Soma is further brought about by the fact that the end of the nether garment of the sacrificer is tucked up with the text — "Thou art Soma's tuck"; for, before consecration the tuck belonged to the man (who was yet unconsecrated), but, after the consecration, it belongs to the consecrated who is Soma.[74] The principle is the same as in wrapping the sacrificer with the shoots of Soma. So, the points are :—

(i) The consecrated = Soma;

(ii) The symbolic death of the consecrated = the symbolic death (in pressing) of Soma;

(iii) The rebirth of the consecrated = the rejuvenation of Soma.

## (F) The Sacrificer (Consecrated) as the Embryo

We have noted that both Soma and the consecrated become the embryo. It is not difficult to see how the sacrificer is called the embryo. The performance of the sacrifice means a new life for the sacrificer; and, as such, he must be born anew. Thus, the sacrificer has a newly constructed hut for him to stay in the day previous to the consecration, the hut denoting the womb from which he is to be born. The black antelope skin is called the 'outer skin' of the embryo etc.[75] The sacrificer (consecrated) is to be born of the sacrifice whose foetus he becomes.[76] He is also said to be the embryo of the Vedas.[77] He is supposed to enter the metres as their embryo.[78] He also is said to *give birth to the sacrifice.*[79] Here we are in a position to add one more point to the three already noted above in Section E.

(iv) The sacrifice = the consecrated; for the sacrifice begets the consecrated (as an embryo) and is in turn born of the one consecrated for sacrifice.

This same point is brought about by such passages as identify the consecrated with Viṣṇu who is identified with the sacrifice.[80] We have noted that the consecrated is identified with Soma that is the material of the sacrifice, and now when he is identified with Viṣṇu it brings forth the same principle of oneness of the sacrificer, the sacrifice and the sacrificial material. Further, *Soma* (the material) is himself identified with Viṣṇu in the same context.[81]

Thus, it is clear that the consecrated — who is symbolically sacrificed at the time of the sacrifice to the deity, in the form of *Soma* or any other offering is reborn with the sap of life. The sacrifice is also killed in the symbolic killing of the sacrificer and is reborn in his rebirth. The sacrifice gives birth to the sacrificer and *vice versa.*

What is true of the sacrificer consecrated for sacrifice is exactly true in the case of the Vedic student who consecrates for the Vedic studies. As the consecrated is supposed to be the embryo of the sacrifice and is born of him, so is the Vedic student the embryo of the preceptor, who is the lord of the rite.[82] As the sacrificer is said to be the 'offerings' offered to the sacrifice and that both are equal in generating one another, so here in the consecration for Vedic-studentship[83] we have the same idea of oneness between the student and the preceptor as the teacher himself is called the Vedic student (*brahmacārin*).[84] We shall fully deal with this point shortly under a separate title.

All these factors are present in the legend under discussion :—

(i) Śukra, the preceptor of Kaca is said to swallow him;[85]
(ii) Kaca comes back alive after the temporary death by being swallowed by the preceptor;[86]
(iii) Kaca brings his own preceptor, who is dead, back to life;[87]
(iv) They come to be of equal prowess — (both being equal to *brahman*).[88]

When Kaca is swallowed by Śukra, it not only suggests the temporary death of Kaca, but also that he has become the embryo of the preceptor from whose belly he comes out. The idea is the same as of the sacrificer being the embryo of the sacrifice. The very fact of being an embryo is enough to suggest oneness of the one who becomes the embryo and the one of whom he is to be born. Oneness in being the embryo is suggested by Śukra addressing Kaca as 'son', after the latter emerges alive out of the former's belly[89] and what else is the 'son' if not the father himself ? The son is only the father's own self reborn.[90] The father is said to enter the wife (his mother!) as an embryo and is said to be reborn in the tenth month from conception.[91] While this idea of rebirth from Śukra makes Kaca his son and suggests the oneness of Kaca and Śukra, the same, hinting at Kaca's temporary oblivion by being swallowed amounting to temporary death, gets well connected with the idea of the preceptor himself being, among other things, death to the student.[92] Thus, the preceptor being both the killer and the generator, is spoken both as Death and the Father of the student. The same principle is expressed by the swallowing and disgorging of Kaca by Śukra.

### (G) Kaca, Soma and Immortality

The main purpose for Kaca's going to Śukra was the gain of the immortality lore, the '*Sañjīvanī*'. This gets explained on the same lines of sacrificial consecration or Vedic studentship. We have noted that the identification of the consecrated with Soma was the main point in the sacrificial rites; also that the sacrificer got his vital sap restored after the *Avabhṛtha* bath as *Soma* also swelled with juice that was extinct from his body during the process of the sacrifice. *Soma* is said to give the life-sap to the ailing man, as we have already noted.[93] The same idea is present in *Soma* being the vital sap of Vṛtra. Cooked rice (*caru*) prescribed for gaining life is called '*saumya*' (that of Soma).[94] In the tale from the *Jai. Br.* we have noted, when Indra and Kāvya Uśanā are running away from the Asuras, Uṣanā Kāvya praises *Soma* as "The supporter of heaven", before he achieves the 'immortal world of the Gandharvas,'[95] thus suggesting *Soma* to be the giver of immortality. Now, *Soma*, who himself is said to be killed in pressing, leads the sacrificer to immortality. *Soma* thus gets a twofold character:—

(i) Being offered as '*havis*' in the sacrifice, i.e. undergoing temporary death (we have already seen that Soma is said to *die* in pressing); and

(ii) Being the harbinger of immortality.

Both these traits can be seen in the character of Kaca who is — (i) killed by being swallowed as a student consecrated for Vedic studies (the Brahmacārin) or the sacrificer who himself is the '*havis*'; and (ii) as the bringer of the Immortal lore to the gods. Viewed from this angle the 'lump of honey' in the tale from the *Kāṭh. Sam*[96] also presents a support. It should be remembered here that it is not the 'lump of honey' that is brought forth; it is the 'lump of honey' when swallowed by Śuṣṇa that brings forth nectar, itself changing its form to that of the Śyena. This also suggests Soma bringing immortality and tallies with the idea of Kaca bringing the lore of immortality when swallowed. It could thus be seen that Kaca characteristically comes nearer to Soma finally, though as a messenger of the gods he resembles Indra and Agni. The same can be seen from the ritual in which the 'Śukra' and the 'Manthin' cups play an important part. Here, some details are to be observed. The Pratiprasthātṛ goes round the altar and pours the residue of Soma (that is the '*Manthin*' cup which he is holding) into the cup of the Adhvaryu (i.e., the 'Śukra cup'). The Adhvaryu, as we have already noted before, pours it into the cup of the Hotṛ for drinking. The cause given is that the draught belongs to the utterer of 'Vaṣaṭ'; and *the Vaṣaṭ being breath, that breath has gone* out of him (the Hotṛ) while uttering the 'Vaṣaṭ'. *Now the draught is breath: thus he pours that breath back into him (Hotṛ)*. If we remember that what is poured is *Soma* itself, it follows, that it is *Soma* that gives the breath, thus giving the very life itself. This corresponds to the idea of Kaca — swallowed and disgorged afterwards — gaining the power to produce life (the *Sañjīvanī Vidyā*), when we remember that the *Soma*-juice is originally from the

'Manthin', which corresponds to the 'eaten' or swallowed. In the context of the Śukra-Manthin cups it is Soma that gives life-breath after getting released from the Śukra cup (that corresponds to the 'eater'), while in our legend it is Kaca that gains '*Sañjīvanī*' after getting swallowed and released from the stomach of his preceptor — Śukra.

Thus it is clearly discernible that Kaca is the under-study of *Soma* that is sacrificed and gives immortality.

Now, the position is this —

(i) Kaca the bringer of immortality comes very close to the student consecrated for the Vedic studies[97] and to the sacrificer, who themselves are symbolically swallowed to represent oneness with the swallower — the preceptor or the (lord of) sacrifice respectively. To put it in another form:— The *havis* = the beast/Soma → the 'Manthin' → the consecrated → the Vedic student → Kaca= All swallowed.

(ii) Śukra, the preceptor comes nearer to Indra, Agni, the Sun, and the 'Śukra' cup, who are all the 'eaters' or the 'swallowers'. Or to put it the other way: Indra → Agni → the Sun → the 'Śukra' cup → Śukra, the preceptor = All swallowers.

Can it be a simple coincidence that the name 'Śukra' be identified with Indra and the sun and Agni who are all swallowers? Or, in other words, is the swallower Śukra (as represented by the 'Śukra' cup or as identified with the swallowers Indra, Agni, and the sun) different from Śukra of our legend? It seems that the Śukra of our legend is *primarily the preceptor in general*, and only secondarily he is the preceptor of the Asuras. In other words, he is deeply rooted in the tradition of the Brāhmaṇa and the Saṁhitā texts and represents the same swallower who is called by various names — Indra, Agni, the Sun or the preceptor; while Kaca represents the same 'swallowed' that bears various names in different contexts; and both these together *represent the principle of oneness of the swallower and the swallowed, as also the principle of continuous life only through symbolic death*. Significant in this connection seems to be the fact that, after Kaca was killed by the Asuras he was mixed with wine (*surā*) and then given to Śukra.[98] *Surā* is mixed with Soma[99] at the Sautrāmaṇī rite and this mixing of Kaca with *surā* also goes to suggest that the idea of Kaca might have been suggested from Soma. Soma again is said to be 'the best of the Aṅgirases';[100] and also the son of Kavi.[101] He is actually addressed as 'Bṛhaspati-suta'[102] which is exactly the position of Kaca. 'Bṛhaspati-*suta*' according to the accent would mean 'pressed by the sacrificer',[103] but it is not altogether improbable that the term might have lost its true connotation and might have been applied later in mythical context to the consecrated who also is said to be appointed by Bṛhaspati for initiation at the time of Vedic studies.[104]

**(H) Swallowing and Initiation (Upanayana)**

This brings us to the rite of Upanayana; for the rite is performed as an introduction of the student to his preceptor. In this rite also the principle of oneness by the symbolic swallowing of the initiate by the preceptor is present, inasmuch as the Ācārya is said to bear the initiate as his embryo —

"The Ācārya becomes the one endowed with the embryo (*garbhī*). On the third day doth the brāhmana take birth with the 'Sāvitrī' ".[105]

We have noted how the *AV* speaks of the Ācārya as Death. The same idea is conveyed by the fact that the 'Brahmacārin' redeems himself from Death by begging.[106] The same idea of temporary death is conveyed by such passages as —

"Now doth he give him to the elements. I give thee to

Prajāpati. To the god Savitṛ do I give thee. To the waters, to the plants do I give thee. Thus doth he give him to the plants and waters. To Heaven and Earth do I give thee. To all the elements I give thee for security (*ariṣṭyai* = non-harm). Thus doth he give him to all the elements for security."[107]

Giving of the initiate to the various elements for security seems similar to Kaca's being given to various wild animals by the Asuras; and his regaining life by the call of his preceptor, who, it could be easily deduced, is supposed to be Death himself and as such has control over the life, either in taking it or giving it back by '*sañjīvanī*'.[108] Though in the legend of Kaca the animals come in the picture to eat Kaca, it is not difficult to see that it is only a modified way of presenting the principle to suit the tale based on the enmity of the gods and the Asuras. Though Kaca seems to die, it is only temporary; and the fact remains that he is, as it were, deposited into the body of the animals only to be taken *back unhurt* (the word used is *a-riṣṭaḥ*). The purpose that is served here in our legend by the *Sañjīvanī mantra* is to be served in the Brahmanical rite by simply adding, after this giving to the elements ('bhūtas' also meaning wild creatures'!), the following:—

"Drink water. Nectar indeed is water. Hence is only said— 'Drink water';[109]

and further on —

'Do not die' is, hence, alone what is said to him, 'Drink water'; nectar, indeed, is water. 'Drink Nectar' is alone that is, thus, said to him. Thus doth he (the preceptor) take *him with nectar both ways.*'[110]

This resembles the *āpyāyana* rite wherein Soma is pressed and the shoots (of the *dead* Soma) are put in the 'Nigrāobhya waters' that rejuvenate them, and brings to our mind the new-moon (Soma), sucked up by the sun, gathering his essence from the plants that had kept it within themselves on the new-moon night.[111]

Now a question — what is the implication of this temporary death?

The temporary death, as a principle, is seen in all the rites we have referred to. It serves to hint at the following points :—

(i) The oblivion of the previous birth (or personality) of the initiate or the consecrated, caused by the preceptor;
(ii) The gain of new power, that is 'immortality';
(iii) The victory over Death.

The temporary phase of death being vanquished by the pupil who attains the new divine (immortal) life can symbolically suggest his victory over Death; more so when he is himself born of Death, his preceptor, who completely envelops him (-swallows him), keeping him within himself and thus makes the initiate a part of himself. To gain immortality it seems quite necessary *to go to Death and vanquish him* by coming back to life. That is why, even the sun is seen to die and come to life conquering Death and gaining immortality.[112] Again the gods themselves are called Death,[113] thus being one with him whom they enter and assimilate. When once this element of Death and being born anew in the *Upanayana,* which is also present in the sacrificial consecration, is understood, it is clear why the initiate at the Upanayana ceremony[114] is called the '*Twice-born*' (*dvijas*). This principle of temporary death at the time of initiation is not peculiar to the Vedic phase of the Hindu religion but is also found among the non-Hindu tribals, as we shall see further on in our discussion.

The next point in the rite of '*Upanayana*' that coincides with our legend is the mention of Śukra and Bṛhaspati in the rite. The place of the initiate's heart is touched by the preceptor before initiation, and he is addressed thus —

"I place thy heart unto duty to me, may thy mind follow my mind; may thou attend to my word, single-mindedly; may Bṛhaspati appoint thee unto me."[115]

It thus suggests that the initiate is to be given to the Ācārya by Bṛhaspati. Now Kaca, as the son of Bṛhaspati stands for the initiate who goes to his preceptor for learning the Vedas. Further it is also enjoined that the *Upanayana* cannot be performed when the Venus is so near the sun that it (Venus = *Śukra*) *cannot be seen*.[116] It thus is clear that the '*Upanayana*' should be performed when Śukra can be seen. Bṛhaspati's influence in the horoscope is good for learning, and hence, if Bṛhaspati (Guru) and *also* Śukra are not seen due to the nearness of the sun, the *Upanayana* cannot be performed.[117] The presence of 'Śukra', the planet, is quite a necessity for the performance of the '*Upanayana*' ceremony. 'Śukra' resembles Śukra in our legend as the lord of initiation to whom Kaca, the initiate, goes for learning the highest knowledge. It should also be remembered that the womb of the preceptor is called the 'womb of immortality',[118] whence the initiate is said to be reborn; and there can be no doubt that Śukra, the preceptor of Kaca, the initiate, fully corroborates with this idea, with the power to impart new life with '*Sañjīvanī*'. Kaca's bringing his preceptor back to life, being equally powerful, is also fully corroborated by the idea underlying the *Upanayana* ceremony when the initiate himself is said to give life to the Ācārya — nay, to the whole world, even to Indra and also to Prajāpati, who is none else than the Ācārya and the initiate himself, thus making the circle complete and establishing the oneness of the initiate and the initiator.[119] Kaca's going to the gods to give them the hope of immortality also is couched in the rite of the *Upanayana*, where we have the initiate substantiating (or supporting) the gods.[120]

Hence, doubtless, the legend of Kaca represents principally the rite of *Upanayana* in the nature of it. The rite of *Upanayana* also, as we have seen, in principle, resembles the sacrificial consecration, the ultimate idea in both being the gain of immortality and the oneness of the sacrifice and the sacrificer. Before we go on to see the rite of Initiation among the non-Hindu tribals, and see how it exactly tallies in spirit with the Vedic rite, it would be good to note here a tale very much similar in spirit with our legend — the tale of Naciketas that occurs in the *Kaṭha-up.*[121] According to it Naciketas is given by his father to Death and from Death here, he learns the highest knowledge. Death, appearing as the one who gives the knowledge to Naciketas, can be well compared with the preceptor in the initiation-ceremony and to Śukra of our legend. Naciketas going to Death and learning the *vidyā* also tallies with the initiate being swallowed and made the embryo by the preceptor — giving him temporary death — and with Kaca of our legend who is swallowed and disgorged by Śukra.

# 3
# EXTENSION OF THE MOTIF

## (A) Some Other Tales

Mārkaṇḍeya saw that the whole earth was engulfed with water, and there was no refuge to be seen anywhere. Mārkaṇḍeya, terrified and confused, praised Viṣṇu who, seeing the sage confused, cast a favourable glance at him and said to him, " Thou hast practised severe penance, O Brāhmaṇa and hast acquired long life. Look thou at me lying on the leaf of the Vaṭa-tree in the form of a child. *I am the very 'Kāla'. Entering my wide open mouth*, take thou shelter therein." Hearing this, the sage entered the mouth of the child-Viṣṇu. Going into the throat *he went right into the stomach*, where he saw the gods, the gandharvas and all the divine ascetics, the whole earth bounded by the four seas and all the villages, mountains etc. *On getting out*, he saw the lord of the universe again in his original form of a child.[122]

It can be seen how the principle of swallowing and disgorging is present here. The lord of initiation can be seen reflected in the child Viṣṇu. The swallowing is preceded by the great deluge which hints at the torture though in a modified form. The gain of the highest knowledge amounts to the oneness with the swallower god, who is the very Death (Kāla), and the whole universe, of which Mārkeṇḍeya — the swallowed — himself is a part. The disgorging alive of Mārkaṇḍeya, who attained long life, indicates the immortality that is to be gained, while the very penance of Mārkeṇḍeya hints at the torture. The realization that the whole universe is inside the belly of the 'child' (Viṣṇu) is the superior knowledge.[123]

The same motif can be detected in a modified form where the period of penance and swallowing (suggestive of death) is replaced by *actual fight* of the initiate with the lord of initiation, gaining a new knowledge and the ultimate gain of the desired boon on the part of the striver. An example of this type is the gain of the Pāśupatāstra by Arjuna from Śiva who comes in the disguise of a Kirāta. In the fight Arjuna is represented as falling into a swoon before finally becoming the recipient of the '*astra*.'[124]

The *swoon* here signifies the temporary death or oblivion, and swallowing, before the final gain of the new knowledge which is the *astra*. The fight signifies the torture and also equality between the striving aspirant and the benevolent divinity. The gain of the *Pāśupatāstra* also suggests the gain of equal power, which reminds us of the idea of Kaca gaining the same lore (*Sañjīvanī*) which is with Śukra. The same idea of torture can be seen in the condition of defeating the Nivāta-kavacas, which Indra sets before Arjuna, prior to the former's making the latter his disciple for imparting the military lore at the latter's request. Oneness of Indra and Arjuna is suggested by the words of Mātali that *Indra himself* was to defeat the Nīvāta-Kavacas in another body, i.e., of Arjuna.[125]

In some of these tales there could also be seen a common motif which, on minutely observing, is of 'swallowing'. The lord divine, whom the aspirant faces before gaining the lore, changes his form suddenly to a huge one, in contrast to which the latter appears just a little one. This is the modified way of expressing the same old principle of the initiate becoming an embryo of the lord preceptor who is to swallow him. The restoring of the divinity's original form indicates the initiate being born anew with equality due to new knowledge. Any number of such tales can be found in *Mb* and the Purāṇas.[126] We shall touch only a few before finally leaving this point.

In the 'Sauptika' Parvan of the *Mb.*[127] we have the account of Aśvatthāman going to kill the children of the Pāṇḍavas, sleeping quietly. As he is about to enter, he sees a huge man at the gate. He is Śiva, who *swallows* up all the weapons of Aśvatthāman. Aśvatthāman tries a sharp sword on the body of the huge man, but that too gets lost into the body of the latter, thus showing its being *swallowed.* Aśvatthāman, dejected at all his fruitless efforts, decides to kill himself by jumping into fire that produces of itself before him, emitting a number of goblins who are unable, however, to terrify him. He praises Śiva and is on the point of offering his body as a faggot to the fire, when Śiva produces himself before him; and, catching him by the arm, offers him a sword and himself gets completely assimilated into the body of Aśvatthāman.

It is not difficult to see the spirit of the whole tale and how it uses the principle already observed. The remarkable similarity of this tale with that of Kaca can also be noted, in the point of the lord's divinity getting completely assimilated into the body of the one who strives. The fire, the goblins and the tiresome fight are all the various sparks of the same main point of torture, before handing over (or giving) the 'boon' — may it be the *military* lore, or some other new knowledge.

Of interest is the tale of Bhīma, who, at the request of Draupadī, goes to fetch the thousand-petalled golden lotuses. When he heads towards the mountain Gandhamādana, he hears a loud thunder, and tracing it, comes ultimately to know that it was produced by Hanūmat, who was residing there. Hanūmat thinks it dangerous for Bhīma to go by that way and hence obstructs the latter's path, moving his tail restlessly, posing to be a sick man, yawning all the while. Bhīma would not mind all this and wants to go by the same path. Hanūmat obstructs him and finally asks him to move his tail aside and go beyond, the reason given being that he (Hanūmat) was sick and old and could not move his own tail.

This Bhīma cannot do even after a great many efforts. Finally, he bows to Hanūmat who is pleased. *Hanūmat, then shows to Bhīma his all-enveloping form;* the latter closes his eyes and, being afraid, requests him to contract the huge form. Hanūmat contracts his form and tells Bhīma the proper way to the lake of thousand-petalled golden lotuses.[128]

Bhīma's gaining the way to the lake of golden lotuses after a lot of struggle purposely created by Hanūmat reveals the main strain of torture, as we have noticed in such tales; while the huge form of Hanūmat goes on the lines of modified swallowing.

And last, but certainly not the least, in this context may be given the tale of Upamanyu.[129] Upamanyu was asked by his preceptor not to drink or eat anything even by begging while in the forest to feed the cows. Upamanyu remained still the same as he formerly was, not getting any weaker. The preceptor asked him how he could manage it. Upamanyu replied that he drank the milk of the cows. He was forbidden to do that and was not allowed to drink even the foam of milk that dripped from the mouth of the calves. Ultimately it so happened that he ate the fruits of the *arka* plant and *lost his eyes.* Thus he wandered and finally *fell into a well.* The evening drew near and when no Upamanyu was seen, the preceptor Dhaumya set forth along with his other disciples to search for him. They all called him and getting his reply, they drew near the well wherein he had fallen. The preceptor asked him to propitiate Aśvinī-kumāras, which Upamanyu did *and got back his eyes.*

Though it appears that the tale is to praise the Aśvinau,[130] it cannot be denied that it depicts the principles of torture before the actual gain of knowledge from the preceptor. It can be noted how this tale comes very near the accounts of the initiation imbibing physical torture among the tribals we shall note later. The well stands here as the one to 'swallow' (and can be compared with the solitary dark forest-hut of the tribals), whence the initiate comes out (reborn) with the gain of new knowledge. The losing of the sight together with the fall in the well signifies the temporary death and oblivion while the regaining of sight stands for the new birth (with the birth of new knowledge). The well wherein Upamanyu falls at once suggests the Death[131] and the regenerator in the same unit, and falls in the pattern of the '*Womb of Immortality*'.

It can thus be seen that in all such tales we have the following points that are only modified traits of one principle of consecration and initiation:

(i) Swallowing conveyed by the idea of enveloping, swoon, the sudden hugeness of form of the lord initiator, closing of the eyes or loss of sight which is suggestive of the principle of temporary death;

(ii) The gain of some kind of new knowledge; and

(iii) Oneness of the initiate and the preceptor.

The Kaca-legend is only one of such tales that uses the same old principle of initiation or sacrificial consecration. This is the primary principle underlying our legend. It is futile to argue whether the legend depicts the traits from the tribal rites of initiation or adheres to the Brahmanical rites of initiation and consecration. The best we can say about this point is that the legend is a finished product of the ancient Vedic rites of consecration and initiation; and most probably, is influenced by the rites of the aboriginals.

**(B) Kaca, Śukra and Śiva**

The legend of Kaca is, surprisingly, not found in most of the Purāṇas. The Purāṇas that refer to the tale do not differ from the *Mb.*[132] But closely similar to our legend, practically in all points, we have the tale of Śukra and Śiva.

According to the account in the *Sk.P*[133] in the fight between Andhakāsura and Śiva, the dead Asuras are restored to life by Śukrācārya with his *Sañjīvanī vidyā*. Nandī, the vehicle of Śiva, knows the trick of the preceptor (of the

Asuras) and informs Śiva. Śiva asks Nandī to go to the abode of Śukra and to bring him a captive. Nandī does as he is asked to do; and when Śukra is brought to Śiva, the latter takes Śukra and simply keeps him in his mouth. Śukra being thus imprisoned, the Asuras die and are not brought back to life. The gods get victory. Śiva then releases Śukra as his semen. *Śukra comes out* with great difficulty with the help of the 'Yoga' called 'Śāmbhava' (*Śāmbhavena Yogena*), and stands before lord Śiva who thus addresses him, "O scion of the Bhṛgus! Like semen hast thou come forth. By this act of thine, art thou *Śukra* (Semen). *My son thou art.* Go thou (thy way)." God Śiva becomes glad seeing Śukra thus come out *from his stomach*, thinking with satisfaction that he did not kill the brāhmaṇa.[134]

The tale, at a glance, could be seen to resemble the Kaca legend. Śukra here undergoes the same fate as Kaca in our legend; and Śiva stands in the place of Śukra. The new knowledge by the help of which Śukra comes out of the stomach of Śiva, and called '*Śāmbhava-Yoga*', can be compared with the gain of the lore of immortality by Kaca. It requires no special efforts to see that all the principles of consecration or initiation are present herein *viz.*, the temporary death at the hands (or in the stomach) of the lord preceptor (the divine lord) — being in the *womb that gives immortality*; and the gain *of new knowledge*.[135] The principle of oneness of the preceptor and the initiate also can be seen in the fact that Śukra is called here 'son' by Siva. This is exactly the same as Śukra's addressing Kaca as 'son'. There is a further similarity found in this tale and the account in the Kaca legend in the fact that, in both, we have the swallower fearing the death of a brāhmaṇa.

At another place in the same Purāṇa, we have this account with a little variation. Śaṅkara calls upon the goddess Kālīśvarī by the Ātharvaṇa chants, whereby all the dānavas get afraid and tell of it to Andhakāsura who resorts to Śukra. Śukra also produces the same goddess by the same chants. The goddess, being pleased, offers to him the lore of immortality (*Amṛtavatī Vidyā*).[136]

Here we have a new point. Both Śukra and Śiva producing the goddess Kālīśvarī suggest that they are of equal prowess; and this reminds us of Kaca and Śukra who becomes equal in prowess after the former gets the *Sañjīvanī*. Kālīśvarī, giving the lore of immortality, resembles Devayānī who, though the daughter of Śukra, causes the final bestowal of the 'lore of immortality' (*Sañjīvanī vidyā*) upon Kaca, with whom she is fully pleased (and actually is in love).

The same Purāṇa has yet other accounts which are almost the same as we have already noted;[137] but one of them has certain important points. According to the account Śukra establishes the '*Śivaliṅga*' named 'Vibhūteśvara' where he learns the '*Sañjīvanī*' lore. The following points are to be noted: —

(i) Śukra performed penance for a thousand years, which is the same as the period of Kaca's stay in Śukra's abode;
(ii) Śukra becomes the planet.[138]

In *Mb.* itself we have an account of the Śukra-Śiva fight. According to it, Śukra stole the wealth of Kubera, Śiva's friend. For this fault of his, Śiva swallowed him; but later was let out at the intercession of Umā. When he was thus released by Śiva, he was accepted as 'son' by Umā. The name Śukra is explained as being born out of Siva's semen.[139]

Though similarity to our legend cannot be seen wholly in this account, two points are to be noted:—

(i) Śukra is swallowed and let out as son; and
(ii) Umā causes him to be released.

The second point reminds us of Devayānī. The relation between Devayānī and Śukra as against Umā and Śiva need not confuse us.[140]

The *Pad. P.* has an interesting deviation in the Śukra-Śiva account. Śiva, according to it, being afraid of killing the brāhmaṇa Śukra, produces from his third eye a kṛtyā and asks her to keep the brāhmaṇa, Śukra, in her vagina. This done, Śiva kills all the Asuras.[141]

It could be seen from the instances given above that the Kaca-Śukra account of swallowing and disgorging exactly corresponds with the Śukra-Śiva account. Śukra is common to both these accounts, but in two different capacities. Śukra in the Kaca legend falls in line with the sacrificial swallower Śukra, Indra etc., as we have already seen; and the tale of Śukra — coming out as semen — has the purpose of explaining the name '*Śukra*' as semen and to praise Śiva as having even greater power than Śukra. Śukra's being the father of Devayānī and the love of Devayānī for Kaca seem to be points added later to the tale which, in reality, originally was only *a tale of initiation* (or consecration). Devayānī, as the daughter of Śukra, features in the Kaca legend as one who was married to Yayāti in a *pratiloma* marriage; and to explain this, probably, she was joined up in the legend to incur a curse which made the marriage with a brāhmaṇa impossible for her. In any case, the Kaca-Devayāni episode is an adjunct to the principal theme, as we have noted. Both Śukra and Kaca seem to be nothing but two forms of Śiva; and this has at least one support. Near the present Kopargaum in the State of Maharashtra, in the island of the river Godāvarī two stones lie side by side and they are called '*Kaceśvara*' and '*Śukreśvara*'.[142] These stones are taken to be only *Śivaliṅgas* and the devotees going there worship them as such. The Bombay Gazetteer records this fact and adds that near the site of the two temples, the tale of Kaca and Śukra is still told and it is the same one as of the *Mb* account of Kaca-Śukra.[143]

We have already seen how 'Śukra' is well settled in the sacrificial context. As noted earlier, Śukra also means 'Soma' which is the name of Śiva thus hinting at the oneness of the swallower and the swallowed. It is difficult to see any propriety of the name of Kaca, which rarely is noted in any other context except as one of the ascetics that attend upon Bhīṣma when the latter leaves his mortal frame in the 'arrow-bed' account.[144] The question still remains as to why Kaca, who occurs so prominently in this legend, appears only as a minor personality elsewhere and has nothing to do with the 'son of Bṛhaspati'. It will be rash to apply any motive to the name 'Kaca' appearing particularly in the legend which explains the principle of initiation or consecration; but, the following discussion might be useful. One of the necessary things at the time of the consecration or initiation is to cut the hair of the initiate or the consecrated, and the shaving of the initiate was done by the Ācārya himself in ancient times.[145] The sun (Savitṛ) is said to tonsure the initiate who is Soma,[146] and the sun is the presiding deity of initiation inasmuch as it is the sun's brilliance that is meditated upon.[147] This indicates the identification of the sun and the Ācārya in tonsuring the initiate. We have seen that the sun is identified also with Śukra, who is the Ācārya. In this way '*Kaca*' (meaning hair) might stand for the 'Tonsured' pupil (initiate). Now, as the preceptor, as noted above, is identified with the sun, he could also be identified with *Rudra-Śiva* in the Śukra-Śiva accounts. It is also supported from the fact that we have another prayer at the initiation with the deity as Rudra.[148] Now, if Rudra-Śiva is taken to be the presiding deity of initiation, it is easy to understand how '*Kaceśvara*' and '*Śukreśvara*' are supposed to be the form of Śiva. Śiva himself is conspicuous with the locks of hair always referred to as 'Jaṭā-jūṭa'.

### (C) Outside India

The remarkable feature of cutting hair at the initiation ceremony is also present in the initiation rites of the tribals even from outside India. Thus, the Urabunna tribe in Australia has a peculiar ritual at the initiation, in which the locks of the *initiate's hair are tied up* by a string and loosened afterwards by taking off the string.[149] In the Unmatuera tribe, the lord of initiation (the initiator) is the *father-in-law*[150] of the initiate. The locks of the initiate's *hair are tied up* and a *girdle of human hair* is wound round his waist.[151] In the Kaitish tribe, the initiation ceremony is marked by the initiate's *head being bitten at the scalp* by other men who must themselves be having *very good heads of hair,* the biting being supposed to be of special efficacy in making the hair of the initiate grow profusely. The name of this particular rite is — '*koparta Kalkuma.*'[152] In the *Mara* tribe also we note the girdle of human hair at the time of initiation and here it is tied (not by the father-in-law, but) by the father of the initiate himself around the waist of the initiate. Along with other gifts given to the initiate at the time of the ceremony, there are also '*hair-girdles*'.[153]

It is difficult to deny the importance of 'hair', either shorn or tied upon the head and around the waist, in the Hindu-ritual at the time of the initiation or the consecration for sacrifice, even granting that it is not quite easy to establish the presence of this feature in the Upanayana or the sacrificial consecration as an influence of the aboriginal rites that might have been in vogue in this land in the times before the impact of the Brahmanical religion.[154] The remarkable feature of the father (or the father-in-law) tying up the hair of the initiate in the tribal rites can also be noticed in the Brahmanical rite when the Ācārya himself shaves the head of the initiate. The whole rite of initiation was, at times, conducted by the father of the initiate himself;[155] and also that there is a constant note of the preceptor calling the initiate his own son.[156] From all this, it will not be wrong to suppose that the name '*Kaca*' (hair) in our legend is significant and, probably, denotes the initiate with the 'shaven' head, or the one with 'hair tied up'. As against 'Śukra', the name of the preceptor, which has a wider application in myths, indicating it to refer to

Śukrācārya, Indra, Sun, Soma and Semen, Kaca is mythically solitary.

A few more instances of initiation among tribes even outside India will show how the motif in them is the same as we have hitherto discussed, and that the Vedic rite of consecration and initiation closely resembles the rite of initiation among these tribes. The whole idea in these initiation-rites is of *temporary death and rebirth,* which makes the initiate 'Twice-born' (*dvija*, as he is termed in the Vedic tradition).

Among the Australian tribes of New South Wales, when the lads are initiated, it is believed that a being called '*Thurmlin*' takes each lad to a distance, kills him and sometimes cuts him up, after which he restores him to life and knocks off a tooth or so as a sign of his having undergone the ceremony.[157]

In one part of Queensland, the humming and irritating sound of the bull-roarer[158] —a wooden plate with a long string, which is swung at the time of the initiatory rites is supposed to be the sound made by the wizard in *swallowing the boys and bringing them back to life* as men.[159] In certain places it is also said that the 'dead' boy *meets a ghost that brings him back to life.* This restoration of the life is done by a performance. An old man with ragged clothes lies down in a 'grave', lightly covered and the original appearance of the ground restored, with the man in the grave holding a bush in the hand as if it is growing on the ground. Other bushes are also stuck into the covered pit to heighten the effect. The novices are then brought near to the edge of the grave. A clan-song is then sung, and gradually the bush gets animated as it were; and finally the man in the grave comes out bringing the lads back.[160]

In the instances quoted above, along with the idea of temporary death and rejuvenation, there also is a point to be noted; and it is of torture. This is suggested by the breaking of the tooth of the initiated. This principle of torture associated with the symbolic death is a common factor in the tribal rites as we shall see presently.

The Congo valley people have a peculiar initiatory rite called 'Ndembo', in which the initiator doctor gets some one to fall down in a pretended fit, and then he is carried away to an *enclosed hut*, "which is outside the town". With him go also other boys and girls that are to be initiated. They all are supposed to be 'dead.' Their parents supply food; and, after a period varying from three months to three years, according to the customs, the doctors shall *bring them back to life.* When thus the children are brought back to life, they pretend to know no one. They do not know (are not supposed to know!) even to masticate food, and friends have to perform that office for them.[161]

It can be seen here how the *dead are reborn*, and how custom forces them to behave like children who know none immediately after they are born. Friends helping these initiates, born anew, to eat, is a clear enough indication of their new childhood.

The people of Rook island, east of New Guinea, hold festivities at initiation, at which one or two disguised men, with heads covered with wooden masks go advancing through the village, followed by all other men. They demand that the circumcised boys who have not yet been *swallowed* by *Marshaba* — the Devil — shall be given up to them. The boys *trembling and shrieking are delivered up to them;* and must keep *between the legs* of the disguised men. Then the whole procession moves through the village again; and an announcement is made that *Marshaba has eaten the* boys and will not disgorge them until he receives the present of pigs etc. All the villagers, then, contribute to the provision which are eaten in the name of the devil *Marshaba*; and then the boys are said to be disgorged.[162]

In the instance quoted just now the idea of swallowing the initiates is quite clear and it is symbolically brought home by the initiate boys and girls walking *between the legs* of the disguised men, which suggests their being in the womb, which is just above the legs between which they are walking. The trembling and shrieking of the initiates denote their horror, and suggest the torture that they are submitted to before initiation. Moreover, in this connection it will be interesting to note that the enclosed hut outside the town, to which the initiates are led, well resembles the hut of the man consecrated for the Brahmanical sacrifice. The carrying to the hut signifies death of the initiates before the rite of initiation, as walking between the legs denotes their being in the womb ready to be delivered after initiation.

In this connection the most interesting account is of the Kakian association. The Kakian house is an oblong wooden shed, situated in the midst of the forest, and is built to admit so little light that it is impossible to see what goes on in it. Every village has such a house. There the boys, who are to be initiated, are *conducted blind-folded*, followed by their parents and relations. Each boy is led by the hand by two men who act as his guardians, looking after him during the period of his initiation. When all are assembled before the shed, *the high priest calls, aloud, the devil.* Immediately a hideous uproar is heard from the hut. It is made by certain men with a bamboo trumpet, and who have previously been ushered unseen into the hut by a 'backdoor'. But, the women and the children think that it is made by a devil and get terrified. Then the priest enters the shed followed by the boys one at a time. As soon as each of the boys has disappeared into the shed, a dull chopping sound is heard, a fearful cry wrings out, and a sword or a spear, dripping with blood is thrust upwards through the roof of the shed. This is a sign that *the boy's head has been cut off, and that the devil has carried him away to the other world.* In some other places, it would be seen, the boys are pushed through an opening made in the shape of a crocodile's jaws or a cassowary's beak, and it is then said that the *devil has swallowed them.* The boys (initiates) remain there, in the shed, for five or nine days. Sitting in the dark they hear the blast of the bamboo trumpet and from time to time the sound of the musket-shots and the clash of swords. Every day they bathe, and their faces and bodies are smeared with a yellow dye, to give them a pale appearance that they have been swallowed by the devil. The novices are told by the priest to behave well to their blood-relations and are *taught the tradition and secrets of the tribe.* In a day or two the men who acted as guardians to the novices return to their village with the glad tidings that *the devil, at the intercession of the priest, has restored the lads to life.*[163]

The principle of symbolic death and new birth is present in the above passage. Here also we have the shed which serves to take the boy away and produce him back giving the old idea of the womb; and it compares with the same old *womb of immortality,* the preceptor who symbolically swallows the initiate and gives him a new life! In all these accounts the underlying principle is the same as in the Brahmanical and Vedic rite of consecration and initiation to Vedic studentship, suggesting the 'second birth' (*dvijatva*) of the boy. It is difficult to believe that in the Brahmanic rite alone swallowing and disgorging are a peculiarity when we have all these examples of tribal rites and of the people of remote places. The question of borrowing from the Vedic fold is a far-fetched one and the only thing that can be said in this connection, to quote Frazer would be, "The simulation of Death and Resurrection or a new birth at initiation appears to have lingered on or at least left traces of itself among the people who have advanced far beyond the stage of savagery. Thus after his investiture with the sacred thread — the symbol of his order — a brāhmaṇa is called 'twice-born'". The same idea is suggested, when Aristotle also says that man is the 'natural' son of god, and that, after initiation, he becomes the legitimate son of god,[165] thus meaning that a man gets second birth by initiation, giving him status in the society.

We have seen that even among the savage tribes, the initiation has an idea of torture of the initiates. A few more examples would make the point clear. Thus, in the Larakia tribe in the Darwin district, the initiation takes the form of a series of tests that are disagreeable to the initiates. The youths are kept in charge of certain old men whose orders they have to obey implicitly. They are tortured, and, without any reason, the elder man will give a knock or a strong blow to the youths. They make them undergo severe manual labour, such as that of cutting down and rolling over heavy logs of wood. The favourite test is to order a few of them to go into the water and bring a crocodile to land. Finally, when the old men are satisfied with the conduct of the youths, they show them the sacred bull-roarer, which is called '*Biddi-Biduba*'.[166]

This *principle of torture at the time of initiation* seems to be present in our legend when Kaca is asked to go to the forest with the cows and is cut to pieces by the Asuras, prior to the final swallowing of him by his preceptor. The same appears to be present in the various tests that the students are said to have been put to as we learn from various tales in the *Mb*.

The examples from the tribal initiation rites have the following points common with our present legend:—

(i) The initiates are swallowed by a great power — representative of the preceptor;

(ii) They are supposed to die, and sometimes are *tortured before the feigned death;*

(iii) They are again brought to life and gain a new, i.e., second birth;

(iv) The initiates get the secret knowledge — i.e. the knowledge of the traditions etc. of the tribe. The secrecy of this knowledge can be compared with the secrecy of the lore of immortality — (i.e. *Sañjīvanī*).

# 4
# SECONDARY NARRATIVES

## (A) The Element of Puberty and Sex

As different from the tales we have mentioned, suggesting the motif of swallowing and disgorging in the gain of some superior knowledge, the present legend has a peculiar point in the love of Devayānī for Kaca, the initiate. Kaca got the *'Sañjīvanī'*, apparently, not so much by serving his preceptor, Śukra, as by his constant attention to Devayānī — the young daughter of the latter; for the gods precisely tell him to please Devayānī and it is by pleasing her that he would be able to achieve his aim of getting the lore of immortality.[167] Kaca remembers this and devotes his time to please the young Devayānī, dancing and singing with her, and by presenting her flowers and fruits. Devayānī also was dancing and playing with the young brāhmaṇa and amusing him in *'privacy'* (*rahaḥ*).[168] This gives a peculiar sexual touch to the whole legend and seems to be quite out of tune with the spirit of the Brahmanical rite of initiation. The description of the love-sport of Kaca and Devayānī does not end here itself. The final stage is the point of separation between these two, Kaca going to the gods unmindful of the amours of the preceptor's daughter and thus fulfilling his object not being distracted by love-sport.[169] This may appear to be a usual love-story; but this part of the legend has to be understood as suggesting —

(i) The influence of sex at the age of puberty; and
(ii) The necessity for the initiate to avoid it.

To understand this fully we have, again, to go back to

the initiatory rite of the tribes. In those rites there is a total restriction on women for danger to their own life. Women are not allowed to witness the rites in certain cases.[170] The initiatory rites among the tribals are performed at the age of puberty, when the initiate is to enter the social order of the society as a *man*; and hence it has a special sexual significance.[171] This goes well with the Hindu custom of the initiate taking his last meal with his mother in the same dish before initiation,[172] even among those who perform the rite according to Brahmanical rites. Among the various taboos laid by the *Smṛtis* upon the initiate, the one which wards him from talking to ladies and from touching the young wife of the preceptor even while bowing[173] hints at the same age — that of puberty — for initiation. It is, probably, this reason why there is no fixed age for the rite and various ages are mentioned for the various *varṇas* giving the maximum age-limit. The maximum age, it may be noted, is the age of attaining manhood; and this might itself have been the proper age for initiation according to some customs in the past; and, when the *Smṛtis* were recast, all these varying customs were brought together giving the various ages for initiation — the rite, however, being necessarily to be accomplished before the marriage.[174] This corresponds to the tribal rite without which no marriage of the boy is possible, and there is contempt of the womenfolk for such a boy.[175] It will be good to note in this connection one of the features of *upanayana* (initiation) prevalent in many parts of India. Just after the ceremony of *upanayana* is over, there is a ritual, according to which the maternal uncle (the natural would-be father-in-law of the boy according to custom) comes forward and asks the initiate, who is supposed to proceed to Kāśī for higher studies, to marry his daughter. The initiate says that he would not do so just then, but would surely (?) marry her after the completion of his studies. The same sort of ritual prevails in Tamil Nāḍu (South India) with the only difference that it is performed just before the marriage. The youth to be married is supposed to proceed to Kāśī; and here the proposed father-in-law goes to him and requests him to leave his intention for studies at the moment and marry his daughter, who is waiting for his hand in marriage. The thread in these two customs is the same. In the previous one, initiation and study are connected with the idea of marriage; and in the latter marriage is associated with the idea of study which is the goal of initiation. The father-in-law (and the maternal uncle who could be the father-in-law) in both these instances can be well compared with the father-in-law of the initiate according to the tribal rites. The same relation seems to be true in the case of Kaca and Śukra. Śukra is silent, but it is Devayānī, who is eloquent on this point; and herself asks Kaca for his hand, which the latter properly rejects. It is thus that the legend of Kaca has the note of sex in it along with the main idea of initiation. The note of sex, as suggested from the last part of the legend, is new to the original initiation rite and comes nearer to the tribal rites. It is corroborated by the customary ritual[176] associated with '*upanayana*' as we have pointed out. In this the Brahmanical rite of *upanayana* seems to be influenced by popular faith both of which are reflected in the legend of *Kaca*.

### (B) Śukra and Sañjīvanī

The word '*sañjīvati*' occurs in the context of the '*Upaṁśu Savana*' and has a faint similarity to the word 'Sañjīvanī'. The stone '*Upāṁśu*' is identified with the sun,[177] and thus can be seen as the controller of the power of revitalizing the dead. When Śukra is identified with the sun, the same power—*Sañjīvanī*—could be said to be controlled by Śukra. Śukra as the semen of Śiva also hints at the same idea. Śukra, in this light, is the essence of life, and lack of mortality. 'Śukra' (semen) is preserver of life. We have already seen how *Soma* is associated with immortality and that Soma is also called Śukra. Soma is also associated with semen.[178]

The same idea is seen in the case of Soma, called Śukra, *giving birth* to Vṛtra when sprinkled in the sacrificial fire.[179] This hints at the generative power of Soma. Śukra the generating power could very naturally be associated with immortality and Śukra, the one who generates, could also be said to be the one who bestows immortality. This association of the generative power and Śukra could also be seen from the fact that all men (beings) are said to be born after the 'Śukra' cup, and, as the cup (i.e. 'Śukra') is employed at the sacrifice, the beings are born again and again.[180] Soma is addressed as 'Śukra' (or rather, the one who has Śukra as the cup) and is invoked to bestow long life, and to protect the progeny.[181] The 'Śukra' and the 'Manthin' cups, both filled with Soma, are invoked to prolong life and confer male offspring.[182] It, thus, could be seen that Śukra is associated with fertility, progeny, new life and creation. Śukra, in this power of his, is identified with the sun who is Savitṛ (the one who generates). The same is the reason why Śukra is said to be the controller of rain. Risley has rightly identified the demon Śuṣṇa with Śukra, both meaning the 'scorching ones'[183] and thus giving the idea of the controllers of rain-water. Rain-water is itself called Śukra in the *Ś.B.*, which says that, when it rains on the Agnihotra-milk, the sacrificer should understand by it the advent of Śukra (pure-juice and semen) in him.[184] Śukra is identified with Indra who is the god of rain and also of fertility.[185] Rain itself is called '*amṛta*'.[186] Śukra, hence, denotes the preceptor who is the second generator of the initiate and the possessor of the lore of immortality; and hence could be invoked at the rite of initiation thus :—

"The *lord of creatures* drank the invigorating essence distilled from food; he drank food and the juice of the moon-plant. By means of scriptures, which is truth itself, the beverage thus quaffed became a prolific essence, the eternal order of universal perception — Indra's organ of sense — the milk of immortality. May this oblation to the Śukra, planet Venus, be efficacious".[187]

It is this power of fertility that is indicated to be bestowed upon the initiate and is called '*sañjīvanī*' and the initiate himself becomes equally powerful,[188] being born from the very womb of immortality[189] which is nothing but the receptacle of the power for procreation and hints at the store of fertility. In this lies the equation, viz., Brahmacārin = Prajāpati = Ācārya[190] — all in possession of the power to procreate, i.e. Sañjīvanī. Looking from another angle also Śukra and Sañjīvanī appear to be well associated. We have noted how Śukra and the sun are said to be identical. Further, Śukra is associated with the highest of knowledge,[191] and we have noted how for the *upanayana,* the presence of the Śukra planet was thought to be necessary. The highest knowledge is symbolised by the 'Sāvitrī' *mantra* at the time of the *upanayana*. If the sun is said to be identical with Śukra, and if the highest knowledge (Brahmavarcasam) is the same as Śukra, or lorded over by Śukra, the natural step is to identify this highest knowledge with '*sañjīvanī*', which is lorded over by him. The importance of the sun in the initiation and consecration[192] ceremony can be seen from the fact that (like Śukra), he is said to take away the very essence of the consecrated.[193] It is the sun who is said to impel the initiate; for the Ācārya says to him — "On the instigation of Savitṛ be the pupil of Bṛhaspati."[194] Śukra and the sun thus being very important at the initiation, it is natural that the power of 'Śukra' i.e., '*sañjīvanī*' and that of the sun — 'sāvitrī', could be taken as identical. Both have the meaning 'producing' ('procreating', 'bringing to life'). As we have noted the power of procreation in the case of Śukra, so is also true in the case of Sun,[195] when he is said to be the lord of 'progeny'. Like '*sañjīvanī*', who actually is said to bring the dead to life, 'Sāvitrī' also figures in the well known story of 'Satyavān-Sāvitrī' as the one who vanquishes Yama and brings her husband to life. '*Sāvitrī*' actually giving new birth to Satyavat, and '*sañjīvanī*' giving new birth to Kaca, are hence definitely identical. The tale of Sāvitrī-Satyavat, it could easily be seen, is the colourful explanation of the main idea in initiation. The effect of the learning of the Sāvitrī *ṛc* is the aim therein. 'Sāvitrī', the essence of the sun, ultimately saves the life of Satyavat. He is, as a matter of fact, '*swallowed*' by Death himself; and disgorged at the intercession of 'Sāvitrī' — the solar power,[196] which is nothing but the same energy the initiate has to meditate upon and is called '*savitur vareṇyam bhargaḥ*'. Sāvitrī, as the mother of the Vedas and of the initiate,[197] can well be compared with 'Sañjīvanī'. The metre Gāyatrī brings Soma from heaven — Soma, the drink of immortality, the very Sañjīvanī[198] and Gāyatrī is the metre of the Sāvitrī *mantra* that is taught to the initiate at the time of the initiation-rite. The initiate is taught the Sāvitrī-Gāyatrī[199] which shows complete identification of '*sāvitrī*' and '*Gāyatrī*'. The very *mantra* is called Gāyatrī *mantra*. Gāyatrī (which is, thus Sāvitrī itself) is said to be the very life-breath.[200] If one cannot chant the Gāyatrī he is dead;[201] she is said to be the very life.[202] Gāyatrī is also the 'lustre of Brahmanical power'[203] — which is also said of Śukra as we have noted already. Thus, it can be seen how Sañjīvanī, the giver of new life, and the vanquisher of death is the Gāyatrī-sāvitrī *mantra* that is taught to the initiate. It is the same 'Amṛtavatī vidyā' which Śukra received from Śiva. Thus, physically as 'seed' (semen) is to rejuvenation, and spiritually as the 'impelling brilliance' is to the 'study of the Vedas,' Śukra is conceptually related to Sañjīvanī.

We have already noted Śukra's association with rain-water (cf. P. 224 f). This reminds us of the God 'Liṅgal' of the Gonds (a tribe in Madhya Pradesh now). Liṅgal is, as the word shows (Liṅgal = *Liṅga* = generative organ) the 'Organ of Creation' and is similar to Śiva, whose semen is Śukra. Liṅgal is the god of fertility and procreation for the Gonds. According to a Gond song this god was killed by three Gond brothers, whose wives were enamoured of him. Some other

Gonds brought him to life with nectar got from Bhagavat, the god. Hence the difference between the two sects of the Gonds as the killers of Liṅgal and as the rejuvenators of him.[204] Liṅgal killed by the Gonds resembles on one hand Śukra that was swallowed by Śiva and was brought back to life; and, on the other, Kaca killed by the Asuras and brought back to life by Śukra.

Risley goes on to mention a yearly ceremony commemorating the birth of the dead Liṅgal; and it is called the 'Water-festival' day. On that day a *boy called Liṅgal* goes about the streets. Women worship him, wash his feet with water and pour volumes of water on his head. The pouring of water on the head of Liṅgal is supposed to bring Liṅgal to life.[205] The worship of Liṅgal (phallus = liṅga = Śiva) by women, and the water playing an important part, suggests that the whole ritual is for fertility. Water here represents 'nectar' that was brought by the other Gond brothers to rejuvenate the dead Liṅgal. Water, bringing Liṅgal back to life, brings to our mind the 'Sañjīvanī', which brought Śukra and Kaca again to life. The close association of Liṅgal with water and the particular significance of this ritual in bringing rain, strikes a parallel in the control of rain by Śukra; and, rain being called seed (cf. p. 205), which is the power to procreate (cf. Sañjīvanī), we can see how Śukra could be said to be the controller of *sañjīvanī* in this light. Hence we can finally put down the control by Śukra of Sañjīvanī as —

(i) Overlordship of initiation and of the *mantra* Gāyatrī-Sāvitrī;
(ii) Overlordship of the power of procreation;
(iii) Overlordship of rain-water which is nectar.

Looking from this angle, it is easy to understand how the Brahmacārin is said to pour seed upon the earth[206] meaning thereby potentiality to procreate; and this again hints at the proper age of initiation and returning home after gaining knowledge. It is also easy to understand in this light why the rites of initiation generally mark the beginning of manhood, and are performed at the age of puberty.

### (C) Devayānī

The name Devayānī is rarely to be found in any other context except that of Śukra and of Yayāti whose wife she is said to be. She is the co-wife of Śarmiṣṭhā with whom she quarrels and competes (*Mb.* I.73 ff.). Devayānī with whom we are concerned here is not so much the wrathful and jealous wife of Yayāti, as the soft and lovely daughter of Śukra. It is not in the scope of this discussion to see whether Devayānī in the Śukra-Kaca episode and Devayānī of the 'Yayāti' episode is the same. If she is the same, it plainly appears that the whole tale of Devayānī and Yayāti is an attachment to the legend of Kaca-Śukra which, in spirit, is an initiation-tale. The name Devayānī seems to have been suggested from the *Devayāna*, which is the time best suited for sacrificial consecration and also for initiation.[207] Devayāna, being thus the path of the gods — the immortal ones — it would naturally be best suited for consecration and initiation where the whole idea is to get immortality. Devayānī, protecting Kaca from death, seems in this light, to be the very spirit of the Devayāna period. We have seen already that Sañjīvanī, as far as initiation is concerned, seems to be Gāyatrī-Sāvitrī. Now, as a bringer of nectar and the giver of life, Gāyatrī comes very close to Devayānī who bestows life upon Kaca — the initiate. The lore of immortality — Sañjīvanī — itself depended on Devayānī; for, without Devayānī, Kaca — the initiate — would not have been re-born. Devayānī thus holds a position between the initiate and the initiator who, here, are respectively a messenger of gods and a preceptor of the Asuras. The position of Gāyātrī also is said to be the same. Gāyatrī is said to have stood in between the gods and the Asuras; further, both these parties invited her; Gāyatrī, however, went to the side of the gods following Agni the divine messenger and the gods thereby were victorious and the Asuras were defeated.[208] This tallies exactly with the position of Devayānī in our legend who, standing between (as a link) her father — preceptor of the Asuras, and Kaca — the god, ultimately sides with Kaca the messenger of gods giving them the ultimate victory. Thus she stands between gods and Asuras. Devayānī and Gāyatrī also come close to each other when we remember that Gāyatrī brought Soma for the gods, and Devayānī caused the lore of immortality to be given to the gods. Devayānī occurs also as an epithet of the nights belonging to the Sun;[209] and when Śukra and the sun are identified, the nights of the Devayāna, personified, could be the daughter of Śukra: These nights naturally are those in the Devayāna. The sacrificial altar is also called 'Devayānī' and is associated with Agni,[210] whom Gāyatrī is said to have followed, as we have just noted. Śukra is identified with the Sacrifice,[211] and hence, Devayānī — the fire-altar — could suggest the idea of being his daughter. Soma is addressed as Śukra and is said to be the one who leads to the Devayānīs.[212] Vāk is identified with the Devayāna path leading to heaven.[213] Now, Vāk is also the mother of the metres, the best among them being Gāyatrī. If Vāk is the Devayāna it can be understood how Gāyatrī (the daughter of Vāk) is the one who goes by that path and is Devayānī, the pervading spirit of that path. Devayānī and Sañjīvanī can thus be seen to be only two phases of the same thing. In the context of this legend of initiation we can say that Devayānī of our legend could be a personification from all these concepts. The Devayānī of the Yayāti legend was a real person. It is not improbable, that this conceptual Devayānī, who represents a pattern of a 'helper to the hero' in myths, got assimilated in the legend of the historical Devayānī. But, it is not necessary to take Yayāti as the inversion of Kaca.

## (D) Wine and the Taboo

The drinking of wine (*surā*) by Śukra and the subsequent taboo is the portion which does not directly form the main part of the legend. About the drinking of *surā* by the brāhmaṇa, there are indications to say that there was a regular custom though it was continuously criticised. The very words of Śukra[214] presuppose that the drinking of wine was a practice for some time. Drinking *surā* can be traced right up to the ṚV. though not without the repudiation of it. Thus Vasiṣṭha, the seer, implores upon Varuṇa to consider that it is *surā* that is to be blamed for the sin that a man commits.[215] This presupposes the drinking of *surā*. Soma's invigorating influence over a man is compared with the intoxication of *surā*.[216] The benevolent are said to gain wine to drink among other things.[217] In the '*Sautrāmaṇī iṣṭi*', it was necessary to hire a brāhmaṇa for drinking wine offered in it and, if one could not be found, the wine meant for him was to be poured on an ant-hill.[218] The difficulty in getting a brāhmaṇa for drinking wine suggests the aversion to drinking, more probably due to its being condemned as unsuitable for the brāhmaṇas. The very fact that a brāhmaṇa was to be found earlier for drinking wine indicates that the custom was quite current in earlier days. In the days of the *Kāṭh. Sam.* the drinking of wine by a brāhman a was looked upon as a sin.[219] The works on Dharmaśāstra generally condemn the drinking of *surā* as one of the five sins: but the *Baudhāyana Dh. Sū.* notes, however, that the drinking of rum was one of the peculiarities of the brāhmaṇas of the North.[220]

The reference to Śukrācārya's drinking of Surā and his subsequent repudiation of the same hints at the prevalence of the practice of drinking wine and a taboo imposed thereon.

## The Element of Deceit

The element of deceit is not clearly marked here. Kaca,

going into the stomach of his preceptor, cannot be said to support this point, for it is an idea associated with the rite of initiation. Kaca does not enter the preceptor's stomach by himself. But this legend is not altogether devoid of the element of deceit. Kaca does not disclose the purpose for his stay in Śukra's hermitage. He, as the messenger of the gods, trying to win the immortal lore from the preceptor of the Asuras, falls in line with Indra who deceives Śuṣṇa and craftily knows the secret of success becoming the louse in the house of Triśīrṣā, the gandharva; and for this reason, Kaca, though a guileless-looking *brahmacārin* here, appears to be having the same guile as is marked in Indra. Thus, in spirit Kaca, the messenger of the crafty gods, is the same deceitful one who softly steals the mind of Devayānī and acquires the lore of immortality, Śukra having the least idea of his intention. Further, he wins the mind of Devayānī, singing and dancing with her in secluded places (*rahaḥ*). This is, obviously, with a plan to please her, as the gods had suggested. But, having achieved the lore, he returns without paying heed to her feelings which he had deliberately aroused. The inversion of this theme occurs in the Vedic myth of the winning of *Soma* (the juice of immortality) by the gods by sending Vāc (a woman = speech), in place of a male (cf. Kaca). They got her back by singing and playing on the lute (cf. Kaca in the case of Devayānī) (*Śat. Br.* III.2.4.2-6).[221]

## Summary and Conclusion

The legend of Kaca uses the main features of sacrificial consecration and initiation or Upanayana. The motif of swallowing that is predominant in this legend can be traced to the Vedic texts where the consecrated is said to be the very material of the sacrifice. The offering of the beast into the sacrificial fire, *Soma* that is pressed at the time of the sacrifice, and the sacrificer himself are all on the same level; and being themselves one with the sacrifice, achieve immortality. The killing of the beast and the pressing of Soma are symbolic death; and only a temporary one. This means also the symbolic death and the rejuvenation of the sacrificer who attains immortality. *Soma* (the sacrificial material) and the sacrificer thus, are put on a common level. *Soma* is swallowed by Indra who is himself said to be the sacrifice and, likewise, (symbolically) the sacrificer is swallowed by the sacrifice and is rejuvenated. This swallowing and rejuvenating with a new vigour is the key-note of the sacrificial rite. The same is seen in the case of the Vedic student — the initiate — who is supposed to be *swallowed* by the preceptor at the Upanayana. The idea of swallowing is closely associated with the idea of the swallowed (student) being the embryo of the preceptor. The student is said to be born anew (and being disgorged as it were) from the preceptor. The preceptor, thus, becomes the father of the student who gives 'new' birth to the initiate. The preceptor and the initiate are said to become equally powerful and immortal; and in this there are references to their oneness. Kaca being swallowed by Śukra presents a similar case. Kaca represents the initiate while Śukra the preceptor. This gains support in the mention of Śukra as the lord of initiation and his identification with the sun and Indra. The *Sañjīvanī* represents the Sāvitrī that the initiate learns.

The motif of swallowing, disgorging and the gain of new knowledge can be seen in the initiation-rites of the tribals, and this gives additional support to the contention that the Kaca legend is the legend of initiation. The peculiarly sexual element in the legend, probably, has been lent from the tribal rites of initiation which mark the age of puberty. The sexual appeal by Devayānī and the avoiding of it on the part of Kaca are well reflected in the Upanayana rites of these days which, on the last day of the rite, bring in the maternal uncle to ask the initiate to marry his daughter, the initiate answering in the negative and wishing to go for studies. The legend of Kaca, to put it finally, involves the principle of initiation. How the motif of swallowing works in the Vedic ritual texts has been amply seen. Swallowing is a mythical superimposition on the belief in complementation and oneness. In later Hindu rituals the same is seen in the act of inhaling of the initiate by the preceptor. The latter sprinkles the initiate with consecrated water with a bunch of sacred grass. He, then, hits the initiate with a flower gently and covers the latter's eyes with a band of cloth (cf. the Kakian practice noted earlier). Once more he is sprinkled with water, and the band is taken off. He, the preceptor, places his palm on the head of the initiate and inhales his breath imagining the initiate inside himself and engulfed with lustre, as he holds his breath. After a while, he releases the breath, imagining the initiate to have come out. He breathes on the heart of the initiate and gives him the sacred thread. In a variant practice the preceptor, after he has inhaled the initiate with his breath, imagines the latter to have entered various creatures (*sarvayoniṣu*). Then he breathes him out.[222] The body of the preceptor acts, symbolically, as representing the womb of all creatures (*sarvayoni*-s). In the Kaca-legend, this way, the stomach of Śukrācārya comes on par with the stomachs of the beasts that 'swallow' various parts of the body of Kaca. Hence, the wild beasts and the stomach of Śukrācārya are two phases of the same concept.

## References

1. *Ś.B.* (*Mādhya*) I.4.1-35ff.; I.7.2.22; *Jai. Br.* I.97; 99 etc. Also *Jai. Br.* 97, 99 etc., Ed. Raghuvira.
2. "वृत्रो ह वा इदं सर्वमास यद् यजूंषि यत्सामानि यद् ह सर्वं वृत्र एवास। तम् इन्द्रो जिघांसांश्चकार। ... अस्मै वृत्रायेन्द्रो वज्रमुद्ययाम, स हायं वृत्रोऽस्माद् वज्राद् उद्यताद् बिभयाञ्चकार। स उवाच मा नु मे प्रहार्षीरिति अस्ति उन्वा इदं मयि वीर्यं तन्नु (ते) (मे) प्रयच्छानीति।" *S.B.* V.5.5.1 ff.
3. *Jai. Br.* Raghuvira, 1954, Nagpur, I-125 to 127.

4. Cf. *Karṇinī vai bhūmiḥ*. The proverb, "The walls have ears" obtains in Hindi and in the Marathi languages.
5. *Śukra* is another reading, which is not very happy.
6. For such a ladder or pillar leading to heaven, cf. the 'Citrā brick' episode, wherein the Asuras are said to pile brick after brick to go to heaven, and Indra snatches away the brick placed by him (*Ś.B.* II.1.2.13ff.; *Taitt. Br.* I.I.2.4 to 6).
   The ladder or pillar here can be compared with the 'Tower of Babel; cf. J.G. Frazer, *Folk-lore in the Old Testament*, Vol. I; for a ladder leading to heaven, see Frazer, *op. cit.*, Vol. II, p. 52 ff.; the verses are *ṚV*, IX.87.2-3.
7. What follows = *Ibid.* I.166 = III.232; cf.
   *kavir vai bhārgavo deveṣu gandharva-lokamaicchat.*
   It is interesting to note how Indra approached the *wife* of the gandharva; the helping susceptibility of the woman to outwit her '*man*' (husband, brother or son) is common in folk-tales. The tale of 'Hiḍimbā and Bhīma' is one example from the *Mb.* The daughter of a demon helps a youth whom the demon wants to kill, K.S.S. Tawny, Vol. II, p. 360; a youth, Campaka, sets free Campakavatī and marries her. See Day *Folk-tales of Bengal*, London, 1912. p. 76 ff.
8. *Kāṭh. Sam.* XXXVII.14 (Satavalekar, 1943). Bloomfield quotes and uses this piece from this story to establish that the identification of Indra with the eagle is one of the secondary tentative starts of the story and criticizes Kuhn for his identification between Indra and Śyena based on this passage. Cf. "Legend of Soma and the Eagle", *J.A.O.S.* XVI.
9. See Hopkins, "Indra as the God of Fertility", *J.A.O.S.*, 36, p. 254 ff.
10. ṚV. VIII.1.28. *puram cariṣṇvam;* cf. floating island in popular belief, Donald Mackenzie, *Myths of China and Japan*, p. 99 f.
11. *Jai. Br.* I.125 *apsu nagaram pāriplavam.*
12. *Jai. Br.* III.232.
13. Cf. *Ś.B.* (*Mādh.*). I.6.1.7; (*Kāṇ.* II.5.3); also (*Mādh.*) I.4.1.34 (Kāṇ II.3.4.24).

14. Hopkins, *Epic Mythology*, pp. 100; 180.
15. *Ibid.*, p. 181.
16. *Ibid.*, p. 106.
17. Cf. also Macdonell, *Vedic Mythology*, p. 102.
18. Cf. *ṚV.* I.1.1.
19. *Mb.* XII.124.19.
20. Cf. also the account of Śibi to test whom Agni and Indra took the form of a pigeon and hawk respectively. It is interesting to note how Indra takes the form of an eagle hawk even here; and can be compared with the episode of the *Kāṭh. Sam.*, we have just referred to above. Indra is said to be the hawk in the Ṛgveda also, IV.27.1. There is, thus, a firmness in the belief in Indra being the hawk.
21. *Jai. Br.* I.161 ff.; *Tāṇ. Br.* XII.6.9.
22. Cf. Weber, *Indische Studien*, III, p. 479.
23. Cf. A.V. VII.38.2.
24. For Agni as the messenger of the gods. See also *Tait. Sam.* II.5.8; also HOS. Vol. XVIII, p. 198. (Tr. by Keith). Bṛhaspati (The father of Kaca) is himself called *Agni*, *Ai. Br.* III.35, where we have Bṛhaspati and Aṅgiras being produced from the burning seed of Prajāpati.
25. Cf. *Ś.B. Kāṇ.* II-6-1.5; *Ś. Br.* (Kāṇva) II.6.1.5 f; cf. Mādh. I.6.3.1-24.
26. Cf. for the same account, see *Mait. Sam.* II.4.3; *Jai. Br.* II.155 etc.; in the *Ś.B.V. 5.5.5.1* ff. we have even metres in the body of Vṛtra. For sacrifice itself in the body of Vṛtra, cf. *Mait.* IV.6.5. For various herbs in *Vṛtra's* body cf. *Mait. Sam.* III-6-3. The *Tait. Sam.* has a variation that Agni and Soma escape out of *Vṛtra's* open mouth II.5.2.

    This shows the all-encompassing nature of Vṛtra (who encompasses, from √*Vṛ*). With the Sun and the Moon coming out of Vṛtra's body, cf. an old American (Wintu Indian) myth recorded by W.T. Olcott, *Sunlore of All Ages*, New York, London, 1914, p. 14 f. In this myth the two luminaries come out of the body of a person who is killed by his son-in-law in a contest. In the Vedic myth Indra is the half-brother of Vṛtra.
27. For *Sautrāmaṇī*, see *Ś.B. Kāṇ.* II.6.1.5; *Mādh.* I.6.3.7; also *Ś.B. Kāṇ.* VII-5-1 ff.; *Mādh.* V.5.4.2 ff.; *Tait. Sam.* II.4.12.1 ff.

28. *Jai. Br.* II.156; cf. *Ibid.* 157, where we have lions, tigers and other animals coming out of Indra's body. *surāvāriṭakā* is difficult; *parisṛk* does not occur elsewhere; *parisṛt* is common; and it was some intoxicating drink. *Karkandhu* and *badara* are types of jujube. *surāvāriṭakā* might, hence, be some intoxicating drink.
29. Vṛtra also is said elsewhere to have been brought to life on the condition that he should be Indra's food. Cf. *Ś.B. Kāṇ.* II.6.1.5 ff; *Mādh.* I.6.3.17.
30. The pattern in all such cases is of complementary rivalry, rather than stark enmity.
31. Cf. *Ś.B.* III.9.4.2. *divi vai somo vṛtro vai somaḥ*; and I.6.3.17 for Vṛtra as food.
32. *Ś.B.* I.6.3.9.
33. Cf. *Mait. Sam.* IV.7.4.
34. Cf. *Tait. Sam.* II.5.3.1.
35. Cf. *Mb.* XIV.11.8 ff; also Hopkins, *Epic Myth.*, p. 129.
36. Cf. *Epic Myth.*, p. 130, where we read that gods created 'yawn' as a great being to destory *Vṛtra* who gaped and out came Indra. Cf Śuṣṇa and Indra.
37. Cf. *Jai. Br.* II.179.
38. Cf. *Jai. Br.* I.233. *annam vai devānām somo rājā.* For similar ideas see *ṚV.* IX.106.8; 108.3; I.91.6; also *Ś.B. Kāṇva*-II.6.2.5; for the moon being drunk by god, cf. *Raghu*, V.6.
39. See Eggeling's remark on the introduction to *S.B.E.* Vol. 26, p. xiii; also *Ś.B.* (*Mādh.*) I-6.4.15 etc.
40. *Ś.B.* (*Kāṇ.*) II.6.2.13 ff.; Mādh. I.6.4.17-19. For Indra = the sun cf. *Jai. Br.* I-8; *Ibid.* II-232.
    See also A.V. XIII.4.46 where the poet suddenly extols Indra in the hymn dedicated to the sun; see Whitney's note on the passage — *Ath. V. Sam., Tr.*, p. 729; *Mait. Sam.* I.10.16; *asau vā-āditya indraḥ.*
41. Cf. *Jai. Br.* I.7; 8.
42. *Ś.B.* (*Kāṇ*) V.2.I ff; V.6.73. (*Mādh.*) IV.2.I. ff; also *Tait. Sam.* VI.4.10.2.
43. Cf. *Ś.B.* V.2.6. (*Kāṇ*); *Mādh.* (IV-2.1.8). The verses prescribed for the Śukra and the Manthin cups in these two branches of *Ś.B.* are, however, different. They are *ṚV.* X.123.1 (for the Śukra at Kāṇva) while the *Mādh.*

has Vāj Sam. VII.12; The *Mādh.* has X.123.1 for the Manthin (moon) cup.

44. Cf. *Mait. Sam.* IV.6.3; *Ś.B.* (*Mādh.*) IV.2.1.1f has it impliedly.
45. *Ś.B. (Mādh)* IV.5.9.4; (*Kāṇ*) V.6.6.4; *Mādh.* IV.2.1-29.
46. For '*Śuṣṇa* and *Śukra*' see also review on Risley's *Tribes and Castes of Bengal, J.R.A.S.*, 1891, p. 359. The root *śuc* has the sense 'to shine', 'be bright', and the root *śuṣ* has also the same, with that of 'drying'. *Śuṣṇa* means also the 'sun' in his terrible parching aspect; he holds waters (*amṛta*).
47. *Mait. Sam.* I.2.4; *ṚV.* XI.109.3 *sukraḥ pavasva devebhyaḥ.* Also *Mait. Sam.* I.6.8. "सोमो वै शुक्रो ब्रह्मवर्चसम्।"
48. The word 'cup' for '*graha*' is Eggeling's.
49. Cf. *Ś.B.* (*Mādh.*) IV.2.1.29; (*Kāṇ*) V.2.1.22.
    It may also be noted that the swallowing of the sun and the moon and again disgorging are present in the case of the solar and the lunar eclipse where the Asura Svarbhānu is the eater; but the idea of swallowing and disgorging in the legend of Kaca comes nearer to the one that we have been discussing, the principle of ultimate oneness of the eater and the eaten being present in the tales of Vṛtra and Indra, the moon and the sun, the 'Śukra' and 'the Manthin'. The same principle plays an important part in the legend of Kaca as we shall have occasion to prove later in our discussion.
    For 'Svarbhānu' swallowing these luminaries, *Ś.B.* (*Mādh.*) V.3.2.2; also *Māit. Sam.* II.5.2. It is a popular myth and occurs in other Vedic texts.
50. *Kau. Br.* X.3; also *Ś.B.* (*Kāṇ.*) II.6.1.5.
51. *Ś.B.* II.6.1.5.
52. *Ibid.*, 3.
53. *Tait. Sam.* II.1.2.7; II.3.11.1.
54. *Ibid.*, II.3.14.1ff.
55. *Ibid.*, II.3.3.3.
56. *Tait. Sam.* II.3.3.1. The union of *Soma* and Śukra (= Agni) is the principle on which the whole system of sacrifice is based. In other words, they are the liquid and drying principles, cf. *Ś.B.* I.6.3.26.

57. Cf. Macdonell, *Vedic Myth*, under Agni or Sun.
58. *Jai. Br.* I.94; also *ṚV* I.69.1.
59. *Gop. Br., Uttar.* III.17 = *Mait. Sam.* IV.7.7, 8.3; *Ś.B.* (*Mādh.*) II.2.2.1; III.9.4.2; etc.
60. Cf. *Jai. Br.* I.82. *krūram iva tad yajñasya kurvanti.*
61. *Ś.B.* (*Mādh*). III.9.4.2-8. *tathāta udeti tathā sañjīvati.* This rebirth is brought about when the pressed shoots of *Soma* are put in water, '*Nigrābhya*'; see Eggeling, *S.B.E.* Vol. 26. P., p. 244.
62. *Ś.B.* III.9.4.7 (*Mādh.*).
63. *Ś.B.* (*Mādh.*) III.9.4.17; (*Kāṇ.*) IV.9.4.14.
64. *Mb.* I.72.
65. P. 173, *Supra*. See also note 68 below.
66. *Tait. Sam.* VI.6.7.1; also *Tait. Sam.* VI.6.9.2 where we have that some parts of the un-'slaughtered' (unpressed shoots of) *Soma* are kept aside in the *graha* lest the sacrificer should also die. This *graha* is called *adābhya* (non-perishable) and *jīvagraha*.
67. For oneness of the sacrifice, the material and the sacrificer, see also *Ś.B.* I.2.2.1 (*Kāṇ.*); (*Mādh.*) III.6.3.21. *havirvā eṣa bhavati yo dīkṣate.*
    Cf. (*Kāṇ.*) IV.6.3-17; *Mait. Sam.* III.6.1.
68. *Ś.B.* (*Kāṇ.*) IV.6.3.16.
    *ubhābhyām agnīṣomābhyām nirmucya svena svatā ātmanā yajate.*
    For sacrificer = the beast; also *Tait. Sam.* VI.I.11; *yadagnīṣomīyam paśum ālabhata ātmaniṣkrayaṇa evāsya saḥ.* Hence it is said, that its flesh is not to be eaten.
69. See note 67 and above.
70. The explanation in the brackets is Eggeling's, *Ibid.*, p. 379. See note 1. "That is, as the Soma plant becomes juicy again, so the sacrificer has his vital sap or spirit restored."
71. *Ibid.* Eggeling, p. 385; *Kāt. Śr. S.X.* 9.6.
72. *Ś.B.* (*Mādh.*) III.3.3.12; (*Kāṇ*) IV.3.3.105.
73. *Ibid.* (*Mādh.*).
74. *Ś.B.* (*Mādh*), III.2.1.15; esp. *atha dīkṣitasya somasya.*
75. *Mait. Sam.* III.6.7; cf. *Ś.Br.* III.2.1.16 f.
76. *Mait. Sam.* III.6.7. *sa vai yajñena jāyate;* Also *Ś.B.* (*Mādh.*) III.2.1.11. *uto jāyate garbho bhūtvā etasmāt yajñāt.*

77. Cf. *Gop. Br.* (Pūrva. III.19).
"अथापि वेदानां गर्भभूतो भवति इत्याहुः।"
78. *Ś.B.* (*Mādh.*) III.2.1.6.
79. Cf. *Ś.B.* (*Mādh.*) III.3.3.12; cf. esp. *sa etam garbham ajījanat.*
80. Cf. *Ś.B. Kāṇ* IV.2.1.17.
For *Viṣṇu* = Sacrifice, see *Ai. Br.* I.4 = 3.15.
81. Cf. *Ś.B. (Kāṇ.)* IV.3.4.14, (*Mādh.* III.3.4.21). The identification at the place is, *Soma* (offering) = Viṣṇu = Sacrificer. The concept is already suggested in *ṚV.* I.164.50. *yajñena yajñam ayajanta devāḥ.*
82. Cf. *A.V.* XI.5.3; also Whitney, *Ath. V. Sam.*, pp. 636-40.
83. The word 'Vedic-studentship' is used by Whitney as a rendering for *brahmacarya.*
84. *A.V.* XI.5.16.
85. *Mb.* I-71.73.
86. *Mb.* I.71.49.
87. *Ibid.* 50.
88. *Ibid.* 57. *sāñjīvanīm prāpya vidyām mahārhām tulyaprabhāvo brahmaṇā brahmabhūtaḥ.*
89. *Ibid.* 48. *putro bhūtvā bhāvaya bhāvito mām.*
90. *Āś. Gṛ. Sū.* I.15.11 *ātmā vai putranāmāsi.*
91. Cf. *Manu Sm.* IX.8; cf. *Ai. Br.* VII-13, esp. *tasyām punarnavo bhūtvā.*
92. *AV.* XI.5.14.
93. See p. 173 *supra.*
94. *Jai. Br.* I.167. The *mantra* of this rite is for getting the mind back from Yama, with Soma's help.
For Soma and immortality cf. Macdonell, *Vedic Myth.*, p. 108; also in later lit. *Soma* and *amṛta* are spoken as one and the same thing. Cf. Garuḍa legend, the chapter on 'Bringing of Nectar.' A boy, after the *upanayana*, is called *Saumya.*
95. Cf. *Jai. Br.* I.126-127. *svāyudhaḥ pavate soma induḥ.*
96. See p. 162, *supra,* and the concerned passage, *Kāṭh. Sam.* XXXVII.14.
97. For the student being very powerful, see *A.V.* XII.5, whole hymn, esp. vv. 7-16.
98. Cf. *Mb.* I-71.33.

*prāyacchan brāhmaṇāyaiva surāyām asurās tadā.*

99. Cf. *Mait. Sam.* II.3.8. *svādvīm tvā svādunā* etc. Also *Tait. Sam.* I.8.21.

100. Cf. Sāma *V. Pūrva* V.5-8.
'त्वं विप्रोऽभवोऽङ्गिरस्तम मध्वां यज्ञं मिमिक्षाण:।"

101. *Ibid.;* RV. IX.10.8. *Kaver apatyam ā duhe.*

102. *S.B.* IV.4.2.12 *bṛhaspatisutasya deva soma; (Vāj Sam.* VIII.9). For Kaca as the son of Bṛhaspati, *Mb.* I.71.15.

103. Cf. *Tait. Sam.* I.4.27-1 and Sāyaṇa on it.

104. Cf. Kane, '*Hist. Dh. Śa,*' Vol. II-Part I, p. 283, for his being appointed by Bṛhaspati; suta means 'son' also.

105. *Ś.B.* XI.5.4.12. For the same idea, cf. A.V. XI.5.3.
The birth after *three nights* tallies with the birth of the one consecrated for the sacrifice and also with the birth of Soma which is kept for three days after purchase; *Kāṭh. Sam.* XII.5.

106. Cf. *Gop. Br.* Pūrva II.3.

107. *Ś.B.* XI.5.4.3, 4; esp. *bhūtebhyaḥ paridadāti ariṣṭyai; ariṣṭyai is from a-riṣṭi,* i.e. 'non-injury'; 'no mutilation'. Kaca is given to the *Śālāvṛka*-s. In the vedic text, Indra gives the ascetics to the *śālāvṛkas.* This expression appears to have become a pattern, for such injury, indicating that the Kaca episode is just a myth, meaning injury, death and rebirth for the initiate. For Indra the *Śalāvṛka*-s and *yātis* (ascetics) see, Dange, *Towards Understanding Hindu Myths,* pp. 223-41.

108. I.71 (Crit. Ed.) 36 ff.
Though in this part of the legend, Śukra does not figure as a 'swallower', the Asuras directly killing Kaca, the fact remains that Kaca is killed and yet is in a position to come out as a whole when Śukra calls him. The episode is narrated mythically. The pattern does not change, though the form changes.
Mark the word, '*ariṣṭaḥ*', which shows that though Kaca was '*killed*' and given to the wild animals (bhūtas), he was only to be ultimately 'unhurt'. So, he was deposited in the wolves, for protected wholeness.
Compare the word '*ariṣṭaḥ*' with '*ariṣṭyai*' in *Ś.B.*, above.

109. *S.B.* XI.5.4.5.

110. *Ibid.*

111. Cf. *Ś.B.* (*Mādh.*) II.4.4.21; here context is of the *sānnāyyā* (coaguled milk) offerings.

112. Cf. *Jai. Br.* I.8, where the sun is said to 'die' at sunset visually; but he is said to enter, in parts, various objects. With faith he enters a brāhmaṇa; in cattle in the form of milk; lustre he places in the fire and so on. As a foetus he stays in the night. He is born in the morning. The offering helps his birth. The word is *ni-mrocati,* i.e. gets shattered goes, or 'dies'.
The idea of being the *Embryo* is to be marked.

113. Cf. *Jai. Br.* I.26-27. Agni is Mṛtyu, called 'Rihan' ('Hurting')... Vāyu is Mṛtyu, called Ajira ('Quick') and so on.
The idea of approaching Death and conquering Him is further on finely reflected in many tales. One such is the famous tale of *Naciketas*.

114. Cf. also *Chānd. Br.* (Calcutta-1958) I.6.21 (p. 78), where the preceptor says catching the navel of the initiate: "O Death, this I give unto thee", and the comment of Guṇasvāmin on it is — "this initiate (*brahmacāriṇam*) . . ."
For full description of Initiation (*Upanayana*), see Kane, '*Hist. of Dh. Sā.,* Vol. II-Part I, p. 277 ff.
Also Apte, *Social and Religious Life in the Gṛhyasūtra*, Bombay, 1954, p. 170 ff.
Also Tilak, *Orion*, p. 155 ff.

115. Kane, '*Hist. Dh. Śā.*', Vol. II, Part I, p. 227.
The initiate is also called 'Bṛhaspati's pupil'. Cf. Apte, *op. cit.*, p. 174.

116. Kane, *op. cit.*, p. 277; see note 642 where he gives the relevant quotations from *Smṛticandrikā*.

117. *Ibid.*

118. Cf. AV. XI.5.7; see below note 119.

119. Cf. *Ibid.* 7.
*garbho bhūtvā' mṛtasya yonau.*
*indro ha bhūtvā-asurāns tatarha.*
Compare with 'Indra' here, with whom the initiate is equalled, Indra of the *Kāṭh. Sam.* who brings nectar that lies in the womb of Śuṣṇa; also with Indra who brings Kāvya Uśanā to the side of the gods.

With the above verse, cf. also *Ibid.* 5.1; also 8. *sa ācāryam tapasā piparti.*

120. Cf. *Ibid.* 3 — *sarvān sa devāns tapasā piparti.*

121. Cf. *Kāṭhā Up-I.* Also *Mb.* XIII (Anuśāsana) 71.

122. *Mb.* III. (Vanaparva), 188. Cf. *Sk. P.* Vaiṣṇava Khaṇḍa (II). 3.27 to 38.

123. Compare with this the Egyptian idea of the 'Divine child". Curiously enough the idea of the 'child' (*Viṣṇu*) on the water of the deluge is exactly similar to the 'Divine Child' (the symbol of the sun) with its finger in its mouth representing the beginning of life from the Abyss (Primeval Waters); see R.T. Rundle Clark, *Myth and Symbol in Ancient Egypt*, London, 1959, p. 36. Cf. Donald Mackenzie, *Myths of China and Japan*, p. 103. See also Dange, Smt. Sindhu S., *The Bhāgavata Purāṇa — Mytho-Social Study*, Ajanta Books International, Delhi, 1984, p. 36.

124. Cf. *Mb.* III Vana-Parvan, 39 to 41.

125. *Ibid. Nivātakavaca Parvan* (i.e. 168) in the Vana Parvan. For Arjuna equal to Indra, see also *Ibid,* Adhyāya, 65-3, etc. etc.

126. Cf. *Mb.* XIV (Aśvam.) 55. The tale of Uttaṅka who meets Kṛṣṇa in the desert; cf. the showing of the '*Viśvarūpa*' to Arjuna by Kṛṣṇa at the time of the battle before telling the Gītā. The same can be noted in the Yaśodā-Kṛṣṇa account where the mother sees everything in the wide open mouth of Kṛṣṇa. The same is true about Duryodhana knowing the real divinity in Kṛṣṇa in the Kaurava assembly.

127. Cf. *Mb.* X (Sauptika) 5-7.

128. *Ibid.* III, Vana Parvan, 151 to 153. The sickly Hanūmān testing the strength and character of Bhīma — the hero — is a motif quite common in folklore. It is common to find such figures — dwarfs, foxes, etc., with pretended weakness, but being immensely useful to the hero in his exploits. cf. Grimm's *Household tales* (Tr. by Margaret Hunt), London 1884, Vol. II, tale 93 where we have a dragon helping the hero; tale 97 has a dwarf doing the job.

129. *Mb.* I.3.33 ff.

130. Cf. also the account of Kaṇva where Aśvinau (dual gods) give him his eyes back. For this and other exploits of Aśvins, see *ṚV.* I.118 and Macdonell, *Vedic Mythology*, under Aśvins.
131. For the well as the semblance of death or the enveloping factor — see the tale of Jaratkāru (*Mb.* I.13) where his parents hang in the *pit*; also *Mb.* III.14 — where the Sage Agasti sees his parents hanging in a pit. See Dange, *Towards Understanding Hindu Myths*, 355 ff.
132. *Bhāga P.* refers passingly to the legend, explaining the *pratiloma* marriage between Yayāti and Devayānī. Cf. IX.18-22; cf. also *Matsya P.* XXV-62, where the account is the same as in the *Mb.*
133. *Sk. P.* II (Vaiṣṇava Khaṇḍa), 16. Here in this Purāṇa the Kaca-Śukra tale does not occur.
134. *Sk. P.* II (Vaiṣṇava Khaṇḍa), 16.75-77.
135. The commentary interprets the word, *'Śāmbhavena'* as *'Śambhuprasāda-labdhena'*, which means — 'obtained by the favour of Śambhu, and is similar to the new weapon or lore obtained from the preceptor.
136. Cf. *Ibid.* VI-Part I.149 ff.
137. Cf. *Ibid.* VII.I.33-3 ff.; also *ibid.* III.15 where the whole account occurs except that of Andhaka.
138. Cf. *Ibid.* 3. See *Mb.* I-71-8 and 58 for Kaca's period of penance.
139. Cf. *Mb.* XII.32 and 54.
140. The pleasing of Devayānī on the part of Kaca and the favour of Umā for Śukra fall in line with the general motif in folk-tales viz. winning of the softer sex to win a powerful adversary. We have hinted at it before. See n. 7, *supra*.
141. Cf. *Pad. P.* VI.18.
142. See P.K. Gode, *Studies in Indian Literary History* (where the author quotes a verse from a manuscript called *Ācārapradīpa*), Vol. II, p. 479. The relevant portion is — *grāme kūrpasañjñike — asti Śukreśvaḥ godā paścimavāhinī vijayate devaḥ kaceśaḥ paraḥ.*

    A Marathi ballad (*povāḍā*) by Paraśurāma (Bombay, 1924, p. 38 ff) is also quoted by Gode, which has *guru śukrakaceśvara godātīravāsī. . .*, *op. cit.*, p. 472. I am indebted to Dr. Gode (who is no more) for this information, p. 482.

143. *Ibid.*, p. 482.
144. Cf. *Mb.* Anuśāsana 26.8; also Sānti, 47-9.
145. Cf. Kane, '*Hist. Dh. Śā.*', Vol. II-Part-I, p. 282. Cf. '*Apast. Gṛ. Sū*' X.668.
146. *AV.* VI.68.3. ab.
147. *ṚV.* III.62.10.
148. This is found in the *Tait. A.* X.1.6 which the author of this book himself was taught as the initiation-*mantra* along with the usual '*Sāvitrī*'. This *mantra* is *tatpuruṣāya vidmahe mahādevāya dhīmahi, tanno rudraḥ pracodayāt.* This is the *mantra* for the Śaivas. The usual *mantra* is *tat Saviturvareṇyam bhargo devasya dhīmahi* etc. (*RV.* III.62.10).
149. Baldwin Spencer and Gillen, "Initiation Ceremonies", *Making of Man*, p. 285.
150. Cf. Śukra as the father-in-law of Kaca, if the latter would have married Devayānī.
151. Spencer *op. cit.*, p. 289; for similar idea, p. 296.
152. *Ibid.*, p. 291.
153. *Ibid.*, p. 299; compare with this, the girdle of Muñjā grass in Vedic. rites. Due to it, it is usual to call the initiate '*Muñjya*' in Marāṭhi. On the same analogy the initiate with the *hair-girdle* can be called Kaca, i.e. 'Hair-boy' — (having-hair-girdle).
154. According to a custom in South India, the pilgrims going to Rāmeśvara (the temple of Śiva) and Palani (the temple of Kārttikeya, the son of Śiva), get hair on their heads completely shorn, irrespective of their being males or females — married and having husbands! Palaṇi is about seventy miles to the south of Coimbatore on the way to Madurai in southern India. The same is at Tirupati.
155. Cf. *Saṁskāra-pradīpa*, p. 407, quoted in Kane, '*Hist. Dh. Sā.*', *op. cit.*, p. 206, no. 480.
156. For father as teacher, see *Bṛh. Up.* V.2.1; *Chānd. Up.* IV.5.5; V.I.I.7; *Mait. Up.* I.2.12.
157. Cf. Frazer, *The Golden Bough,* Vol. II, London, 1890, p. 348.
158. For the 'Bull-roarer' and its shape, see A. Lang, *Custom*

*and Myth*, London, 1884, p. 33. For swallowing in initiation, *ibid.*, p. 53 ff.

159. Frazer, *op. cit.*, p. 342.
160. *Ibid.*, pp. 344-45.
161. *Ibid.*, p. 345.
162. *Ibid.*, p. 352.
163. *Ibid.*, p. 356.
164. *Ibid.*, p. 357.
165. Aristotle quoted by A. Coomaraswamy in his article — "The sun-kiss", *J.A.O.S.* (No. 60), p. 50, note 13. For the 'Not-dying' gained by sacrifice, *Ibid.*, p. 51, note 17.
166. Baldwin Spencer and F.I. Gillen, "Initiation ceremonies" in the *Making of Man* (Modern Library), 1931 p. 284; cf. the story of Upamanyu, noted earlier.
It will be interesting to note here a popular saying at the '*Upanayana*' as it is performed in the Vidarbha region of Maharashtra (India). It is often common to hear the elderly people telling the 'baṭu' (initiate) that his thigh is going to be cut and a live frog is to be inserted inside, the thigh being stitched again! Well, it is never done and remains only a joke. But why should the joke be current at the cremony? It appears to be a relic of the principle of 'Torture' and might have formed a part of the tribal ritual which influenced the Braḥmanical rite though only in jocular saying. The insertion of the frog might have been, in all probability, an actual rite. The frog indicating the male organ, probably, hints at the time of the rite, puberty.
167. Cf. *Mb.* I.71.14. *devayānyām hi tuṣṭāyām vidyām tām prāpsyasi dhruvam.*
The emphasis in the words '*hi*' and '*dhruvam*' is to be marked.
168. Cf. *Ibid.* 22-24.
169. *Ibid.* 77, the whole Adh. (i.e. 1-23).
170. Cf. A Lang, *Custom and Myth,* p. 33. With this can be compared the restriction upon those who have undergone the ceremony of Upanayana not to utter the 'Sāvitrī' (Gāyatrī) before women.
171. Frazer, *Golden Bough,* Vol. II, p. 258.

172. Cf. Kane, *Hist. Dh. Ś.*, Vol. II, Part I, p. 283; also Rajabali Pande, *Hindu Saṁskāras*, Banaras, 1949.
173. Cf. *Manu*. II.179; 212, 215.
174. Cf. *Yājña*. I.2.3, 14 and 37. Also cf. *Manu*. II.38; even to this day, the Mārawāḍi and other Vaiśya communities have their 'Janeu' (*Upanayana* = the sacred thread ceremony) just a day before the marriage.
175. B. Spencer and F. Gillen, in the *Making of Man*, 1931, p. 282.
For contempt for men without *Upanayana* at age later than the one prescribed, cf. *Manu*. II.39 and *Yājña*- I.2.38, where they are called '*Vrātyas*' and '*Sāvitrīpatitas*'. In *AV* XV, the Vrātya is a respectable person, but belongs to a non-Vedic fold. However, even a Vedic is advised to respect him. The *Sāvitrī-patita* is one who has not learnt the sacred *mantra*, praising the sun (= Savitṛ), taught to the Vedic student at *upanayana*.
176. For this feature in Upanayana see also Rajabali Pande, *Hindu Saṁskāras*, p. 228. Pande calls this a 'late feature'. We have seen that this feature is not quite late and is well set in the tradition of the savage tribes, though it is later than the Brahmanical rite of Upanayana.
177. *Ś.B.* III.9.4.2 (Mādhya); (Kān. I.9.4.2.) —
*upāṁśu-savanaḥ sa vivasvān āditya nidānena, ghnanti- uta vā enam yad abhiṣuṇvati tathā . . . sañjīvatī.*
178. Cf. *Jai. Br.* I.259.
*yad havirdhāne somam rājānam abhiṣuṇvanti yaja- mānam eva tad retaḥ kurvanti.*
179. Cf. *Ś.B.* (Kāṇva) I.6.3.8. *yo draṇakalaśe śukraḥ pariśi ṣṭaḥ āsa.*
180. Cf. *Ibid.* (*Kān.*) V.6.7.3; (*Mādh.*) IV.5.5.7.
*atha śukrapātram anu prajāḥ prajāyante* etc.
Eggeling renders the word 'prajāḥ' as men. It will be better to take it to mean 'progeny'.
181. Cf. *Mait. Sam.* I.2.5
*āsmāko'si, śukraste grahaḥ prajāḥ pāhi.*
182. *Ibid.* I.3.12.
183. Cf. *J.R.A.S.*, 1893 p. 276 ff.
184. *Ś.B.* (*Mādh.*) XII.4.2.10.

185. For Śukra = Indra, see no. 45, *supra.*
186. For it see *ibid.;* Hopkins Keith, *Religion and Phil. of the Veda* and *Up.*, II, p. 331.
187. Cf. Moor, *Hindoo Pantheon*, p. 282.
188. Cf. *AV.*, XI.5.12.
189. *Ibid.* 7. *gabho bhūtvā' mṛtasya yonau.*
190. Cf. *Ibid.*
191. Cf. *Mait. Sam.* IV.6.3 = IV.6.8. *tejo vai sukro brahmavarcasam;* elsewhere we have *somo vai Śukro brahmavarcasam;* cf. *Ibid.* I.6.8.
192. The sacrificial consecration and the initiation have practically the same underlying idea. We have already seen it. For more particulars, see Keith, *Rel. and Phil. of the Veda*, Vol. II, p. 370.
193. Cf. *Jai. Br.* III.359.
     The sun himself is said to be 'Dīkṣiṭa', hinting at the oneness of the consecrated and the deity, *Ibid.*, III.358.
194. *Rel. Phil. Vedas*, p. 370.
195. Cf. *savitā vai prasavānām iṣṭe* for *Śukra*, see n. 180 *supra.*
196. For the tale of Sāvitrī-Satyavat, see *Mb.* I.241-48; III-293-10 ff; *Rām.* II.306 etc. It is *Sāvitrī* (the solar energy) that stands before king Aśvapati and gives him a daughter made of *her own brilliance.* Hence it could be seen that 'Sāvitrī' — the wife of Satyavat and the daughter of Aśvapati, is only the personification of the solar energy.
197. Cf. Hopkins, *Epic Myth*, p. 86; *Mb.* III.100.34; Read also *Manu*, II.170, where Sāvitrī is said to be the mother of the initiate, while the preceptor is his 'father'.
198. Cf. *Jai. Br.* I.288; *Ś.B.* (*Mādh.*) III.2.4.1; *Mait. Sam.* IV.I. etc. See legend of Garuḍa, A, "Garuḍa and the Bringing of Nectar".
199. Cf. *Ś.B.* XI.5.4.13.
200. Cf. *Jai Br.* I.99.
201. *Ibid.* I.103.
     Cf. also *Ibid.* I.110; I.132; I.266; 269; 272 etc.
202. *Ibid.* I.292; also *Mait. Sam.* III.4.4. *āyur vai gāyatram* and *prāṇo vai gāyatram.*
203. Cf. *Jai. Br.* I.232; II.131; *Mait. Sam.* III.2.6; 4-6.

For Śukra see note 191, *supra*.

204. Cf. *J.R.A.S.*, 1893 review on Risley, p. 272.
205. *Ibid.*, p. 274.
206. *AV.* XI.5.12.
207. There is no one opinion about the time for initiation. In all probability, the original time fixed was the Devayāna but later according to circumstances it changed.
208. *Ś.B.* (*Mādh.*) I.4,I.34-35.
209. Cf. *Mait. Sam.* I.4.3. *yā terātrayaḥ savitar devayānīḥ* = *Tait. Sam.* I.6.6.4; III.5.4; Kāṭh. *Sam.* V.6.4.
210. Cf. *Mait. Sam.* II.8.13; = *Tait. Sam.* IV.4.6 = Mānava. *Śr. Sū.* VI.2.2. *agner yānyasi . . . devayanī asi.*
211. Cf. *Jai. Br.* I.94. *yajño vai śukraḥ.*
212. Cf. *Mait. Sam.* I.33.36; *Tait. Sam.* III.9.9; III.3.33; Kāṭh. *Sam.* XXX.6; Vāj. *Sam.* VIII.48 to 50; Mānava *Śr. Sū.* VII.1.1. etc.
213. Cf. *Jai. Br.* II.298.
214. *Mb.* I.71.54-55, "Who, being a brāhmaṇa, will drink wine henceforth etc."; that Śukrācārya drank it is proof enough.
215. Cf. *ṚV.* VII.86.6.
216. *Ibid.*, VIII.2.12.
217. *Ibid.*, X.107.9.
218. Tait. Br.I.8.6.2; cf. also *Kāṭh. Sam.* XII.12, also Śānk. *Śr. Sū.* XV.15.14.
219. *Kāṭh. Sam.* XII.12.
Cf. " तस्माज्ज्यायांश्च कनीयांश्च स्नुषा श्वशुरश्च सुरां पीत्वा सह लालपत आसते। पाप्मा वै माल्व्यम्। तस्माद् ब्राह्मणः सुरां न पिबति। पाप्मना नेत् संसृज्या इति।"
220. *Baudh. Dh. Sū.* I.22; also Kane, *op. cit.*, p. 965.
221. See Ch. III, 3(E), n. 113, *infra*.
222. For more instances see Dange, *Encyclopaedia of Puranic Beliefs and Practices*, Vol. III, p. 913 f. The idea in the initiate 'entering' various creatures may be compared with the idea of giving the Vedic initiate to various creatures. Cf. *atha enam bhūtebhyaḥ paridadāti*; and, this for *ariṣṭyai*, i.e. for protecting him from harm; see n. 107 *supra*.

## III
## Churning of the Ocean

*The sacrificial pressing of Soma into the 'Kalaśa' by the 'adris', the Ṛg-Vedic idea of the release of the celestial waters, and the popular ideas of the creation of the world and the advent of rain blended together to form the legend of the CHURNING OF THE OCEAN.*

# 1
# THE LEGEND

## (A) At Mb.

The gods came together on one of the high peaks of the mountain Meru and began thinking as to how to gain nectar. Nārāyaṇa said to Brahmā, when all the gods were thus engrosed in anxiety, "May this ocean — *'Kalaśa'* — by name be churned with the help of the Asuras, whereby nectar would spring forth. Let all the herbs and the precious stones be put into it. Then (O gods!) churn the ocean and you will get nectar"* (I. 17).

The gods then tried to uproot the mountain, Mandara, which was endowed with all the creepers and was the resort of the Apsarases and Kinnaras etc., and was eleven thousand *yojanas* in height with an equal portion of it under the waters. When the gods were unable to uproot it even with all their might, they resorted to Viṣṇu, who was sitting with Brahmā and said thus, "May you both decide upon our well -being. May you make efforts to uproot the mountain Mandara for our good." Saying, "That will be done", Viṣṇu, along with Brahmā, urged the king of serpents to uproot the mountain. Ananta, the mighty one, the king of serpents, then, did uproot the king of the mountains with all its forests and forest-dwellers. Then the gods approached the Sea with the mountain and said to him (standing) on its shore, "We shall churn thy waters for the sake of nectar." The lord of waters said, "If you keep my share also in nectar, then shall I undergo the strain of churning with the mountain Mandara." The gods (agreed and) with the Asuras asked the

**Mb.* I.17 to 19 (*Crit. Ed.* I-15 to 17).

king of tortoises to be the prop of the mountain, Mandara. When the tortoise-king accepted the request, Indra pressed the mountain on the bank of the former with a device (*yantreṇa*). Making the churning-rod of the mountain Mandara, and Vāsuki the churn-rope, the gods began churning the ocean, the receptacle of waters, for *amṛta*; and likewise did the dānavas, the nāga kings and the great Asuras, all coming together. At the mouth of Vāsuki were the Asuras, and the gods stood by the tail where the god Nārāyaṇa himself was. Then the god Nārāyaṇa, taking up the head of the nāga (Vāsuki) hurled it down again and again. From the mouth of Vāsuki that was being hurled up and down again and again, smoky and fiery winds began constantly coming out. Those same multitudes of smoke became masses of clouds full of lightning, and began showering rain-water upon the gods tired during the act of churning. The mountain-tops began showering heaps of flowers upon the host of gods and Asuras. There arose a great sound like the rumbling of the clouds from the ocean that was being churned by the gods and the Asuras. Various kinds of aquatic animals, being crushed by the great mountain, were destroyed in the salt water (of the ocean). The mountain pounded to extinction various animals — the dwellers of the region. As the mountain was whirling continuously, the trees from the mountain-tops fell (into the ocean) along with birds (residing on them). The fire caused by their mutual compact began blazing anon and it enveloped the mountain Mandara like a dark cloud with its lightnings. It burnt there all the elephants and lions that ran out and all animals and other beasts of various types perished in it. Indra pacified with rain the fire that was blazing hither and thither. There flew forth fluids from various trees and various medicinal liquids into the waters of the ocean. With those nectar-like and powerful fluids and with the milk that oozed out from trees, and with the essence of gold, the gods became immortal. Then the whole water of the ocean got turned into milk, mixed with the various and the best of juices. Then from milk came out ghee. Then the gods said to Brahmā sitting (nearby), "We are all, except Nārāyaṇa, well tired, O Brahman!, and as yet there is no nectar; and the churning of the sea has been going on for a long time!" Then, Brahmā said to Nārāyaṇa,"Do thou give them strength. Thou alone art the last resort herein." Viṣṇu said, "I shall give strength to all those that have joined in the work. May all (of you) churn vigorously the ocean 'Kalaśa". On hearing the words of Nārāyaṇa, all those mighty ones (the gods and the Asuras etc.) rendered the water of the ocean again turbid (due to vigorous churning). Then came forth from the ocean that was being churned, the *moon* with a hundred rays, clear, brilliant, cool-rayed. Then came out *Lakṣmī* from the ghee — Lakṣmī, the white-garmented. Then *Surā* and then the *White steed*. Then *Kaustubha*, the divine gem, sprang forth from the ghee, and shining with its rays went to the chest of Nārāyaṇa. Srī (Lakṣmī), surā, the moon, and the steed, swift as mind, went by the sun-path where the gods were. Then, Dhanvantari the god with beautiful form came out with a white pitcher in which there was *amṛta*. Seeing this wonder, there arose a loud roar among the dānavas for nectar — all saying, 'This is mine, this is mine.' (And they took it in their custody). Then came out the elephant *Airāvata* with four white tusks and huge in form. He was appropriated by Indra, the wielder of the Vajra. Then came out the poison Kālakūṭa due to intense churning, suddenly enveloping the whole world, and burning like a smoky fire. By smelling it, the three worlds got dazed. The lordly god (*Śiva*) put it in his throat (mouth) and thenceforth he was called, it is heard, Nīlakaṇṭha — (the one with blue throat). Seeing this whole wonder the dānavas lost all hope and became great enemies of the gods for nectar and Lakṣmī. Then, Nārāyaṇa, resorting to guile, took the form of an enticing belle and went to the dānavas. Those foolish ones gave that nectar to her being enamoured of her.

Then the daityas and the dānavas donning their armours and taking their various weapons ran to attack the gods. The god Viṣṇu (however) with Nara took away nectar from the king of the Dānavas for the gods. All the hosts of gods, then drank nectar from Viṣṇu, right in the tumult of the battle. Then, when the gods were drinking nectar, Rāhu (also) drank it in the disguise of a god. When it (nectar) had just reached the throat of the Dānava, the sun and the moon told it (to Viṣṇu) desiring the good of the gods. Then his head was chopped off by the god (Viṣṇu) with his disc, even as he was in the act of drinking *amṛta*. That head of the demon, resembling the peak of a mountain falling down, being cut by the disc (of Viṣṇu), produced a terrible sound. The headless body (also) fell rolling on the ground, shaking the earth with its mountains and forests. Striking enmity with the sun and the moon, eternally does Rāhu, since then, eclipse them. Then followed the fierce battle to win nectar in which the gods and the demons fought with various weapons and devices. When the battle was thus raging, Nara and Nārāyaṇa both fought with their weapons— the bow and the disc respectively. Gaining the ultimate victory, the gods placed the mountain Mandara back at its own place. Indra, with the gods, then gave that nectar to Nara to keep it safe (I. 18).

### (B) The Purāṇas

The legend of the 'Amṛtamanthana' is mentioned in various Purāṇas. The accounts tally in almost all main features, varying only in the motive for the churning and the number and the names of gems that came forth from the ocean and such other minor points.

The *Agni P.* mentions it in the context of the 'Kūrmāvatāra' (the Tortoise-incarnation).[1]

According to the *Viṣṇu P.* the whole heavenly world got powerless due to Indra's incurring a curse for the insult he inflicted on the sage Durvāsas in throwing away the garland given by him. The gods went to Brahmā who asked them to resort to Viṣṇu; and Brahmā himself went along with all the gods to Viṣṇu who was on the Northern shore of the milky ocean.[2] It does not refer to the killing of Rāhu, and the whole point is the deception of the Asuras as such by Viṣṇu taking the form of Mohinī, the belle.

The *Bhāg. P.* has the gods resorting to Bali, the king of the Asuras, to help them in churning the ocean.[3] In both the *Viṣṇu* and the *Bhag.P.* Viṣṇu himself takes the form of the tortoise, and in this point these accounts vary from that of the *Mb.* where the gods go to solicit the help of the 'King of Tortoises'. In the account of the *Bhāg. P.* the mountain Mandara is not uprooted by Śeṣa (Ananta) as we see in *Mb.* It is up-rooted by the gods and the Asuras coming together with all their force; but the golden mountain, being thus carried to the shore of the ocean slipped from their hands and crushed many gods and Asuras under its weight. Seeing them all with their arms and necks broken, Viṣṇu brought them back to life with a glance of his eye; and putting the mountain on the *back of Garuḍa* even with his hand, and mounting the bird, went with the gods and the Asuras to the ocean. Suparṇa (Garuḍa), placing the mountain in the water of the ocean, went away after being allowed by Viṣṇu.[4] There is another interesting variation in this account. When Viṣṇu took the form of a belle and took away *amṛta* from the Asuras, the latter argued that the gods and the Asuras were all the sons of Kaśyapa and hence were brothers of each other. Hence Mohinī should distribute nectar equally amongst all of them.[5]

The *Viṣṇu Dh. P.* mentions the whole account in short.[6] Here Rāhu takes the form of the sun.[7] Here we are told that the Asuras had Prahlāda as their king; and he gave away nectar to Viṣṇu in the female-form being urged by the Asuras that were enamoured of her.[8] Again it is not Rāhu himself, having enmity with the moon and sun, that eclipses the two; but it is Viṣṇu who gives the boon to the Asura that the latter would cover the two luminaries on the Parvakāla;

and that this time would be auspicious for performing penance and muttering the *mantras.* Viṣṇu, moreover, bestows the boon of immortality upon Rāhu saying that the latter had tasted nectar and as such could not be expected to die.[9]

The *Rāmāyaṇa* gives in short practically the same account as of the *Mb.* only pointing out how the thousands of '*apsarases*' became only common belles due to their being discarded by the gods and the Asuras.[10]

The *Hari V.* [10a] has practically the same account as that in the *Mb.* with only minor differences. According to it, the gods and the Asuras come together on the mountain *Gandhamādana* (and not on Meru). They smell a flower and, while pursuing the source of the same, come to the decision of churning the ocean.

We shall have to return to the various accounts further in our discussion; but the main points that are common to all the accounts can be jotted down as follows:

(i) The devas and the dānavas come together to *churn out nectar*; but ultimately, on gaining it, they fight;

(ii) *Nectar* is referred to as *Soma* (as different from Soma = the moon);[11]

(iii) Other gems also come out with nectar, but it is a secondary motive; for *amṛta* is the main cause of the contest between the gods and the Asuras;

(iv) Nectar is with the Asuras as soon as it is churned off and the gods take it back to heaven.

(v) Viṣṇu is the main incentive for the churning, the whole support, and it is he who takes it back by *resorting to deceit.*

# 2
# THE CHURNING

## (A) Soma and Samudra

In the legend under consideration *amṛta* is said to be churned out of the ocean (*Samudra*). The name of the ocean churned for getting *amṛta* is given by the *Mb* as '*Kalaśa*'.[12] This name of the '*Samudra*' probably hints at something more than a mere name. This reminds us of the fact that '*Samudra*' is also the name of the vessel that is used for pressing the Soma in sacrifices. *Soma* is said to rush to this 'Samudra' with a roaring sound.[13] *Soma* is requested to enter Samudra.[14] He is invoked to increase '*Samudra*' in volume.[15] 'Samudra' is said to be the abode of *Soma* (Indu) wherein he makes a terrible noise.[16] The receptacle of *Soma* called 'Samudra' has also another name, '*Kalaśa*'.[17] *Soma* was brought by Śyena Suparṇa from heaven,[18] which also is called 'Samudra'.[19]

Thus we get the following points about '*Samudra*'.

(i) Samudra = *Antarikṣa,* i. e. the heaven; or mid-region;
(ii) Samudra = *Soma-Kalaśa;*
(iii) Samudra = terrestrial ocean.

Now, let us see the association of the mountain and the *Soma*. *Soma* is said to be hidden in the mountain and is called '*giriṣṭhāh*'.[20] Connecting these ideas together we get to understand that *Soma*, which is in the mountains, comes to the '*Kalaśa*' which is *Samudra*. The pressing stones also are called *adri* which means *giri* (mountain).[21] Soma is said to be milked (pressed) by the ten fingers by means of the *adris.*[22] Sāyaṇa commenting on the word '*giri*' takes it to mean 'the pressing stone'.[23] The word '*giri*' is applied also to the mountain.[24] Thus in this context the words '*giri*' and '*adri*' have two meanings : —

(i) *The mountain* whence Soma is brought to be pressed into 'Samudra', i. e. the *soma-kalaśa;*

(ii) The *pressing stones* by which *Soma* is pressed into the 'Samudra', i. e. the *soma-kalaśa.*

Thus idea of *'adris'* or the *'giris'* producing *Soma* resembles closely the idea in our legend where the mountain, Mandara, is used as a means to churn out *amṛta* which is another name of Soma.[25]

The point to remember in this connection is that Soma (nectar) is produced from the impact of the *adri* or *giri* (the mountain or the pressing stones). It should not be argued that in the sacrificial pressing of Soma, the juice goes from the 'adris' to the Soma-kalaśa which is 'Samudra', while in the account in our legend nectar goes up from the Samudra below. Even in the account of the churning as it occurs in the *Mb.*, there is an indication to show the downward march of the juices before nectar actually came up. These juices themselves were as good as nectar and can very well be taken to have caused nectar to come up from the ocean. It is because of these nectar–like juices from the various plants that the gods and the demons got vigour and the gods got immortality.[26] *Mb.* and Purāṇas are one in that portion of the account which states that the *ocean was the milky one. Mb.* however, strikes a stronger note in saying that the ocean was not originally milky, but it turned milky and full of ghee due to the juices that dripped from the various plants.[27] The juices of the plants thus mixing in the *'milky Samudra'* bring to our mind the juice of Soma being mixed with milk in the '*Samudra*' — (*Soma-Kalaśa*). It is true that in the pressing of Soma, there is no indication of 'churning'. However, in *ṚV* itself there is an indication of churning, where we have *Soma* formerly 'churned' out (from the mountain; *adreḥ*), by Śyena.[28] This flight of the bird Śyena in the air (with *Soma*) can be compared with Dhanvantari coming out of the ocean, especially when both — the aerial region (Antarikṣa) and the ocean — have the name 'Samudra'. It is not improbable, hence, that the whole idea of the churning of nectar from the ocean (the terrestrial Samudra) is taken from the pressing of *Soma* in the sacrifice on the one hand and on the other, influenced by the bringing of *Soma* from the aerial region. It seems that the idea began with the bringing of *Soma* from heaven (the Samudra) by Śyena and was developed on the analogy of the pressing of *Soma* by the '*adri*' or '*giri*' into 'Samudra', the *Soma*-vessel. The word '*adri*' meaning the pressing stone, and the mountain and 'Samudra' meaning the aerial region as also the *Soma-kalaśa* and the ocean, might have lost the ancient meaning retaining only the popular ones and the whole idea of pressing *Soma* was expressed in the changed form as we have in the *Mb.*[29] The upward movement of Soma (*amṛta*) is not peculiar to the churning legend alone. We get in the *ṚV* ideas similar to this one — that the nectar-like juices drop into the ocean and nectar goes up. Thus Soma is said to *shine in the heavens* after crossing the three worlds.[30] It is said to gather into the Soma vessel and then, after being pressed, *ascends to the heavens.*[31] Soma, prattling like a child, *wants to ascend to the heavens* with waters that increase milk etc.[32] *Soma* is said to *ascend to heaven* assuming a white form.[33] Its juice protects the sacrificer and goes to the heavens (*ṚV.* IX. 97.2). Being praised by people Soma goes to heaven which is his former abode (IX. 97.6).

### (B) The Release of the Gems

The gems that came out of the sea are said to go to the gods by the path of the sun.[34] It, thus, can be seen that *the gain of nectar is associated with the release of the gems,* most of which are luminaries — or denote brilliance. The *Viṣṇu*

*P.* states that after the fight for *amrta* was over with the ultimate victory of the gods, the sun and the other luminaries began revolving along their fixed path.[35] This presupposes their being obstructed by certain other forces; and the gain of *amṛta* with the success of the gods removed this obstruction. This is similar to the Vedic idea of the release of the celestial waters, and with them, the release of the luminaries.[36] Any number of passages could be quoted to support this idea. Thus, Indra is said to have released the waters and *at the same time* he placed the sun in the sky.[37] He is said to have set in motion the floods of waters of the sea and generated the sun.[38] The waters at another place are said to be *released from the mountain* and this is followed by the release of the sun ascending to the heavens.[39] Indra won the light and the divine waters.[40] This idea of the release of waters from the mountains and the release of the sun appear to be similar to the release of the various juices from the mountain Mandara and the release of the luminaries from the ocean churned with it. The setting in motion of the waters by Indra and the sudden release of the luminaries also hint at the idea of churning the sea and the subsequent release of the various luminaries. The belief of the celestial waters and light flowing together is quite an ancient one,[41] and the same seems to be reflected in the churning of the ocean and the release of the gems. This association of the waters and the luminaries is not restricted only to the Vedic literature. The Egyptian goddess of the sky — Nut — is sometimes represented by a figure in which a band of stars is accompanied by a stream-band of waters.[42] Like the luminaries that are hidden in the waters of the ocean and come up as soon as the water of the sea is churned, or moved vigorously, we have in the *ṚV* another idea, similar to that of *Mb.*, of poison and nectar being in the waters. It is where the sacrificer speaks about Soma telling him that all medicinal herbs are contained in the waters.[43] The association of the luminaries and the waters can also be seen from the fact that, not only the sun and the moon, but even the stars are supposed to travel in boats across the firmament,[44] which, hence, could bear out its similarity to the ocean. Nectar and the luminaries can be seen to be associated with one another from the *Ṛ V*. Thus we read of *Soma* mixing with water, generating the heavenly bodies and the sun.[45] After being born, *Soma* gives strength to the sun.[46] These references are enough to show how the waters, the luminaries and Soma (nectar) are associated. The getting of *amṛta* is, as a matter of course, the gain of new life for the heavenly bodies — the gods, the stars and the other luminaries — alike. Hence also are the gods said to be devoid of lustre being devoid of nectar, and get joyous at its advent, as it brings with itself a trail of luminous objects. It is easy to understand, in this light, how the gain of *amṛta*, with the gain of the luminaries from the ocean-waters, signifies victory to the gods and the gain of the kingdom of heaven. It is in this capacity also that *Soma* (*amṛta*) is called the restorer of heavens (*svarvid*),[47] and the creator of the heavenly bodies from the waters.[48] We have already seen how Soma rises into the heavens. In the same context we also get to know the birth–place of Soma — the *yoni* — which Sāyaṇa identifies with the vessel (*kalaśa*) which[49] is also called *samudra*. Now when Soma and *amṛta* are completely identified it is easy to understand how *samudra* (the terrestrial ocean) later came to be the birth-place of *amṛta*; and, when the word Samudra came to be known in its restricted sense of the terrestrial ocean with *amṛta* hidden in it, it could lead to the idea of the churning of the ocean to produce nectar from it, the fittest churn-staff being the '*giri*' or the '*adri*', with the original meaning, viz. the 'pressing stones', forgotten. We have seen how the account in the 'churning-legend' has the water turned into milk and that again to *ghṛta*, before the actual advent of nectar. This corroborates with the Vedic idea of Soma's *yoni* being 'ghṛtavat' (full of *ghṛta*[50]). To complete the idea of the Soma-plant being pressed in the sacrifice, as it were, the 'churning' speaks of the various plants being put into the ocean to help *amṛta* spring forth rapidly.[51]

Thus the whole idea of the 'churning of the ocean' appears to have been handed down from the Vedic times, suggested from the sacrificial pressing of the Soma-plants by the pressing stones —*adris* — into the *samudra*. The luminaries coming out as soon as the waters were released, seem identical with the ocean-waters producing the luminaries when it was vigorously churned and moved. To put it finally, the following ideas seem to have been responsible for the '*churning of the ocean*' as it appears in the epic:

(i) The pressing of *Soma* by the '*adris*' and pouring it into the *kalaśa samudra*;
(ii) The waters releasing the heavenly bodies and light;
(iii) The upward movement of *Soma* from its *yoni* — the *soma-kalaśa, samudra.*

## (C) The Moving Mountain

The idea of removing the mountain from its abode and carrying it to a distance is not an uncommon one. Probably the idea goes back to the Vedic time where we have references to the mountains constantly moving from place to place. One of the exploits of Indra is to settle the mountains.[52] The same idea followed up in the later texts, where we have the mountains being called the sons of Prajāpati and constantly moving.[53] This quality of the mountains of changing their place could have easily given birth to the idea of their being lifted from their place and removed, being finally settled. Thus we have in the *Rām*. Hanūmat uprooting and carrying the Droṇagiri[54] and in the *Bhāg. P.* Kṛṣṇa lifted up the mountain Govardhana.[55] The moving mountains are also to be found in the tribal mythological thought.[56]

## (D) Fire, Rain and the Churning

*Mb.* says that the impact of the trees on the mountain used as the churn-staff produced fire, enveloping all quarters; further that Indra quenched the fire with rain.[57] In *Śup. Ad.* and also in *Mb.*, Garuḍa is said to have seen a fire around the place of *Soma*; and he quenched the same by waters brought by his 'ninety times nine' mouths before actually capturing, Soma.[58] The same account of Garuḍa's quenching the fire is followed by the Purāṇas. We have also a reference to fire encircling the place of Soma in the *Jai. Br.*,[59] where Soma is said to have been guarded by the gandharvas who are called '*agnayaḥ*' and are identified with the '*dhiṣṇyāḥ*' — i. e. the 'fire-altars'. The main current in all these ideas can easily be marked viz. the association of fire and Soma (*amṛta*). The account of fire being produced at the time of churning is conspicuously absent in the *Viṣṇu* and the *Bhāg. Purāṇas* which give the account in detail. The *Viṣṇu P.* mentions the rain, but it says that it was caused from the clouds that were formed from the poisonous vapours coming out of the mouth of Vāsuki. This rain refreshed the gods that were at the tail-end of Vāsuki.[60] It is difficult *not* to see any relation between the accounts of the Soma haraṇa and the churning of nectar in this connection. The exploit of the bringing of Somā by Śyena-Suparṇa explains, according to Bloomfield, the bringing of rain by the lightning,[61] thus having fire and rain in association. Keith maintains that the whole of the Soma sacrifice is a spell for bringing rain-water.[62] This seems to be supported by the loudly resounding 'earth-drums', giving the semblance of rumbling clouds, used at the *soma*-pressing at the sacrifice, and the '*dhiṣṇyāḥ*', the fire-altars; and the same idea, most probably, is represented in the account of the churning of nectar, with its fire and rain, or the clouds showering rain.

# 3
# THE CHURN-STAFF AND THE ROPE

## (A) Tortoise

All the accounts of the 'churning' are one on the point that the tortoise is the main support for the churn-staff (Mandara). The *Mb.* account has the gods and the Asuras going to the king of the tortoises to request him to perform the needed supporting act.[63] The Purāṇas have Viṣṇu himself taking the form of a huge tortoise to support the staff.[64] The *tortoise* is an important figure in mythology, and even Viṣṇu had to assume its form. The tortoise is, thus, the embodiment of the creative power. This identification of Viṣṇu and the tortoise could be traced even in other places. In the *Mārkaṇḍeya P.* we have Viṣṇu supporting the country in the form of the tortoise.[65] A live tortoise is placed in the altar which is the representation of the earth, elsewhere.[66] This position of the tortoise in lying at the altar-base and its position at the 'churning' explains its role as the very creator.[67] It will be interesting to note here that the tortoise plays this very important part in creation in the mythology of the tribals also. Thus, according to a Birhor tradition, the primeval waters first produced a lotus through the stalk of which the sun lord ascended to the top; and having taken his position on the full blown petals of the lotus, he caused earth to be brought out to him by a *tortoise*.[68] Risley points out that the tortoise (along with the serpent) was accepted as ancestor by almost all the original people in India.[69] This may be corroborated by the fact that a caste called 'Kurmi' is found in Bengal and Orissa. This fact has been noted by A. Lang also who refers to Risley to say that the Jagannath Kumhars of Orissa have the tortoise as one of the totems.[70] From this it seems probable that some ancient inhabitants of this land believed in the tortoise as the great creator and when the belief got assimilated into the Vedic religion the tortoise was identified with Visnu and Prajāpati. The tortoise gained this importance, probably, due to its resemblance to the (cosmic) egg, from which Brahmā is said to have originated, its two shells giving the idea of the upper and the lower world (heaven and earth) which can also be seen in the case of the egg.[71] It is interesting to note the similarity between the Birhor tradition referred to above, and the idea of Brahmā coming out of the navel of Viṣṇu,[72] in both the lotus-stalk playing an important part as an offshoot of creation. The sun, in the Birhor tradition, it may be noted, does the same work as is said of Viṣṇu, in causing the tortoise to work for creation — the tortoise in the Birhor tradition creating the earth, while the epic one, urged by Viṣṇu, creating the very nectar necessary for the created to live long, thus indicating the continuity of creation. In the churning-legend we have the gods asking the tortoise to work up for nectar, and also Viṣṇu himself taking its form. The latter idea is the same as the tortoise working up with the energy of Viṣṇu. The Birhor idea of the sun sitting on the lotus also tallies with the Purāṇic account of the churning where Viṣṇu himself is said to press the Mandara from above.[72a] More so when the sun is said to be only another form of Viṣṇu and they are identified. Now Viṣṇu, as the tortoise in the ocean, presents another interesting point. Viṣṇu (the sun) on the top, and Viṣṇu, (the tortoise) at the lower end of the churn-staff, gives a complete idea of the whole creation being lorded over by Viṣṇu, and the same idea can be seen where Viṣṇu is said to have given his prowess to the gods and the Asuras,[73] thus practically the whole process being in his control. In the present context the tortoise is particularly suited to be at the lower end of the churn-staff. Not only is it apt to give the idea of being at the source of all beings and creation, but also, due to its shape, it indicates the lower wheel of the churn-staff of which the sun (Viṣṇu) is the other at the top. Thus, the two forms of Viṣṇu (i. e. the one indicating the sun at the top and the other, the tortoise) represent two wheels — the upper and the lower. The lotus, on the other hand, has always been a symbol of the sun and of creation.[74] Thus the churn-staff comes to be united with two wheels at the two ends. The idea is very much similar to that in the *Jai. Up. Br.* [75] that the heaven and earth are firmly fixed and are kept apart, by the column of atmosphere, like two wheels, attached to an axis.[76] The sun which is believed to stand over the navel of the earth at the top of the axis expresses the same idea as Viṣṇu at the top of the Mandara, with the tortoise at the bottom. The tortoise at the bottom of the churn-staff and the sun (Viṣṇu) at the top can also be compared with practically the same idea expressed in Viṣṇu at the bottom and the lotus (the sun) at the top with Brahmā on, the whole picture, again symbolising creation. The staff of the Mandara seems, thus, to be another form of the idea of the lotus-stalk coming out of the navel of Viṣṇu sleeping in the Milky sea (the ocean in our legend) and the lotus-stalk coming out of water in the Birhor tradition. The idea in the lotus-stalk having Brahmā at the top is closer to the idea in the churning legend inasmuch as in both of these we have Brahmā and Viṣṇu having a combined effort for creation. The gods, it may be noted, go to Brhamā who directs them, and goes with them, to Viṣṇu for churning the ocean.

The figure of the tortoise is a common feature to be found in Hindu temples. Generally it is in the central place in the temple.[77] Even in the Agni-cayana at the sacrifice, *a live tortoise* is buried in the lowest layer of the bricks as noted earlier. Sometimes, however, the tortoise in the temple is simply represented by a hexangular figure. Its position is generally in front of the main shrine of the god and gives an idea of the pivotal position of the creature in the 'churning'.

Not only is the tortoise thus represented in the temples of the Hindus of India, but it also plays an important part in some of the Balinese temples. In some such Balinese temples it is usual to find the whole structure of the temple resting on the figure of a tortoise, whose head, four legs, and the small tail appear to be emerging out, as it were, from the basement of the building. It is also of no little interest to note that, the temples that are built upon such a basement of the tortoise, are called *Meru*, and have a 'Padmāsana of the sun' atop. The creature represents the *'fire-tortoise'* called *'Kūrmāgni', 'Bedwāgni' or 'Bedwānala'* (Sanskit, *Vaḍavānala*), on which the earth is supposed to rest.[78]

The following points are to be noted from this description :—

(i) The tortoise is represented as an auspicious creature on which rests the whole temple-structure, indicating thereby the whole earth and the abode of gods resting on it. This is very similar to saying that the tortoise is the main support of creation and comes very close to the idea of the Birhor tradition in which the creature actually brings up the earth. It also strikes a remarkable similarity with the tortoise which is the main support of the Mandara — the churn-staff — and is the very pivot — or the very navel of creation;

(ii) The 'Meru' resting on the tortoise suggests the Mandara mountain in our legend; Meru is the 'spine' of the universe;

(iii) The 'Padmāsana' dedicated to the sun-god brings out its similarity with the lotus-stalk with a full blown flower on the top of it with the sun on it, as conceived in the Birhor tradition, and also the lotus-stalk coming out of the navel pit of Viṣṇu, with Brahmā atop.

It will, thus, be seen how the whole idea of the churning of the ocean represents the act of creation, in a way, and is found, with a few variations, in the ideas[79] we have just mentioned.

### (B) Vāsuki

We have noted the remarkable similarity between the 'Meru' and the 'Padmāsana' of the Balinese temple on the one hand and the churning-mountain with Viṣṇu (the sun at the top) on the other. We have also noticed that the tortoise is common to both — the churning, as the support of the mountain Mandara, and the structure of the 'Meru'. Now, the whole structure of the 'Meru' has also a gigantic serpent figuring into it, which brings it closer to the 'churning' legend. The serpent is said to contract the too violent movements of the 'Fire-tortoise' (Kūrmāgni). Vogel rightly remarks that the gigantic (serpent) represents the world serpent. The 'Meru' of Pur Badur at the foot of the great volcano has two such nāgas.[80]

Though the Serpent at the basement of these temples with the tortoise may not have any direct resemblance to Vāsuki, the churn-cord in the churning of the sea, it has a definite indication of resemblance. We have noted how the churning of the ocean stands as the symbol of creation. We have also noted how the tortoise is associated with the idea of creation. The same is true of the serpent. It will be good to recall here Risley's finding about the castes in Bengal and Orissa and his conclusion that both the serpent and the tortoise were supposed to be the most ancient ancestors by the people of this land, thus hinting at the serpent's share in the creation of the world. The serpent is often associated with progeny and is worshipped by women as the giver of it.[81] Hence, it is quite natural that he should find an important place in the churning legend which symbolizes creation. The serpent in this legend, thus, seems to be a general one and the name Vāsuki seems to have found place in it only as the great serpent-king known to mythology. The serpent in the churning legend has another important point to present. We have noted how the vapours coming out of the serpent's mouth were said to be turned into clouds which showered rain. This has a suggestion which supports the 'creative' aspect of the legend. The serpent as the controller of rain is an idea common to many a mythological thought,[82] and, hence it is from this point of view also that the serpent in the churning legend is appropriately utilised.

### (C) The Gems

The gems that came out of the ocean are not all the same in the various accounts of the 'churning'. According to the *Mb.* the gems number eight in all and are — (i) the moon, (ii) Lakṣmī, (iii) Surā (wine), (iv) the white steed Uccaiḥśravas (v) Kaustubha, (vi) Dhanvantari with the pitcher of *amṛta,* (vii) Airāvata and (viii) Kālakūṭa, the poison.

The Rāmāyaṇa has only six —viz. (i) Dhanvantari, (ii) the Apsarases, (iii) Vāruṇi (the wine), (iv) Uccaiḥśravas, (v) Kaustubha and (vi) *amṛta.*

It can be marked that the *Rām.* takes *amṛta* and Dhanvantari as two different ones and not associated with each another. It drops Lakṣmī, the moon, Airāvata and the poison. It should be noted, however, that in certain recensions of the *Rām.* in place of *amṛta* we have *Soma,* but that does not signify the moon; for, in that case, nectar would be left out. Dhanvantari is not said to have come out with the pitcher of nectar. But, in yet other recensions we get the whole account of the *Mb.*[83]

In the account of the *Agni. P,*[84] the moon, the horse and the Airāvata are not mentioned but, we have the tree Pārijāta, the cows (desire-yielding) and the Apsarases in addition, the gems in all being eight in number as in *Mb.*

In the *Viṣṇu P.*[85] also eight is the number of the gems, but no mention is made of the horse, the Kaustubha and Airāvata, while as in the *Agni P.,* we have the Pārijatā, the cow Surabhi (only one and not many cows), and the Apsarases.

The *Bhāg. P.*[86] has ten gems in all. It leaves out the moon, retaining all others as in *Mb.* and adding Kāmadhenu, Pārijāta and the Apsarases as in the other accounts.

It will be interesting to see how the Indian motif of the legend of the Churning of the Ocean appears elsewhere. We have noted that the account of the churning of the ocean gives *kalaśa* as the name of the ocean. Now the *kalaśa* means a vessel; and it is exactly in this form that the Zuni Indian myth (America) has it. In this myth the Primeval Mother is said to have a terraced bowl in which she poured some water in the beginning of Creation. She, then, spat into it[87] and whipped the liquid rapidly with her forefinger. It soon formed into foam and rose up to the brim of the pot. The Mother blew up the foam, which went into the skies and returned as spray into the churning-spot. "See", said the Mother, "the bowl is, as if, the world; the rim its farthest limits . . . whence white clouds shall rise, float away and, bursting, shed spray, that my children shall drink the Water of Life".[88]

The vessel of the Primeval Mother is the Ocean (*Kalaśa*) in the *Mahābhārata*-myth; and it is indicative of the generative pot. The motif of the churning and spraying is present in the account of *Mb.* in the fact, that the churning of the ocean generates huge masses of smoke from the mouth of the serpent Vāsuki, forming into clouds and showering rain.

In the Japanese mythology, the semi-divine personae — Izanagi and Izanami (brother and sister) — are said to have been told by the senior gods to "make and consolidate" the "drifting island". They were given the "*ama-no-tama-bo-ko*" (the celestial jewel-spear). The pair stood on the "floating bridge of Heaven" which is said to be the Rain-bow or the Heavenly Rock-boat, and pushed down the "*tama boko*" till it reached the ocean. According to the Japanese text — *Ko-ji-ki* — they stirred the brine until the water began to get curdled. When the water got thickened the pair withdrew the spear. Some substance attached to the end of the spear now dropped off and fell in the ocean below. And the first ever island was formed.[89] In a Japanese illustration of the churning myth,[90] in its variant form, the churning-mountain rests on a tortoise, and the supreme god rests on its summit. This god on the summit holds in one of his arms a water vase, which is similar to the description of the god Dhanvantari [91] holding a pitcher of *amṛta* in his hand. In the Japanese version, we have just noted, the sun emerges from the churned-up ocean.

The complex Hindu churning-myth also reached Old America. Unlike the Zuni myth noted above, we have here the tortoise, which shifts the myth from its simplicity as marked in the Zuni myth. But the thing that is remarkable is that the tortoise is on the summit of the mountain-pestle. The serpent-rope is, however, in the proper place. Two dark gods, like the Hindu Asuras, hold one end of the serpent, while the other one is held by an elephant-headed god.[92] The churning of the gems from the ocean has an interesting parallel in Old America, where two gods churn gems and gem-strings, indicative of children.[93] The primordial ocean, according to the Egyptians of the ancient times, was not nothing. It was full of the "*Waters of Life*". It was known as NUN and was the "Father of Gods" [94]

## (D) A Few Interpretations

Held [95] holds that the whole legend of the 'churning of the ocean' is only an expression of the principle of '*Pravṛtti*' and '*Nivṛtti*'. He says, "We presume that the word *Pravṛtti* (turning forward) is suggestive of the churn-staff moving from left to right when the churn-cord is pulled by the gods[96] and the word '*Nivṛtti*', as implying the 'turning back' again, the turning of the churn-staff from right to left, when the churn-cord is pulled by the demons." He compares with this turning the '*right turn*' in the ritual of producing fire, when the officiating priest gives the fire-drill three turns to the right, and his turning the fire-drill back again as enjoined. But as to whether or not there be any connection between the idea of *'Pravṛtti'* and *'Nivṛtti'* on the one hand, and the turning of the churn-staff on the other, Held himself is doubtful, as is clear from his admitting the fact, due to lack of evidence.

While it is not altogether improbable to establish or suppose any connection between these ideas, it seems far remote to assume that it would be the main idea in the churning of the ocean. Nivṛtti is associated with Death, when the work of creation should be supposed to end, as opposed to Pravṛtti. On the other hand, the whole process of the churning of the ocean is to obtain the juice of immortality meaning the nullification of Death which is associated with Nivṛtti. Both the 'forward' (left to right) and backward (right to left) movements *together* help the advent of nectar. Hence it would not be proper to associate the 'backward' pull with 'Nivṛtti'. The whole process, as we have already seen, is a symbolic act of creation. Held's comparison of the three pulls to the right by the officiating priest in producing fire also does not seem to fit in the context here, unless we definitely know what the three backward pulls signify. As a mater of fact it would be better, and proper, to take all the left-to-right and the back-again pulls helping create-fire, the whole act symbolizing creation. We have seen how in the 'churning' myth the idea is similar to the one in the lotus-stalk and the creation of the universe or the earth. Hence, the 'churning' should not be taken as an isolated case. In all the ideas we have referred to, i.e. the 'churning', the lotus-stalk with Brahmā atop, the Birhor tradition with the lotus-stalk, and also the idea of the primeval waters producing a lotus and Prajāpati's making up the earth with mud-particles brought from below, one principle is common. While the lotus symbolises creation, it also symbolises the sun (and in the Birhor tradition he is actually there), which suggests the nullification of Death and the very power to procreate, as is suggested from the name *Savitṛ*. The same idea of creation is to be found in churning, as is seen from the bright gems that come up. Savitṛ and immortality go hand in hand; and the gain of nectar is the same as gaining the light of the sun or the very essence of the sun-power.[97] The main idea, thus, seems to be the gain of immortality and, with it, the continuation of creation. It is the main idea of the gods that sat in conference on the top of Meru. It is, thus, off the mark to understand Death or Nivṛtti by the backward turn of the churn-staff. It is also not sure whether it is the gods that gave the forward (left to right) turn, as there is no clear indication of it in the legend anywhere. One thing, however, can be said about 'Nivṛtti' here. Nivṛtti can be said to be the state *before the churning* began, when the whole water of the ocean (i.e. the primeval water) was calm and serene without any sign of life, wherein all the luminaries — the moon, the Lakṣmī, the Kaustubha etc. — were hidden. This also goes well with the anxiety of the gods about getting the juice of life. This state of affairs is exactly similar to the one when the waters are said to be blocked, or in captivity, and the sun and the whole life and light are said to be in the *lap of Nivṛtti* (*nirṛti*).[98] This state is to be broken and the planting of the perpendicular mountain in our legend, or the lotus-stalk in the other accounts, is symbolic of this change as a start to creation. Nivṛtti is thus the state before the actual churning began and when the waters are churned, it all is a process of creation and the gain of immortality — all the turns helping this process, irrespective of their being 'forward' or 'backward' and caused by the pull by the gods or by the Asuras. All these turns in the churning thus signify life, with its action (*gati*).

Oldham[99] makes a cut and dry work of the whole idea of the churning, fixing his attention on Vāsuki, the churn-cord. According to him the churning by means of the Nāga king Vāsuki, "*no doubt* refers to the commerce carried on by this chief or his subjects in distant lands on both sides of the mountain Mandara lying east-west."

Oldham does not support his statement by definite facts. The predominance of the Nāga clans in the various parts of India cannot be denied,[100] but to say that the churning with the king of the nāgas (Vāsuki) is symbolic of the commerce of the Nāga-king and the nāgas, is not quite acceptable, though the idea in itself is quite a fine piece of fertile imagination.[101] This opinion of Oldham presents certain doubts. If Vāsuki on both the sides of the churn-staff (Mandara) represents the commerce and control of the king of the powerful nāga clans, it is not quite clear why he is given such a position that seems to be a lowly one. The indications of the churning legend also go against this hypothesis of Oldham; for, as partaker in the gains of the churning, the Nāgas never feature though amongst those who churned the ocean they are mentioned.[102] In all probability the Mandara does not have any geographical implication here; but means simply a mountain, irrespective of its position. The mountains Meru and Mandara are often coupled together as the highest of the mountains without any special reference, in such cases, to their geographical position. The mountain Mandara comes in this legend not primarily as the Mandara that lies East-west as Oldham thinks; but only as a mountain. The mountain might have crept in the account on the analogy of the *'adri'* or *'giri'*, the *'pressing stone'* but later on, when the original implications of the words *giri* (the pressing stone) and *samudra* (the vessel of Soma) gave place to their secondary ones, the *giri* (mountain) that could churn the great *samudra* (ocean) came to be identified with Mandara, the mountain famous for its height. Both the Meru and the Mandara, figure in the legend, and the Mandara alone was chosen as the churn-staff, probably, because 'Meru' was to be left out being the place of the gods in consultation. That the name Mandara does not have any special significance other than that of its height, can also be seen from the fact that the Balinese temples, representing the whole structure of the 'churning', as it were — complete with the tortoise, the serpent and the mountain — have the word 'Meru' attached to them, and not Mandara. The snake Vāsuki also does not seem to have any historical significance in the legend, and is to be taken primarily as the world serpent — the source of creation and the controller of rain.[103] Vāsuki is brought in simply because of its being well known and does not seem to have any more importance than the serpent 'Ananta — Śeṣa,[104] who is employed to uproot the mountain.

It is, thus, clear that the serpent Vāsuki and the mountain Mandara, together with the tortoise, represent the creative principles, as the lotus-stalk and the tortoise in other tales.

Geldner thinks that the legend of the churning of the ocean has a probable origin in the *Ṛgveda* (V. 2. 3) where the words *'amṛtam'-viprkvat'* occur with which the high priest at the sacrifice throws ghee in to the fire. The word *amṛtam* used for ghee, according to him, gives the idea of nectar separating itself in the process of churning.[105] He opines, that the coming out of the horse *Uccaiḥśravas* in the 'churning' is also indicated in *ṚV* (I. 163.1).[106] The idea of the horse (called Uccaiḥśravas), is quite an old one, and his coming out of the ocean is indicated even in the *Ś. Br.*, where the horse is said to be beyond the sea.[107] Sāyaṇa gives a twofold meaning of *samudra* — (i) the aerial ocean and (ii) the sun.[108] Sāyaṇa takes Purīṣa to mean water.[109] Thus the idea of the horse being born from the water or from *samudra* (the aerial region) is complete. *'Samudra'* as the birthplace of the horse is also mentioned in other Vedic texts. Thus we read in the *Tait. Sam.* that *'Samudra'* is the 'yoni' of the horse, and *samudra* is his kin.' [110] The same occurs in the Ś. Br.[111] The *Vāj. Sam.* clearly refers to the horse being produced from the water.[112]

The horse Uccaiḥśravas, probably, is the same horse referred to above and may be originally the sun coming out of waters in the *antarikṣa* and later was called Uccaiḥśravas, coming out of the waters of the ocean.

### (E) The Element of Deceit

The defeat of the Asuras by the gods after nectar was captured is the last phase of the legend of 'churning'. This victory is won chiefly by Viṣṇu by resorting to deceit and capturing nectar from the Asuras. We have referred to this point in the variations of the account that are found in the Purāṇas. The main point in short is that Viṣṇu, taking the form of a woman went to Asuras and, enticing them by her (!) beauty, wrested nectar from them. Rāhu, the Asura, took the form of a god; and, sitting in line with the gods, tried to drink nectar; but no sooner had the drink entered his throat, than Viṣṇu cut his head off, thus rendering him devoid of *amṛta*. Thus, the deceit is twofold:

(i) Deceit by the gods — represented by Viṣṇu; and
(ii) Deceit on the part of the Dānavas, Rāhu representing them.

The idea of sending a woman to entice the enemy for the gain of *amṛta* is not special to the churning legend. The same idea could be found in the *Ś. B.*, where we have Soma ultimately won by the gods by sending Vāk (speech). According to the account, while Gāyatrī was carrying Soma to the gods from heaven, the gandharva Viśvāvasu stole him (Soma) from her. The gods were aware of this. They thought, "The gandharvas are fond of women; let us send Vāk (speech) to them, and she will return to us with Soma." They, accordingly sent Vāk to the gandharvas. The gandharvas came after her and said to the gods — "Soma shall be yours and Vāk ours". The gods agreed to it and further said to the gandharvas, "If she (Vāk) comes back to us, do not carry her back by force." When the gods got Soma thus, and the gandharvas took Vāk, the gods allured Vāk by singing and playing on the lute and she left the gandharvas and came over to the gods.[113]

The tale bears a close similarity to the account of our legend where Viṣṇu — the female — brings back nectar. The points that are common are follows:

(i) Vāk (female) carried *Soma* to the gods, as Mohinī carried nectar;

(ii) *Soma*, as soon as it was on its way to the gods, was captured by Viśvāvasu, the gandharva; in our legend *amṛta*, as soon as it was churned out, was taken away by the Asuras.

The other point, where the Asura Rāhu takes the form of the sun and sits in the line of the gods to take part in the drinking of nectar and is ultimately thrown away has also a very fine parallel in the Brāhmaṇa texts. It is the tale of Śaṇḍa and Marka. These Asuras come in the context of the 'Śukra' and the 'Manthin' cups. They are addressed and called for drinking Soma and are said to be ultimately duped and thrown off without Soma. Thus we have in the *Ś. B.* — "Śaṇḍa and Marka are Asura and Rakṣas; for them (are the 'Śukra' and the 'Manthin' cups) taken; to the gods are (those cups) offered."[114]

Here the fact that the Soma-offering is taken for these Asuras is similar to Rāhu's sitting in line with the gods and taking a mouthful while, the throwing away of these Asuras resembles Rāhu's head being chopped off. Śaṇḍa and Marka are also said to be the preceptors of the Asuras.[115] It is not improbable that both these ideas in the churning legend, i.e. the sending of Mohinī and the defeat of the Asura Rāhu[116] have their root in the Brahmaṇa accounts just referred to.

## SUMMARY AND CONCLUSION

The idea of the churning of the ocean is not a new one and can be traced in the Vedic literature, as we note in Vedic passages, where Soma, spoken as *amṛta,* is said to be rising up to the heaven from the *'Samudra'* which is the name for the Soma vessel. The *'Samudra'* meaning the Soma-vessel also is called 'Kalaśa' which tallies with the name of the ocean in *Mb* that was churned by the gods and the Asuras to get *amṛta*. The mountain (Mandara) is a changed form of the pressing stones called *'adri'* or *'giri'*. The juice of the Soma plant presssed into the vessel of *Soma* seems to have suggested the idea of the various fluids dripping into the ocean from the mountain Mandara. The idea of these fluids changing the whole water of the ocean into milk and further into *ghṛta* is parallel to the idea of Soma getting mixed with the milk in the vessel of Soma, and seems to have been suggested from it. The aerial atmosphere being called *'Samudra'* also might have suggested the idea of the churning inasmuch as the heavenly bodies move in it. The Vedic idea of the various luminaries being free to move as soon as the waters are released, most probably, suggested the idea of the gems coming out of the water of the ocean that is vigorously moved in the process of churning. The phase of the ocean — still and serene before the vigorous movements of churning, concealing the gems in its depth — looks very much similar to the state of the streams of waters that are held captive (and hence are to be released) with all the luminaries kept hidden by some demon. The stirring of the ocean is symbolic of the beginning of the act of creation. The mountain Mandara, reminding us of the Vedic *'adri'* or *'giri'* stands also as a symbol of creation and resembles the first lotus-stalk that comes out of the primeval waters. The tortoise and Vāsuki, are also symbols of creation. Vāsuki, as also the mountain Mandara, do not signify any particular entity; it is the world-serpent signifying the creating spirit like the tortoise. The serpent and the tortoise, it is probable, have been the gift of popular belief. The legend of the churning, as it is given in *Mb*, thus, seems to have its roots in the Vedic literature, especially in the sacrificial ritual of the pressing of Soma. This original idea got influenced by the popular belief about creation and the whole account got a bit of fashioning up when it was actually incorporated in the Mahābhārata.

## The Motif Underlying the Three Legends

We have studied three legends from the *Mb.* up-till now. These legends present some common points which are: —

(i) Nectar or immortality (*Soma*) or the lore of immortality is with somebody who is inimical to the aspirants of it;
(ii) It has to be gained by cunning and deceit;
(iii) The aspirant has to undergo severe strain; and
(iv) The ultimate supremacy is of the aspirant who is successful. The same applies to the gods who aspire for it.

All these points with a bit of variation here and there could be found to be present in all the three legends. If we view the Garuḍa legend from this point of view, we see that *Soma* was with Indra, who is a god; it was protected by gods. Now a question might be asked as to how we could say that Garuḍa was inimical to the gods when later Viṣṇu favours Garuḍa, and Indra gets reconciled with him? But, looking minutely, the position is as follows : —

(i) Garuḍa goes to fetch nectar not of himself, but as he is forced by the nāgas;
(ii) The nāgas (or the serpents) then come to be in the possession of nectar;
(iii) Indra takes it back with Garuḍa's consent. Garuḍa's fight with Indra to get nectar is only apparent, the main fight being with the nāgas who put it as a condition for the freedom of Garuḍa's mother. Thus the main point is the gain of nectar to have freedom from the enemy; and, in this way, we can see how the nāgas are virtually instrumental in the gain of nectar. The point becomes clearer when the nāgas are actually in the possession of nectar, while Indra

and Garuḍa (now on the same side) wrest it from them resorting to trick and bring it back to the side of the gods. Nectar was to be brought back to the gods, from the nāgas, lest the latter should become immortal. Here we have the old note of the constant competition for immortality. The supremacy of Garuḍa, the aspirant for nectar, over Indra and the gods on the one hand and over the nāgas on the other can also be marked.

Very much similar to this legend is the legend of the churning, and hence we shall note that before the legend of Kaca. The Asuras and the gods, together, churn the ocean with great strain. Nectar comes out and is at once appropriated by the Asuras. Viṣṇu resorts to deceit and takes *amṛta* away from the Asuras. The further similarity of the motif in this legend with that in the legend of Garuḍa is seen when Rāhu is introduced. Rāhu takes the form of a god and sits in the line of the gods. Nectar is actually served to him and then, *when it was yet to reach his throat*, it is cut. This is exactly what happens in the Garuḍa legend. The nāgas, the enemies of the gods because of their possession of nectar, are shown the pitcher of nectar. They are almost in the possession of it; and, when they are in a state of complacency over the gain, they are deprived of it. Viṣṇu taking away *amṛta* from the Asuras, can be compared here with Indra taking it from the nāgas. Viṣṇu is actually identified with Indra later even in the legend of Garuḍa in taking nectar away from the nāgas, in one place in the *Sk. P.,* as we have already noticed while discussing that legend. In the 'churning' legend also, it could be noticed, the gods, after great physical fight and the employment of deceit gain *Soma* (*amṛta*) and subsequently dupe the Asuras. This is quite similar to Garuḍa's gaining superiority to the nāgas after capturing *amṛta* (*Soma*)

Kaca's account is quite simple. He undergoes torture

before gaining the lore of immortality. The gain of the lore of immortality by Kaca, the son of Bṛhaspati, leads the gods to ultimate victory over, and superiority to, the Asuras, as also it leads Kaca to superiority to Śukra, the enemy-priest.

The gain of immortality as suggested by the capture of *Soma*, or by the gain of the lore of immortality, is a principle not peculiar to these three legends. It is an underlying principle throughout the Vedic literature and we have seen how the very aim of sacrificial consecration and the initiation for the Vedic study is to gain immortality, the same being present in the expressions, common in the Vedas, where the poets always aspire for the light of the sun, and hate to be away from him, or being devoid of his light. This principle is the supreme principle of life; and, to gain immortality, it is no evil even to cheat the forces that block it. Numerous places are to be found in the Vedic literature where we have the sacrifice running away from the gods and they have to get it back coaxing it or cheating the Asuras. There seems to be a constant struggle for supremacy between two forces inimical to one another and that supremacy is to be gained either by acquiring nectar, or the lore of immortality or the very sacrifice which leads to immortality, or heaven. The same is the principle expressed in a variety of tales. We have already pointed this fact by referring to various tales — that of the gods who created two illusions (or devices) competing with each other, that of Indra, who tried to get nectar from the mouth of Śuṣṇa, that of Indra, who knows the secret of the success of gods and ultimately urges Uśanā to create a pillar leading to heaven and see the immortal world. The same is true about the tale of the 'Citrā-brick', where Indra demolishes the column erected by the Asuras to reach heaven, the abode of immortality, thus leaving the Asuras devoid of immortality and making the chances for the gods to acquire it brighter. The same also is true of the account of Śaṇḍa and Marka, as we have already noted.

One more point, common to these three legends, is that

rival forces come together in the gain of immortality. The nāgas and Garuḍa cause nectar to be brought. It is the competition between these two — or rather Kadrū and Vinatā — that is responsible for the advent of nectar. This is clear when we know that the gods are said to actually create these rival forces for the aim, i.e., for the gain of nectar. The Asuras and the gods — rivalling with one another before and after the gain of nectar — actually come together to 'churn' *amṛta*. Kaca and Śukra — the preceptor and the initiate— likewise, can be seen to unite (as *'garbha'* and *'garbhin'*) for the gain of the lore of immortality.

In these tales of cunning, contrivance and deceit to gain immortality there is the desire to negate death, at the basis. There is indication of the central problem: Can man be immortal? However, the legends treated here do not speak of the gain of immortality on the part of the humans. Though Kaca is said to be a mortal (*Mb*. I. 76. 47, where Śukra tells Devayānī, "A girl like you should not grieve for a mortal" *na trādṛśī martyam anuśocate*), he is not an ordinary mortal; and the gain is ultimately for the gods. This is a clear message of these legends.

The unsuccessful quest for the gain of immortality, or for the means to acquire it, places these legends in line with such other accounts as of the mighty bird, Zu, or of Gilgamesh. In the former case, the bird steals the 'tablets of Destiny', outwitting Bel, the lord of the gods. The moon-god is sent to attack Zu. Later, the sun-god contrives a plan. He asks the serpents and their mother for help. A wild bull is killed. The serpents, alongwith their mother, conceal themselves in its entrails. When Zu sees the bull, he begins to devour it. When, ultimately, he reaches the entrails, the serpents attack him. They bite off his pinions and ruin his claws; and they throw the bird in a pit. As the clay tablet is mutilated, it is difficult to know what heppened to the 'tablets of Destiny'. But it could be understood that they were recovered by the gods, and Destiny remained a closed secret for mortals.

We could see the pattern, and read 'nectar' in place of the 'tablets of Destiny'. In the account of Gilgamesh, this hero is the king of Uruk. He steals the 'plant of immortality' to revive Enkidu (who is his alter ego), who is dead. However, a serpent seizes it on the way, when Gilgamesh places it on the ground and goes to fetch water. The plant of immortality is lost. In the Hindu context, when the myth of the gain of *Soma* is told, the actors are all divine —, or supra-mortal. In the legend of 'churning', the actors are not mortals. When the myth of the gain of *Soma* is employed to glorify rituals (as in the texts noted in our discussion of the legends), the pressed out *Soma* is drunk by the priests and the sacrificer. But they are not *mortals*. On the plane of the ritual, they are supra-mortals — semi-divine!

## References

1. *Agni P.* IV.1 ff.
2. *Viṣṇu P.* 1.9.
3. *Bhāga. P.* VIII.6.
4. *Ibid.*, 35.39.
5. *Ibid.* IX.7.
6. *Viṣṇu. Dh. P.* I.40 ff.
7. *Ibid.*, I.42-43.
8. *Ibid.* 26 and 27.
9. *Ibid.*, 42.33 ff.
10. *Rām.* I.45.15 ff (Mylapore, Madras, 5, 1958).

10a. *Hari V.* Bhaviṣya Parvan, 30.

11. Cf. *Viṣṇu Dh. P.* I.42.46.
    *pītaśeṣam athādāya somam. . .*
    Also *Rām.* I.45.27, where we have a variant reading as *somo devas tathaiva ca.* in the place of *tathaivāmṛtam uttamam.*
    The *Hari. V.* has (cf. Bhaviṣya Parvan-30.6 ff).
    *mathnīmaḥ somajam jalam.*
12. *Mb.* I.17.12. *mathyatām kalaśodadhiḥ.*
13. Cf. *ṚV.* IX.107.21. *samudre vācam invasi.*
14. *Ibid.*, IX.63.23. *indo samudramā viśa.*
15. *Ibid.*, IX.29.3. *vardhā samudram.*

16. *Ibid.* IX.26.6.
17. *Ibid.* IX.17.4; 18.7; 8.1. etc.
18. Cf. Garuḍa legend for various quotations for Somāharaṇa, *supra.*
19. *ṚV.* X.98.5.
20. Cf. *RV.* IX.62.4; also IX.18.1.
    Also
    "अंशोः पीयूषमपिबो गिरिष्ठाम् ।"
21. Cf. *ṚV.* IX.39.6. *harim hinvanti adribhiḥ.*
22. *Ibid.* 80.5.
23. Cf. on *ṚV.* IX.95.4; 98.9.
24. Cf. *ṚV.* I.154.2; 180.2.
25. *ṚV.* IX.74.4.
26. *Mb.* I.18.27.
27. Cf. *Viṣṇu P.* IX.77 *'Kṣīrābdhau';*
    *Bhāg.* P. VIII.6.22 *'Ksīrodadhau'.*
    *Mb.* I.18.18.
    Cf. also *Hari V.*, Bhaviṣya Parvan, 30.27.
28. Cf. *ṚV.* IX.77.2. *śyeno mathāyat.*
    also *Ibid.* I.93.6. In the first half in the line fire is said to have been brought by Mātariśvan from heaven; in the second half Śyena is said to have 'churned' Soma (*amathnāt*).
29. In this connection, I recall my talk with (now late) Dr. P.K. Gode of the *B.O.R.I.* (Poona) who mentioned about a painting which depicted the 'Amṛta-manthana' as is found in the account of *Mb.* In this painting, in place of the ocean, the churn-staff was actually placed in a big tub-like thing. This painting could not be traced by me. (I believe in its existence relying upon Dr. Gode). The big tub comes very near to the idea of the *Soma-kalaśa* (which is the 'Samudra' in the *Mb* legend). See Appendix F.
30. *RV.* IX.17.5.
31. *Ibid.* IX.40.2 and Sāyaṇa on *dhruve sadasi, dyuloke* (heaven)
32. *Ibid.* IX.74.1.
    *svar . . . siṣāsati* and Sāyaṇa — *somaḥ svaḥ svargalokam sambhaktum icchati.*

Probably because of this quality of being in the heaven — attributed to *Soma* — and arriving on earth and again going up back, he is called the supporting pillar of the Heaven and Earth; for the idea see, *ṚV.* IX.74.2, *divaḥ skambhaḥ*; also IX.87.2. *viṣṭambho divo dharuṇaḥ pṛthivyāḥ*.

33. *Ibid.* IX.74.7; on the advent of Soma and its imagery, see Dange, *Images from Vedic Hymns and Rituals*, pp. 85-92.
34. *Mb.* I.18.37; cf. *yato devās tato jagmuḥ*.
According to the *Viṣṇu P.* even the sun goes up with his full light after the gain of *amṛta* — (note 35). This presupposes complete darkness everywhere before the 'churning' of the ocean, which itself would be a big mass of darkness. This is exactly what the Egyptians of old believed, R.T. Rundle Clark, *Myth and Symbol in Ancient Egypt*, pp. 50, 52; the name is Nun.
35. *Viṣṇu P.* I.9.113.
*tataḥ prasannābhaḥ sūryaḥ prayayau svena vartmanā jyotīṁṣi ca yathāmārgam..* .
36. Cf. Tilak, *Arctic Home in the Vedas*, Poona, 1956, p. 250.
37. *ṚV.* I.51.4; also 52.8 etc.
38. *Ibid.* II.19.3.
39. *Ibid.* I.32.4; VI.30.5.
40. *Ibid.* III.34.8.
41. *Arctic Home,* p. 249.
For fuller discussion on this point see the chapter "Vedic Myths — The captive waters."
42. *Ibid.*, p. 258.
43. *ṚV.* I.23.20. Poison may not be supposed to be bad. It can also serve as a medicine. Its place among the gems speaks for its goodness.
44. Cf. Lockyer, *The Dawn of Astronomy*, p. 35., referred to by Tilak in the *Arctic Home*, p. 258.
45. *ṚV.* IX.42.1.
46. *Ibid.*, IX.97.31.
47. *Ibid.* IX.84.5, *svarvidam*; also IX.8.I; — 106.4.
48. *Ibid.* IX.2.1.
49. *Ibid.* IX.40.2; note 31, *supra*.
50. Cf. Soma addressed to, *ṚV.* IX.82.1.
For the *Mb.* idea, see I.18.18.

We are not concerned about the meaning of the word '*ghṛta*'. Suffice it to mark that the word '*ghṛta*' remained in literature with the restricted meaning, like '*giri*'. It may be noted, the words used in the legend are *payaḥ, ghṛta* meaning 'water', 'milk' and 'ghee'. Cf. *Vedic Index*, p. 250.

51. *Bhāg*. P. VIII.6.22.
*Viṣṇu P.* I.9.77.
The *Mb.* does not have this point.
The churning generates the life-sap (*amṛta*) and sets the light-principle in order. It is thus the motif for *order*. It gets associated with rain as we have noted; and in this it is an aspect of *ṛta*, which means both cosmic order and rain in the Veda.
52. Cf. *ṚV.* II.12.2.
53. *Mait. Sam.* I.10.13.
54. *Rām.* VI.74.67.
55. *Bhāg. P.* X.25.
56. The Kharia tribe believes in the moving mountains and worships mountains; cf. Crooke, *Popular Religion and Folk-Lore of North India*, Vol. I, p. 62.
57. Mb. I.18.15.
"वासुकेरथ नागस्य . . . मुखात् ।।
ते धूमसंघाः सम्भूताः मेघसंघाः सविद्युतः ।
अभ्यवर्षन् सुरगणान् श्रमसन्तापकर्षितान् ।।"
58. Cf. I.4 A *supra* (The Garuḍa Legend).
59. Cf. *Ibid.* n. 196, *supra; Jai. Br.* I.287.
60. Cf. Viṣṇu *P.* I.9.87.
61. For a full discussion see Bloomfield, 'The Legend of Soma and the Eagle', *J.A.O.S.*, XVI.
62. *Rel. and Phil. of the Veda*, p. 331. See also Eggeling, Introduction to *S.B.E.*, Vol. XXVI, p. xiii for various opinions.
63. I.18.11-12.
64. *Viṣṇu P.* I.9.88; *Bhāg P.* IV.II.6.8.
65. Cf. ref. to it by Gonda, *Aspects of Early Viṣṇuism*, p. 127.
66. Cf. *Ś.B.* VII.5.I.6; this is at the Agnicayana ritual. The altar in it has five layers; and the tortoise is placed in the lowest layer; for altar = earth, cf. *Ś.B.* I.2.5.7; also III.7.2.1.

67. For tortoise = Prajāpati, see *Ś.B.* VII.5.1.5.
68. Gonda, *Aspects*, p. 71.
69. Review, *J.R.A.S.*, 1893, p. 257 ff.
70. A Lang, *Myth, Ritual and Religion*, London, 1913, Vol. I, p. 80 (quoted from 'Primitive marriage in Bengal'!, *Asiatic Quarterly* No. 3).
71. *Ś.Br.* VII.5.1.1–2.
72. Brahmā coming out of Viṣṇu's navel is a commonly known idea. Cf. *Hari V.* Bhaviṣya Parvan, Adhyāya-II-12. For a fuller study of this motif see Dange (Mrs.) S.S., *The Bhāgavata Purāṇa — Mythosocial study*, pp. 45-58.
72a. Cf. *Bhāg. P.* VIII.7.12; *Viṣṇu P.* I. 9.90.
73. *Bhāg. P.* VIII.7.11.
74. Cf. Kramrisch, *'The Hindu Temple'*, *P.* 403; also Rundle Clark, *Myth and Symbol in Ancient Egypt*, *P.* 61; 66 ff.
75. Cf. *Jai. Up. Br.* I.20.10.
76. *Ibid.*, also Gonda *Aspects*, p. 95.
77. A number of examples can be given. One such tortoise can be seen at the famous temple of the goddess Ambā at Kolhapur, just in front of the inner hall of the main shrine. The position of the hexangular figure is also almost in the same place.
78. Vogel, *The Indian Serpent Lore*, p. 284. The tortoise under the lowest layer of bricks in the sacrificial altar and the tortoise at the base of the Balenese 'Meru' present a very similar idea, both supporting the divine structure. The tortoise in the 'Meru' is called *'Kūrmāgni'* and is similar to the tortoise under the sacrificial *fire in the altar.*
79. With this cf. *Tait. Br.* I.1.3.5 where we have the account of the primeval waters *producing a lotus-stalk,* and Prajāpati diving in the form of a boar, fetching earth and spreading it on the leaf.
80. Vogel, *Indian S.L.*, p. 284.
81. Various 'Nāga-kals' (nāga-stones) are placed beneath the peepal tree (called also 'nāgabandhu') by married ladies desirous of children; cf. Vogel, *Indian Serpent Lore*, p. 270. I have personally noticed several such Nāga-kals placed beneath the peepal tree on the shore of the sea behind the temple of Rameśwaram. These stones mostly

show two serpents intertwined with each another and are said to have been placed there after the fulfilment of the desire for progeny. A serpent seen in dream by a woman indicates progeny; cf. Dr. Barua's paper, "The Serpent-lore of Assam", *J.U. Gauhati*, Art No. 1958. Manasā, the snake-goddess (Sister of Vāsuki) is believed to be the giver of life, Risley, *J.R.A.S.*, 1892, p. 249 ff; also Vogel, *Indian Serp. Lore*, p. 278. For Manasā as the controller of life see Appendix C.

The serpent as a symbol of creation was the idea in ancient Egypt. He was the lord of the universe and a phase of the god Atum. See Rundle Clark, *Myth and Symbol in Ancient Egypt*.

The serpent in the Old Testament is also connected with creation inasmuch as he is the cause of the fall of Adam from heaven into this Earth for creation were.

82. Cf. Werner, *Myths and legends of China*, p. 208.
    See Oldham, "Serpent worship in India", *J.R.A.S.* (1891), p. 376 where he mentions about the propitiation of the nāga for fine weather and also rain. Cf. Hastings, *Encl. Rel.* and *Ethics* under 'Serpent'.
83. Cf. *Rām.* I.45.15 ff (Mylapore-1958).
84. *Agni P.* IV.9 ff.
85. *Viṣṇu P.* I.9.90 ff.
86. *Bhāg. P.* VIII.7.
87. According to the ancient Egyptian belief, the land is the *spittle*, Rundle-Clark, *Myth and Symbol in Ancient Egypt*, London, 1959, p. 41. The spittle symbolizes the body-moisture which is the potent principle of creation. The same is to be noted in the creation of beings from the tears of deities etc. Atum's tears create beings (*ibid.*, p. 90); barley and also rain came from the eye of Prajāpati in the ancient Hindu myth (*Maitrāyaṇi Sam.* IV.6.3); in the Japanese mythology Izanagi's eye produces the moon (W.T. Olcott, *Sun-lore of All Ages*, New York — London, 1914, p. 24).
88. Donald Mackenzie, *Myths of Pre-Columbian America*, p. 175; also Cushing, "Zuni Bread-Stuff", *Indian Notes and Monographs*, Vol. VIII, New York, 1920, p. 23 f.
89. Donald Mackenzie, *Myths of China and Japan*, p. 350.

90. Donald Mackenzie, *Myths of Pre-Columbian America,* p. 190.
91. The concept of the god Dhanvantari is, without doubt, suggested from the sun. The etymology of this word is interesting. The word *dhanvan* indicates in the *ṚgVeda* a vast region understood to be the "sandy desert" (see *Vedic Index of Names and Subjects*). It is to be noted, however, that the word comes with Savitṛ, at *Ṛgveda* II.38.7; at V.53.6 we have *anu dhanvanā yanti vṛṣṭayaḥ*. At I.116.4 the word *dhanvan* is associated with the sea whence the Aśvins rescue Bhujyu. Now commonly the firmament is believed to be the ocean, which is, hence, the *dhanva*; and the *dhanvantari* is the traverser of the sky-ocean, fr. *dhanva* + √ *tṛ*. Dhanvantari is said to be holding a white pitcher, *Mb. Adi.* 18.38. The sun has been well set in the ancient Hindu belief as the receptacle of waters and the fluids that procreate as also heal. See Dange, *Pastoral Symbolism from the Ṛgveda* (Ashtekar Vedic Research Lecture Series, Vol. III, 1968), University of Poona Publication, 1970, Ch. "Aspects of the Fiery Fluid"; also *ṚV.* I.23.17; see also by the same author, *Vedic Concept of 'Field' and the Divine Fructification*, Bombay Uni., 1971, pp. 190-211.
92. D. Mackenzie, *Myths of Pre-Columubian America*, p. 191.
93. *Ibid.*, p. 209; see plate opposite p. 232, figs. 2 and 3.
94. Rundle Clark, *op. cit.*, p. 36.
95. Held, *The Mahābhārata*, p. 145 ff.
96. It may be marked that the 'Left to right' turn is called '*Pradakṣiṇa*' and is auspicious. Cf. *Raghu*, II.71; also *Ibid.*, III.14.
97. For the sun-power and fertility or lack of death, cf. "Sun-Kiss" article by Ananda Coomaraswamy, *J.A.O.S.*, Vol. 60, p. 46 ff.
98. Cf. Tilak, '*Arctic Home*', p. 250 ff. for the '*Captive Waters*'.
99. "Serpent Worship in India", *J.R.A.S.*, 1891, p. 368. See also *The Sun and the Serpent*, p. 59 (by the same author).
100. Cf. Garuda-legend where various references are given.
101. Oldham would have, probably, gained support from the fact that the little island near the coast of Kathiawad, is

called 'Kaccha' (which etymologically goes well with Kathiawada) and might suggest the *tortoise* in the legend. The location of the Mandara-East-West (according to Oldham) could well be supposed to give the idea of the mountain resting on the tortoise (island). *Viṣṇu*, taking the form of the Kaccha is actually said to be as spacious as an island in the *Bhāg. P.* VIII.7.9.

But Oldham does not seem to have noticed this fact. Oldham obviously fixes his attention on the serpents in India in his article and in his book and casually refers to Vāsuki as the churn-rope in the great 'churning'. Hence, his remark may not be taken as quite a careful one.

It may be interesting to note also, that Oldham thinks '*Mandara*' to be symbolically representing a *Ship*. Cf. *The Sun and the Serpent*, p. 59. It is difficult to understand how 'Mandara' could be the 'Ship' in this context. For Mandara see *Vāyu Purāna*, 49.50 where we have the etymology-*mandā* = 'water'; *dara* = cut; so water churner.' Oldham does not mention this ref. from the *Vāyu P.*, nor does he give this meaning of '*Maṇḍā*' = water to support his opinion. He does not likewise give any reason for the length of the Mandara from east to west. See, however, Rasbihari Bose, "Mandara Hill', *Indian Antiquary*, Vol. I, 1872, p. 56 ff. He takes it to be near Bhagalpore in North India.

102. Cf. *Mb.* I.17-29 (*Crit. Ed. B.O.R.I.*), *daityā nāgottamā-stadā.*

Oldham, however, supposes the Daityas, Asuras etc. as only Nāgas.

103. For Vāsuki as a historical person see, Oldham's article in question (*J.R.A.S.*, 1891). For serpents controlling rain see note 82 supra (Present chapter). See also Appendix E.

104. For Ananta Śeṣa, cf. *Mb.* I.18.7.

105. Cf. Geldner referred to by Keith in *Rel. and Phil. of the Veda*, p. 624; Keith mentions also various other views here.

The words are, *dadāno asmā amṛtam viprkvat.*

106. *Ibid.* Cf. *ṚV.* I.163. *udyan samudrād.*

107. Ch. I.4, n. 201, *supra.*
108. Cf. *samudrāt, antarikṣanāmaitat;*
*yad vā samudra ādityaḥ.*
109. Cf. *puriṣād udakāt.*
110. *Tait. Sam.* VII.5.25.2.
111. *Ś.B.* X.6.4.1.
112. *Vāj. Sam.* XIII.42.
"अश्वं जज्ञानं सरिरस्य मध्ये।"
With the Sun-horse from the ocean can be compared the Avestan idea of the star-horse Tir or (Tiśtrya) fighting the black horse Apaośa in the cosmic ocean (that is the mid-region) named Vouru kaśa.
113. Cf. *Ś.Br. (Mādh.)* III.2.4, 3-6. This is an inversion of the Kaca legend, where it is the male that is sent.
114. Cf. *Ś.B. (Mādh.)* IV.2.1.4; for the same idea, cf. *Mait. Sam.* I.3.10-12.
115. *Tait. Sam.* VI.4.10.1. Sāyāṇa takes these two as the sons of Śukra, the preceptor of gods. See *Sāyaṇa* on the above passage.
116. For *Rāhu* swallowing the moon and the sun, cf. *ṚV.* V.40.5-9; *Ś.B.* V.3.2.2. In the Vedic texts it is Svarbhānu, not Rāhu.

# APPENDICES

# Appendix A
# GARUḌA AND THE NĀGI

It has been pointed out, that in the sculptures from Khmer there are certain figures of two-hooded serpents having one head encircling a figure of Garuḍa, thus showing the ultimate oneness of these two and hinting at the Garuḍa-serpent motif which supports the two-fold division of society. Notice has also been taken of certain statues of Garuḍas having serpents in their mouth and it has been said that these probably were worshipped by a section of Nāgas. It will be interesting to take notice in this context, of a statue which helps our contention. It is a statue from Sanghao in the Calcutta Museum reproduced by Thomas in his book *'Epics, Myths and Legends of India'* (Bombay, no date of publication, Plate LI opposite p. 70). In it, we see a nāgī with Garuḍa (the caption given is 'Garuḍa and Nāgī'); but the nāgī in human form is represented as standing with crossed legs and is quite at ease. From the back of the whole of her figure a huge Garuḍa is seen, his head towering high above the head of the nāgī and looking like a huge hood. The tip of the feathered tail of Garuḍa, touches the heels of the nāgī's feet from behind. In the beak of Garuḍa is seen a big cobra whose tail supports the right hand of the nāgī, while the palm of her left hand is resting firmly on her waist. The expression of the nāgī is not a disturbed one; on the other hand, it appears that she is quite at ease. It should be marked here that in this statue the nāgī is not represented as being eaten by Garuḍa, while she and Garuḍa both seem to form one complete whole. It will be good to remember that the combined Eagle-serpent motif has been a very favourite one in all ages. The traditional antagonism of the serpent and the Eagle is also found represented in the golden goblets of the archaic Sumerian past. Zimmer[1] rightly opines that this twofold symbol of eagle and serpent is possessed of a vitality that outlasts ages. He gives an explanation of the symbol stating that the eagle stands for the '*unbounded spirit*' free from the fetters of the earth, the higher spiritual principles released from the bondage of the earth; while the serpent is an embodiment of the water of life from the earth.

This explanation comes very near to the whole idea in the Brāhmaṇas and the *Suparṇādhyāya* where Kadrū is said to be the Nāgī and is identified with the earth. The Nāga-Garuḍa motif in *Mb*, and earlier in the *Suparṇādhyāya*, could properly be taken to express this symbolic dualism found in various faiths and lands; as such, Garuḍa need not have been suggested from the Vedic Suparṇa about whose association with Nāga (serpent) little could be found in the Vedic literature. This motif of the double-figure, whatever explanation we might give for it, most probably, came from the original faiths and could very well give the idea of a dual social system as we have already hinted at in the case of the nāgas. That the motif is older than the story in *Mb.* can be seen from the fact that an amulet from Harappa[2] also displays a figure of Garuḍa flanked by two nāgas. On the obverse of the amulet a bird with spread wings is shown and on each side of it there is a snake of sinuous body. This motif could be even older than the Harappa civilization, or might even have been borrowed from the aboriginal tribes or clans then existing. We have already seen, that the various people in India were called by a common name 'Nāgas';[3] and, as such, it could be safely admitted that this dual motif in *Sup. Ad.* and *Mb.* was a gift of the people called the Nāgas, who seem to have a dual system of social organization. Zimmer refers to Garuḍa and the Nāgas, saying that Garuḍa represents the mystic power against serpent-poison and hence is popular in worship and folklore. We add that Garuḍa, being the mythic power controlling snake-poison, could natually be supposed to be respected and deified by the *sarpas* (nāgas) who learnt the *sarpa-vidyā*. This also goes to hint at how Garuḍa could be the deity of a sect of the nāgas. Even while accepting the widespread symbol of the Eagle-serpent, it must be remembered that Garuḍa and Nāgas are referred to as groups of people in *Mb.* and must be taken as such. The *Sup. Ad.* and the other texts also do the same.

How this motif of the dual figure of the eagle and the serpent lingered even through civilized ages could be seen from the vision of saint Hildegard recorded by Charles Singer[4] wherein the Eagle and the serpent prominently appear.

## References

1. *Myths and Symbols in Indian Arts and Civilization*, New York, 1947, p. 73 ff.
2. Cf. Fr. Heras, *Studies in Proto-Indo-Mediterranean Culture*, St. Xavier's College, Bombay, 1953, Fig. 219, opp. page 369.
3. Also Oldham, *'The sun and the serpent'*, London, 1965, p. 47. Oldham observes that there were no tribes named Nāgas; but they were so called by the Brāhmaṇas because the former worshipped the snakes. This is hard to accept. Cf. also Fausboll, *Indian Mythology according to the Mahābhārata*, London, 1903, p. 41, where nāgas are included among the Asuras. See also Slater, *Dravidian element in Indian culture*, London, 1924, p. 75.
4. *From Magic to Science*, Dover, 1958, p. 216, see figure 102. The motif was known in ancient Egypt also; cf. R.T., Rundle Clark, *op. cit.*

# Appendix B
# 'RĀMAṆĪYAKAM', THE ISLAND OF THE NĀGAS

The nāgas are carried by Garuḍa on his back both according to *Sup. Ad.* and *Mb.* Father Heras interprets this as an Indian invasion of Egypt. He refers to the tale in *Mb.* and sees in this the invasion of Egypt by the *nāga soldiers under the leadership of Garuḍa.*[1] How the Rev. Father was led to this conclusion is difficult to know. He refers to the statues where the nāgas and Garuḍa are seen together. Then he refers to the passage in *Mb.* and straightway concludes that the carrying of the nāgas by Garuḍa on his back is symbolic of Garuḍa's leaderhip of the nāgas. The nāga-Garuḍa motif is found also in Egypt, as he mentions, on the helmet of the Egyptian kings[2] and such other articles. This leads the Father to think that India lent to Egypt the double motif of nāga and Garuḍa; and this was done, according to him, because of an invasion by the nāgas (nāga-worshippers) under one who was from the Garuḍa tribe. He accepts the view of Oldham that the Garuḍas formed a tribe separate from the nāgas, but holds that the leader of the nāgas who invaded Egypt was one from the Garuḍa tribe.

The hypothesis of the Rev. Father is open to question. First of all, the very passage from *Mb.* (I. 26 ff.) upon which the whole structure of his argument stands, does not support his views. In the passage there is not the right indication to show that Garuḍa was the leader of the nāgas. The passage clearly shows that Garuḍa carried the nāgas on his back, not as their leader, but as a slave to set his mother free from slavery. In the face of this clear textual mention of Garuḍa's slavery, it seems far from the truth to suppose that the account is a symbolic leadership of the nāgas on the part of Garuḍa. The nāga-Garuḍa motif is, as we have seen, common to many people, and when Heras says that it is the nāgas of India who, under the Garuḍa leader, lent it to Egypt, his statement needs be taken with care.

Father Heras further points out, as a support to his view, the presence of a village by name El-Rahmaniya in north Egypt.[3] He identifies it with the island Rāmaṇīyakam where Garuḍa was asked by the nāgas to take the latter. This also seems to be a very bold step without looking into the actual passage properly. In *Mb.* the abode of the nāgas — Rāmaṇīyakam — is said to be in the midst of the ocean (*samudra-kukṣau*). One wonders whether the village in north Egypt would hold this description even with all its greenery and foliage which comes in the description of the Rāmanīyakam. Taking his idea firmly, Heras interprets the pasage in *Mb.*, where the nāgas are said to be scorched as they are carried by Garuḍa to the sun and the subsequent rain on the request of Kadrū, to indicate a really long journey though a desert which is on the way to Egypt. This is to see too much in the passage. The scorching heat and the journey to the sun by Garuḍa, more porperly, symbolize the sun-bird nature of the bird, while the rain on the request of Kadrū is symbolic of the power of the nāgas over rain, the instances of which we have amply seen.[4]

Oldham takes 'Rāmaṇīyaka' to be on the Malabar coast. Lavaṇa who dwelt in the Rāmaṇīyaka, according to him, was a king of this coast.

About the Rāmaṇīyaka it may be noted that *Mb.* states it to be an island. Nīlakaṇṭha commenting upon it also takes it as such.[5] This goes well with its situation as described in *Mb.* as 'in the midst (*kukṣau*) of the ocean.' *Mb.* has Kadrū asking Garuḍa to lead the Sarpas to another *island.* All this refers to a cluster of islands near one another. There is also an indication of the fact that the nāgas that went on Garuḍa's back went to the Rāmaṇīyaka for the first time,[6] while there were other nāgas already in the island; for, it was called the abode of the nāgas. If we suppose with Heras that Garuḍa led the nāgas to Egypt and, hence, the Egyptians got the symbol of the eagle and the serpent, we are to presume that there were no nāgas (or nāga worshippers called the nāgas) in Egypt. But this is against the text of *Mb.* and *Sup. Ad.* (the latter of which Heras does not refer to). *Mb.* and *Sup. Ad.* clearly state that these later nāgas went to a place that was already an abode of the nāgas. This fact and also the position of Rāmaṇīyaka (i. e. being an island) rules out the possibility of its being *a village in north Egypt*. Nor can it suit the Malabar coast. Most probably Rāmaṇīyaka was somewhere in the Bay of Bengal and might have been another name of Nicobar; or Rāmaṇīyakam might have been the island Nicobar itself so called because of its beautiful (*ramaṇīya*) surroundings. The name of Nicobar in ancient times was *Nakkavaram*, and the same is also identified as the ancient Nāgadvīpa.[7] Etymologically *'Nakkavaram'* can be *Nāga-puram* and is actually said to be the Nāgadvīpa. If we remember that the nāgas and the Makaras (Nakra) are generally interchanged in sulpture, as we have already seen, it is easy to understand how *Nakkavaram* (originally *Nakrapuram*) can be *Nāgapuram*. Thus, etymologically and also by the tradition recorded in sculpture the nāga and Nakra (Makara) being interchangeable, *Nakrapuram* (Nicobar) could be the *Nāgadvīpa* or the abode of the nāgas to which the nāgas were taken by Garuḍa. This sounds well when we know that these islands called 'Dvīpāntara' were only a part of ancient India that was the *'Jambudvīpa'* proper.[8] Nicobar suits well in this context, as Rāmaṇīyaka was said to have been, according to *Mb.* itself, prepared by Viśvakarman as the abode of the Makaras (i.e. the Nakras.[9] Hence Nakrapuram-Nakkavaram). It was already populated by certain Nāga clans when the nāgas carried by Garuḍa went there for the first time.

We have noted how the position of this Nāgadvīpa (Nicobar) suits the description in *Mb.* for, the island of Nicobar is to one side, aloof, in the ocean (*samudrakukṣau ekānte*); not only that, but it is said to be surrounded by water (*sāgarāmbu-parikṣiptam*). At another place in *Mb.*, the Jambu-dvīpa is described as the divine hare with Tāmra-parṇa as the head (or tip) and having the '*Kaśyapadvīpa*' and the '*Nāga-dvīpa*' for his two ears.[10] Tāmraparṇa is identified with the modern Ceylon, and if this is the head portion (*śiras*) with the mouth extending to the southern peninsula, the island of Kaśyapa (modern Kaccha) could be one ear and the other would *roughly* be the island Nicobar, though far remote from the mainland. The idea in the passage seems to denote two ends of the Jambudvīpa proper; and the exact similarity to the place of the ear need not be stressed.

A word about 'Lavaṇa'. The nāgas brought by Garuḍa on his back are said to have seen the terrible Lavaṇa. Oldham[11] and also Nīlakaṇṭha both think it to refer to Lavaṇa, the Asura. Oldham further states that Lavaṇa was the lord of the western coast. I disagree. Probably the passage in question has no reference to Lavaṇa — the demon. It simply implies that the nāgas saw the terrible ocean. Lavaṇa means ocean, and as it was seen by these nāgas for *the first time,* they thought it to be terrible (*ghora*). The passage refers to the exodus of the nāgas all right; but it seems more probable that the nāgas spoken of in this particular passage went to the island that was somewhere in the Bay of Bengal which was called in ancient times by the name of '*Mahodadhi.*'[12] *Mb.* clearly mentions '*Mahodadhi*' in this context;[13] and hence the westward exodus to Egypt, as thought by Heras, is not convincing, not tenable. So is Oldham's opinion that Rāmaṇīyakam was on the Malabar coast. It can then be rightly supposed that the Spisode of Rāmaṇīyaka indicates the migration of the nāgas from the main-land to the island of Nicobar (the ancient Nāgadvīpa) that was in the *Mahodadhi* (the modern Bay of Bengal).

Of interest it may be to note that Mookerji mentions the '*Ramaṇṇadeśa*'[14] as extending from Rangoon to Pegu on the west coast of Burma. This '*Ramaṇṇadeśa*', according to him, was the general name given to the various settlements of the Mons who were also known as the *tailaṅgas* (from Āndhra Pradeśa) and migrated to Burma. They had a Hindu kingdom in the 6th century A.D. Is it not probable that, in times before the 6th century A.D., the islands nearing the coast of Burma, including the Nāgadvīpa (Nicobar), and the coast itself, had the name 'Rāmaṇīyaka', from which '*Ramaṇṇadeśa*' was formed —, and was a cluster of colonies of the nāgas before these Mons migrated to Burma? The answer is 'Yes'. But, the 'Rāmaṇīyaka of *Mb.* is surrounded by the water of the ocean; and, hence, excludes the coast of Burma and hints prominently at the island of Nicobar which is nearer to the Burmese coast than the mainland of India and is still surrounded by the waters of the ocean.

With all this discussion, we may add that *Rāmaṇīyaka* meaning '*beautiful*', may only be an epithet of the island populated by the nāgas — the Nāgadvīpa — Nicobar.

We have maintained that the carrying of the nāgas on back by Garuḍa is only an expression symbolic of the status in the dual social organism. The going to Rāmaṇīyaka indicates probably an exodus of the nāga clan to this island of Nicobar at the time when in the social order of the nāgas, the members knowing the Gāruḍā-vidyā were not much respected and are here symbolically described as lower than the other magicians among nāgas. That the nāgas themselves were snake-charmers, we have seen. We may further remark that the nāga magicians, or snake-charmers, probably, had two main deities viz., Garuḍa and Manasā (the snake goddess). Garuḍa got further identified with Śiva who is called 'Suvarṇa-pataṅga Rudra'.[15] Garuḍa is also called '*Tryambaka.*'[16] The antagonism between the sects of Śiva and Manasā can be seen from the tale of Behulā and Manasā in Appendix C.

## References


1. Cf. *Studies in Proto-Indo-Mediterranean Culture*, p. 361 ff.
2. The serpent (cobra) symbol on the crown is as old as the idea of the primeval waters according to Egyptian faith. The cobra adorns the head-crown of the highest god — *Atum*, cf. R.T. Rundle Clark, *op. cit.*
3. *Ibid.*, p. 368.
4. For more instances see also Hastings, *Enclyclopaedia of Religion and Ethics*, under 'serpent', p. 401 (h); also p. 415.
5. See Nīla, '*rāmaṇīyakam dvīpa-viśeṣakam.*
   See *Mb.* I.27.1 *jagmatustam dvīpam āśu vai.*
6. Cf. I.27.2 *pūrvam āgatāḥ.*
7. Cf. R.K. Mookerji, *Ancient India* (Allahabad, 1956), p. 484; and the map opposite.
   For Nāgadvīpa and nine *dvīpas* of Bhārata, see also Vasudevasharana Agarwala in *J.B.R.S.*, XXIII, Part I, pp. 133-37.
8. *Ibid.*
9. *Mb.* I.27. *tam dvīpam makar-āvāsaṁ vihitaṁ viśva-karmaṇā.*
10. Cf. *Mb.* VI.6.55 and 56.
    पार्श्वे शशस्य द्वे वर्षे उक्ते ये दक्षिणोत्तरे।
    कर्णौ तु नागद्वीपश्च काश्यपद्वीप एव च।।
    ताम्रपर्णशिलो राजन् श्रीमान्मलयपर्वतः।
    The Gorakhpur Ed. gives the reading *tāmra-parṇaśiro* while the Citraśālā Press has *tāmraparṇasilo.* as above.
11. Cf. *The Sun and the serpent*, p. 60, Nīlakaṇṭha, Com. on *Mb.*
12. Cf. *Ancient India* — Map opp. p. 484.
13. Cf. *Mb.* I.22.4, also I.25.1.
14. *Ancient India*, p. 488.
15. Cf. *Agni P.*, 297-5.
16. Cf. *Mantraśāstra*, Part II, Paradi, 1957, p. 26, "*namo bhagavate Garuḍāya tryambakāya*".

# Appendix C
# THE STORY OF BEHULĀ AND THE SNAKE GODDESS

A merchant lived in Campakanagar. He was a devotee of Śiva, and would not pay worship to Manasā — the snake-goddess. He would not accept the superiority of Manasā. Manasā told him in many ways to worship her; but he refused. So the goddess decided to trouble him. Manasā told him that, if he did not worship her, she would bite his newly wedded son. The merchant, however, ordered a special device to be prepared to avoid all possibilities of snakes coming inside the nuptial chamber. Manasā was on the watch and threatened the carpenter with loss of life if he did not keep a crevice through which the snakes could go inside. The son of the merchant slept in the nuptial chamber with his wife Behulā. When he was asleep, Behulā, who kept awake, saw a serpent coming through the crevice and caught it. Many serpents crept in and Behulā caught them; but, ultimately, she was overpowered by sleep and Manasā herself came and killed her husband. Next morning the corpse was tied upon a raft and left in the river. Behulā also sat by the side of her husband. As it went on floating on the water of the river for some days, Behulā saw a washerwoman on the bank. The washerwoman, seeing that a small boy troubled her in her work, killed him; and, when her work was over, brought him back to life by sprinkling some water on the body. Behulā saw this and turned to the woman for help. The washerwoman promised to bring back to life her husband only if Behulā would change her father-in-law to worship

Manasā. Behulā agreed and took her husband, who gained life, back home. She requested her father-in-law to worship Manasā. He accepted on the condition, that he would offer flowers to Manasā by the left hand turning his face away. Manasā also agreed to this; and, along with Śiva, Manasā got to be worshipped though she got a lower position inasmuch as she got worship by the left hand, while Śiva by the right.

The tale suggests, in a way, the rivalry between Śiva and Manasā. The rivalry possibly hints at the fact that both Śiva and Manasā are invoked to nullify the snake-poison. Manasā is represented with a seven-hooded serpent above her head. She is also called Viṣaharī Devī, while Śiva is identified with Garuḍa who is invoked to nullify snake-poison.

The story of Behulā is very famous in Bengal. (For the figure of Manasā with seven hoods of a serpent see *Humpi Ruins* by Longherst, Delhi, 1933, p. 30 figs. 8 and 9).

For further information on Manasā, see B. S. Vidyāratna, '*Manasā-Maṅgal*' (Bengali).

## Appendix D
## GARUḌA AND THE KHILA SŪKTAS OF THE ṚGVEDA

We have noted that the name Garuḍa is not mentioned in the Vedic literature proper, the first mention being in the *Tait. Āraṇyaka*. However, amongst the *Khila Sūktas* of the *Ṛgveda* we have reference to Garuḍa in certain places.[1] We have also reference to the birth of Garuḍa and the sudden effects of it, such as tremor in the mountains, fear among the three worlds etc. The verses are exactly the same as of *Sup. Ad.* and one wonders if they are not originally from *Sup. Ad.* That Garuḍa could never have been suggested from the Vedic Suparṇa seems clear enough even here. We have noted that Suparṇa's association with snakes or poison is next to nil in the Vedic literature, except for the passages from the *AV* which we have already critically studied. Garuḍa, on the other hand, is constantly associated with the serpents. This is seen even in the *Khila* hymns; for, in the same hymn where Garuḍa is praised, after a few verses we have the praise of the serpents with a reference to the sacrifice of Janamejaya.[2] We have references to Agasti, Narmadā, Mādhava, Mucukunda etc. in the same place. Obviously these are later additions and do not prove Garuḍa's existence in the body of the main Vedic texts. The only thing probable in this connection is that these were at a very late period, fabricated, and interpolated in the *Ṛgveda,* the indication of which we get from *Sup. Ad.* itself where at the end, Garuḍa is said to have won the boon of getting admitted into the Vedic texts and of being an object of study for the Brahmins.[3] The Khilas further refer to Vainateya also, and he is asked to drink Soma. Both Vainateya and Indra are invoked in the same line,[4] which indicates their equality. Possibly this line is suggested from *Sup. Ad.* where Indra and Garuḍa fight and Garuḍa is victorious and they both become friends.

## References

1. Cf. *Khilla*-II.2.2 ff.
2. Cf. *Ibid.* 5.
   भो सर्प शृणु भद्रं ते दूरं गच्छ महायशाः।
   जनमेजयस्य यज्ञान्ते आस्तीकवचनं स्मर।।
   For the same stanza with a very slight change, see *Mb.* I.58.25.
3. Cf. *Sup. Ad.* XIV.30 ff.
4. Cf. VI.21, *Vainateya somam piba somam pibatu vṛtrahā*.

# Appendix E
# THE MĀṄGAS AND THE MĀṄGA-GĀRUḌĪS

Enthoven (*Tribes and Castes of Bombay,* Vol. ii, p. 434, Bombay, 1922) in his survey states that Māṅga-Gāruḍīs are a sub-caste of the Māṅga. Māṅga-Gāruḍis are, according to him, a class of wandering jugglers or snake-charmers. He also gives information about the tattooed marks on the hands of the Māṅga-Gāruḍis. The marks are mostly of a cypress, a scorpion or a snake. They have a mark III tattooed on every finger of the right hand except the thumb. At the back of the hand, there is to be found the figure of a sunflower.

We may add that the sunflower probably indicates their originally being the sun-worshippers. That the Māṅga-Gāruḍīs are a sub-caste of the Māṅgas seems parallel to the Gāruḍīs being a sub-caste of the nāgas. Enthoven further remarks that the Māṅga-Garuḍīs were so called because they were *originally* snake-charmers. It seems more probable that originally they were Māṅgas and came to be named Gāruḍīs because of their indulging into magic generally and snake-charming particularly. This goes perfectly well with the Garuḍas primarily being only nāgas and being later called Garuḍas because of their knowing the 'Sarpa-vidyā' (= 'Gārudā vidyā'). In the story of Mataṅga from *Mb.* also we have Mataṅga primarily a human being — *a Cāṇḍāla* — and then gaining *'bird-hood'* which indicates his gaining supernatural powers, thus hinting at forming a new sect in the old whole. The knowledge of snake-charming gave the Māṅga-Gāruḍīs a different name, and a different status. The two nāgas overpowered by Gāruḍa, were the followers of Mataṅga according to *Sup. Ad.* which hints at their being of another sect (cr phratry) of the nāgas. This sect seems to be present in the Māṅgas (Mataṅga = Māṅga) of to-day. The Māṅga-Gāruḍīs being a sect of the Māṅgas (= the Mataṅga-nāgas) it is natural to take the Garuḍas of old to be only a sect of the nāgas.

Thurston records a caste named Gāraḍī, whose main occupation is snake-charming. This caste is found in Mysore and also in Telugu province. (Cf. *Castes and Tribes of Southern India*, vol. ii, p. 268.) Pandit Satawalekar poses a question as to 'how can we admit the serpents as the progeny of Kaśyapa'.[1] He thinks that Kaśyapa came from the Caspian Sea and thus doubts whether the nāgas (from India) can be his progeny. But there remains no doubt if we look to Risley's findings, as we have already noted in our discussion. The serpents and the tortoise (Kaśyapa?) were thought to be the ancestors by many people in India according to him. The totem tortoise probably got identified with the Kaśyapa, whosoever he may be. When in *Mb.* we have Garuḍa and the serpents as sons of Kaśyapa, it probably reflects an aboriginal conception which still is found to be present in India according to Risely.

## Reference

1. *The Rāmāyaṇa*, Araṇya-Kāṇḍa, Pardi, 1950, p. 436 ff.

# Appendix F
# THE CELESTIAL CHURNING

We have hinted at the possibility of the whole idea of the churning of the ocean, as it appears in the epic, being adapted from the Vedic idea of the release of the celestial waters and the pressing of *Soma* in the sacrifice. It will be good in this context to note a passage from 'Mihira Yashta' (89-90) mentioned by Shapurji Kavasji Hodiwala.[1] According to the passage —

> Ahura Mazada appointed Mithra to be the officiating priest to prepare *Haom.* Mithra first prepared Haom on the Albuz mountain in a celestial mortar decked with stars and made of heavenly substance".

Hodiwala takes the heavenly mortar to mean the moon surrounded by the stars. It seems better to take by the celestial mortar not the moon, but the whole of the firmament decked with stars. The moon is not actually decked with stars. The stars surround him. The general tendency again is to identify the moon with *Soma* (Haom); and hence, to have the moon to prepare *Soma* in, does not seem to convey the exact sense. There is another interesting point. The mortar for pressing *Soma* in, suggests also the pestle. The pestle for pressing *Soma* being the same '*adri*' or '*giri*' and being perpendicular in the action of pressing comes nearer the mountain Mandara that is the churn-staff. If the mortar is the firmament which is also said to be '*Samudra*', the pestle can be the Mandara, when the celestial '*Samudra*' gave place to the terrestrial one. The gems that went up in the churning can well be the stars revolving while the celestial pressing was in progress.

The heavenly mortar and the pestle can well be compared with the painting mentioned on p. 266 note 29, *suprā*, where in place of the 'ocean', a big tub-like thing (very similar to the mortar) is said to have been painted.

That the churning of the ocean has been suggested from the release of the heavenly waters and the luminaries can be seen also from the fact that, according to the Vedic conception our world with the atmosphere above it is shut off by the vault of the sky from the transcosmic region (which extends beyond it) of the heavenly light-waters, the seat of immortality, and the ultimate fountain-head of life".[2] This ultimate seat of immortality, which is at the bottom of the celestial Light waters, can be compared with *amṛta* that also is at the bottom of the terrestrial ocean with all other gems.

## References

1. S.K. Hodiwala, *Indo-Iranian Religion*, Bombay, 1925, p. 11.
2. Cf. Maryla Falk, "Serpent and the bird", in *Bhāratīya Vidyā,* Vol. IV, Part 2, p. 201 ff. The same article would be useful to have an idea that Vāsuki in the churning legend is the world-serpent. For the world-serpent, see also Zimmer, *Myths and Symbols*, New York, p. 73; also Singer, *From Magic to Science*, Dover, 1958, p. 216.

# Bibliography

## Sanskrit Texts (with abbreviations)

### Samhitās


(*AV*) Atharvaveda-saṁhitā; Ed. S.D. Satawalekar, Pardi, 1957.

(*Kāṭh. Sam.*) Kāṭhaka-saṁhitā; Ed. S.D. Satawalekar, Aundh, 1943.

(*Mait. Sam.*) Maitrāyaṇī-saṁhitā; Ed. Leopald Von Shroeder, 1923; S.D. Satawalekar, Vik. Saṁvat, 1998.

(*RV*) Ṛgveda-saṁhitā; Ed. Vaidika Saṁśodhana Maṇḍala, Pune, 1933-1951.

(*Sama V*) Sāmaveda-saṁhitā; Ed. Pt. Ramaswarup Sharma, Moradabad, 1912.

(*Taitt. Sam.*) Taittirīya-saṁhitā; S.D. Satawalekar, New print, Sam. 2039; Ānandāśrama, Pune, 1948.

(*Vāj. Sam.*) Vājasaneyi-saṁhitā; Ed. Pt. Rama swarup Sharma, Moradabad.


### Brāhmaṇa and Āraṇyaka Texts


(*Ait. Br.*) Aitareya-Brāhmaṇa; Ānandāśrama, Pune, Part-I 1930 : Part-II 1970

(*Chand. Br.*) Chāndogya-brāhmaṇa; Calcutta, 1958.

(*Go / Gopatha Br.*) Gopatha-brāhmaṇa; Gastra, Leiden, 1910; Jivananda Vidyasagar, Calcutta, 1891.

(*Jai. Br.*) Jaiminīya-brāhmaṇa; Ed. Raghuvira and Lokesh Chandra, Nagpur, 1954; reprint, Motilal Banarsidass, Delhi 1986.

(*Ṣaḍ. Br.*) Ṣaḍviṁśa-brāhmaṇa; Leiden, 1910.

(*Śat. Br. Ś.B. Ś.Br.*) Śatapatha-brāhmaṇa (Mādhyandina); Kashi Sanskrit Series, 2nd print, Varanasi,

Chaukhamba, V. Samvat, 1997; (*Kāṇva*) Raguvir and Caland, 1939.

(*Taitt. Br.*) Taittirīya-brāhmaṇa; Ed. Ānandāśrama, Pune, 1979.

(*Tāṇḍya M. Br. / Tān. Br.*) Tāṇḍyamahā-brāhmaṇa; Chinnaswami Shastri, Kashi Sanskrit Series, 1936.

(*Taitt. Ār.*) Taittirīya-āraṇyaka; Calcutta, 1871.

**Upaniṣad Texts**

(*Bṛhad. Up.*) Bṛhadāraṇyaka-upaniṣad; Gita Press, Gorakhpur.

(*Chānd. Up.*) Chāndogya-upaniṣad; Gita Press, Gorakhpur.

(*Kaṭha Up.*) Kaṭha-upaniṣad; Gita Press, Gorakhpur.

(*Kau. Up.*) Kauṣītaki-upaniṣad; Gita Press, Gorakhpur.

(*Mait. Up.*) Maitrāyaṇī-upaniṣad; Gita Press, Gorakhpur.

(*Muṇḍ. Up.*) Muṇḍaka-upaniṣad; Gita Press, Gorakhpur.

**Sūtra Texts**

(*Āpast. Gr. S.*) Āpastamba-gṛhya-sūtra; ed. Chinnaswami Shastri, Benares, 1928.

(*Āśv. Śr. S.*) Āśvalāyana-śrauta-sūtra; Ānandāśrama, Pune, 1917.

(*Āśv. Gṛ. S*) Āśvalāyana-gṛhya-sūtra; Ed. with Marathi Tr., Shivaram Shastri Shintre, Mumbai, 1938.

(*Mānava Gṛ. S.*) Mānava-gṛhya-sūtra; Ed. Knauer, Petersburg, 1897.

(*Śāṅkh. Śr. S.*) Śāṅkhāyana-śrauta-sūtra; Ed. A. Hillebrandt, Calcutta, 1888.

(*Baudh. Dh. S.*) Baudhāyana-dharma-sūtra; Dharmasūtra Texts, Vols. I-II, Calcutta, 1908-9.

(*Gau. Dh. S.*) Gautama-dharma-sūtra; Dharmasūtra Texts, Vols. I-II, Calcutta, 1908-9.

(*Vas. Dh. S.*) Vasiṣṭha-dharma-sūtra; Dharmasūtra Texts, Vols. I-II, Calcutta, 1908-9.

**Epics**

(*Rām.*) Rāmāyaṇa; Ed. Chinnaswami Shastri/Subrahmanya Shastri, 2nd. Ed., Mylapore, Madras, 1958.

(*Mb.*) Mahābhārata; Ed. (with the com. of Nīlakaṇṭha-Nīla), Chitrashala Press, Pune; Crit. Ed., BORI, Pune; and Gita Press, Gorakhpur. The last is mainly used., V. Samvat 2013-15.

**Purāṇa Texts**

(*Agni P.*) Agni-purāṇa; Ed. Ānandāśrama, Pune.

(*Bhāg. P.*) Bhāgavata Purāṇa; Ed. Gita Press, Gorakhpur.

(*Gaṇ. P.*) Gaṇeśa-purāṇa; Ed. Venkateshwar Press, Mumbai.

(*Garuḍa P.*) Garuḍa-purāṇa; Ed. Venkateshwar Press, Mumbai.

(*Harivam P.*) Harivaṁśa-purāṇa; Ed. Gita Press, Gorakhpur.

(*Mārk. P.*) Mārkaṇḍeya-purāṇa; Ed. Venkateshwar Press, Mumbai.

(*Matsya P.*) Matsya-purāṇa; Ed. Venkateshwar Press, Mumbai, Anandāśrama, Pune.

(*Pad. P.*) Padma-purāṇa; Ed. Venkateshwar Press, Mumbai.

(*Sk. P.*) Skanda-purāṇa; Ed. Venkateshwar Press, Mumbai.

(*Śiva P.*) Śiva-purāṇa; Ed. Venkateshwar Press, Mumbai.

(*Vā / Vāyu P.*) Vāyu-purāṇa; Ed. Venkateshwar Press, Mumbai.

(*Viṣṇu P.*) Viṣṇu-purāṇa; Ed. Gita Press. Gorakhpur.

(*Viṣṇu Dh. P.*) Viṣṇudharmottara-purāṇa; Ed. Venkateshwar Press, Mumbai.

**Other Texts in Sanskrit**

Bṛhatkathāmañjarī; Ed. Kāvyamāla, 1901.

Kādambarī; Ed. Nirnayasagar, Mumbai, 1948.

Mantraśāstra; by Śaṅkarācārya, Paradi, 1957.

Nāgānandam; Ed. M.R. Kale; Nirnayasagar, Mumbai, 1919.

Nirukta; Ed. Nirnayasagar, Mumbai, 1930.

Raghuvaṁśam; Ed. Nirnayasagar, Mumbai, 1916.

Rājataraṅgiṇī; Ed. Mumbai, 1892.

Śākuntalam; Ed. A.B. Gajendragadkar, Surat, 1950.

Śiśupālavadham; Ed. Nirnayasagar, Mumbai, 1940.

Suparṇādhyāya; Text (in Roman script) used by J. Charpentier, Uppsala, 1920.

The *Zend Avesta*, in SBE. Tr. by James Darmesteter, Motilal Banarasidass, Delhi 1988 (1882).

**Others**

Agrawala, V.S. : About the Dvīpas of Ancient India, *JBORS*, Vol. XXIII.

Allan, A.H., 1901 : "Vaṭasāvitrī-vrata", *JAOS*, 21-2.

Anand, Subhash, 1966 : *Story as Theology*, International Publications, New Delhi.

Apte, V.M., 1954 : *Social and Religious Life in the Gṛhyasūtras*, Popular Prakashan, Bombay, 1954.

Banerji, R.D., 1930 : *Prehistoric Ancient and Hindu India*, Blackie and Son (India) Ltd., Bombay, Madras, Calcutta; Reprinted 1950 (1934).

Barnett, L.D., 1922 : *Hindu Gods and Heroes*, London.

Barnett, L.D., 1929 : "Studies in Indo-European Psychology", *JRAS*, LXI.

Barth, A., 1914 : *The Religions of India* (Eng. Tr. by Rev. J. Wood; first pbn. 1882).

Berden, Francis, F., 1989 : *The Aztecs*, Chalsea House Pbn., New York, Philadelphia.

Barua, B.K., 1950 : "The Serpent Lore in Assam", *J. University of Gauhati*, Art No. IX, Gauhati.

Bloomfield, M., 1896: "The Legend of Soma and the Eagle", *JAOS*-16.

Boisselier, J., "Garuḍa dans l'Art Khmer", *Bulletin* d l' *Ecole Francaise*, Tome XXXIV-51.

Bose, Rasbihari, 1872 : "Mandara Hill", *Indian Antiquary*, Vol. I.

Briggs, L.P., 1951 : "The Syncretism of Religion in the South-East Asia", *JAOS*-71.

Cavendish, Richard, 1994 (1989): (Ed.) *Legends of the World*, Barnes and Noble Books, New York.

Chakrawarty, Chandra, : *Ancient Races and Myths*, Calcutta.

Charpentier, J., 1920 : *Die Suparṇasage,* Uppsala.

Coleman, Charles, 1832 : *Mythology of the Hindus*, London.

Coomarswamy, Anand, 1940 : "The sun-kiss", *JAOS*-60.

Coomarswamy, Anand, 1928 : "Letter on Erākapatta", *JRAS*-LX.

Cox, G.W., 1870 : *Mythology of the Aryan Nations,* London.

Crooke, W., 1896 : *Religion and Folk-lore of North India.*

Cushing, 1920 : "Zuni Breadstuff", *Indian Notes and Monographs*, Vol. VIII, New York.

Dange, Sadashiv A., 1970 : *Pastoral Symbolism from the Ṛgveda,* Uni. of Poona, Poona.

Dange, Sadashiv A., 1971 : *Vedic Concept of 'Field' and the Divine Fructification,* Uni. of Bombay, Bombay.

Dange, Sadashiv A., 1987 : *Puranic Myth and Culture,* Ajanta Books International, Delhi.

Dange, Sadashiv A., 1986-1990 : *Encyclopaedia of Puranic Beliefs and Practices*, Navrang, New Delhi (Vols. I-V).

Dange, Sadashiv A., 1996 : *Towards Understanding Hindu Myths*, Aryan Books International, New Delhi.

Dange, Sadashiv A., 1997 : *Images from Vedic Hymns and Rituals,* Navrang, New Delhi.

Dange, Sadashiv A. and (Mrs.) Sindhu Dange, 1994: *Critiques on Sanskrit Dramas*, 2nd Ed., Aryan Books International, New Delhi (First Ed., Moradabad, 1969).

Dange, (Mrs.) Sindhu S., 1984 : *The Bhāgavata Purāṇa — Mythosocial Study*, Ajanta Books International, Delhi.

Dasgupta, S.N. and De, S.K., 1947 : *A History of Sanskrit Literature*, University of Calcutta, Calcutta.

Date, G.Y., 1948 : *Sulabha Marāṭhī Hindi Viśvakosa*, Pune.

Day, 1912 : *Folk-tales from Bengal,* London.

Dixitar, R.R., 1951 : *Puranic Index*, Vols. I-II, Madras.

Dowson, J., 1961 (1953) : *A Classicial Dictionary of Hindu Mythology and Religion*, London.

Dubois, Abbe, J.A., 1906 (1897) : *Hindu Manners, Customs and Ceremonies* (Tr. English by Beauchamp, H.K., fr. French).

Elvin, Verrier, 1947 : *Muria and their Ghotul*, Oxford.

Enthoven, R.E., 1920 : *Tribes and Castes of India*, Vol. I; and 1922: *Tribes and Castes of India*, Vol. II, Bombay.

Falk, Maryla, 1943 : "Serpent and the Bird", *Bhāratiya Vidyā*, Vol. IV-2.

Fausbøll, V., 1903 : *Hindu Mythology According to the Mahābhārata*, London.

Fausbøll, V., and Davids, Rhys, 1877 : *Jātakas*, Vol. I.

Fausbøll, V., and Davids, Rhys, 1879 : *Jātakas*, Vol. II.

Fausbøll, V., and Davids, Rhys, 1883 : *Jātakas*, Vol. III.

Fausbøll, V., and Davids, Rhys, 1887 : *Jātakas*, Vol. IV, London.

Francis, H.T. and Thomas, E.G., 1954 : *Jātaka Tales*, Jaico, Bombay.

Frazer, J.G., 1810 and further: *The Golden Bough*, Vols. I-VII, New York.

Friderisch, 1876; 1877 : "The Island of Bali", *JRAS*, Vols. VIII & IX.

Geldner, K.F., 1978 : Der Ṛigved, Vols. I-III HOS.

Gode, P.K., 1954 : *Studies in Literary History*, Vol. II, Sindhi Jain Series, Bombay.

Goldenweirer, Alexander, 1931 : *In Making of Man New York*.

Gonda, J., 1954 : *Aspects of Early Viṣṇuism,* Utrecht.

Hariappa, H.L., 1953 : *Ṛgvedic Legends through the Ages,* Deccan College, Poona.

Hastings, J., 1908-1921 : *Encyclopaedia of Religion and Ethics*, Vols. 1-2 + Vol. 13. Index, London.

Haug, M., 1878 : *Essays on the Religion of the Parsis*, London.

Held, G.J., 1935 : *The Mahābhārata*, London, Amsterdam.

Heras, Fr. H., 1953 : *Studies in Proto-Indo-Mediterranean Culture,* Bombay.

Hodiwala, S.K., 1926 : *Indo-Iranian Religion*, Bombay.

Hope, A.R. and Monrieff, : *Classical Myth and Legend*, Gresham Publishing Co., London.

Hopkins, E.W., 1901 : *The Great Epic of India*, New York.

Hopkins, E.W., 1910 : "Mythological Aspects of Trees and Mountains in the Epic", *JAOS*, 30.

Hopkins, E.W., 1915 : *Epic Mythology,* Strassberg.

Hopkins, E.W., 1916 : "Indra, the God of Fertility", *JAOS*, 36.

Jacob, John, 1909 : *Hindu Tales* (Tr. Eng., Meyer), London.

Kane, P.V., 1968-1977 (1941; Reprint) : *History of Dharmaśāstra*, Vols. I-V, BORI, Poona.

Kellet, E.E., 1927 : *Story of Myth*, London.

Keith, A. B., 1989 : *The Religion and Philosophy of the Veda and Upanishads*, Vols. I-II (*HOS*, Cambridge, 1925), Reprint, Motilal Banarsidass, Delhi.

Keith, A. B., 1967 : *The Veda of the Black Yajus School*, entitled Taittirīya Saṁhita, Vols. I-II, Motilal Banarsidass, Delhi (*HOS*, 1914).

Kramrisch, Stella, 1916 : *Hindu Temple*, Calcultta.

Lang, Andrew, 1884 : *Custom and Myth*, London.

Lang, Andrew, 1897 : *Modern Mythology*, London.

Lang, Andrew, 1913 : *Myth, Ritual and Religion,* London.

Law, B.C., : "Non-Aryan Tribes in the Ṛgveda", *ABORI*, XXIII.

Lindsay, 1951 : "Makara in the Old Buddhistic Sculpture", *JRAS*, LXXXIII.

Longherst, A.H., 1933 : *Humpi Ruins*, Delhi.

Mackenzie, Donald : *Myths of Pre-Columbian America*, Gresham Publishing Co., London.

Mackenzie, Donald : *Myths of China and Japan*, Gresham, London.

Macdonell, A.A., 1897 : *Vedic Mythology*, Strassberg.

Macdonell, A.A. and Keith, A.B., 1958 : *Vedic Index of Names and Subjects*, Vols. I-II (London, 1912).

Majumdar, R.C., and Pusalkar, A.D., 1952 : *Classical Age*,
Majumdar, R.C., and Pusalkar, A.D., 1952 : *Vedic Age*,
Majumdar, R.C., and Pusalkar, A.D., 1954 : *Age of Imperial Unity*, all Bhāratīya Vidyā Bhavan, Bombay.

Max Müller, F., 1907 : *Chips from a German Workshop*, Vol. II (Vols. I-IV), Longman's Green and Co., London.

Max Müller, F., 1926 : *History of Sanskrit Literature*, Calcutta.

Meeds, Margarette, 1929 : *Coming of Age in Samoa*, London.

Meeds, Margarette, 1942 : *Growing up in New Guinea*, London.

Meyer, J.J., 1954 : *Sexual Life in Ancient India*, Calcutta.

Mitra, Sarat Chandra, "Cult of the Godling Naga", *JBORS*, Vol. XXIII.

Monier-Williams, M., 1990 : *Hinduism*, London.

Mookherji, R.K., 1956 : *Ancient India*, Allahabad.

Olcott, W.T., 1914 : *Sunlore of All Ages*, New York.

Oldham, C.F., 1891 : "Serpent Worship in Ancient India" *JRAS*, XXIII.

Oldham, C.F., 1901 : "The Nagas", *JRAS*, XXXIII.

Oldham, C.F., 1905 : *The Sun and the Serpent*, London.

Pande, Rajbali, 1949 : *Hindu Samskāras*, Banares (Varanasi).

Pargiter, E.F., 1922 : *Ancient Indian Historical Tradition,* Oxford Uni. Press, Oxford.

Penzer, N.M., 1952 : *Poison Damsel and Other Tales*,

Penzer, N.M., 1952 : *Ocean of Story*, Vols. I-X.

Perry, W.J., 1931 : "Coming of the Warriors", *Making of Man*, New York.

Rapson, E.J., 1955 : *Cambridge History of India*, Delhi.

Renou, Louis, 1947 : *Vedic India*, Calcutta.

Rundle-Clark, R.T., 1959 : *Myth and Symbol in Ancient Egypt*, London.

Slater, 1924 : *Dravidian Elements in Indian Culture*, London.

Sukhthankar, V.S., 1957 : *On the meaning of the Mahābhārata*, Bombay.

Thomas, P., : *Epics, Myths and Legends of India*, 9th ed., Bombay.

Thurston, E., 1909: *Castes and Tribes of South India*, Vols. I-II, Madras.

Tilak, B.G., 1955 : *Orion*.

Tilak, B.G., 1956 : *Arctic Home in the Vedas*, Poona.

Vaidya, C.V., 1905 : *Mahābhārata — A Criticism*, Bombay.

Viyogi, 1958 : *Jātaka-Kālīna Bhārtiya Sanskṛti*, Patna.

Vogel, J. Ph., 1926 : *The Indian Serpent Lore*, London.

Werner, E.T.C., 1922 : *Myths and Legends of China*, London.

Westermark, 1901 : *The History of Human Marriage*, London.

Wilkins, W.J., 1882 : *Hindu Mythology — Vedic and Puranic*, Calcutta.

Zimmer, H., 1946 : *Myths and Symbols in Indian Art and Civilization*, New York (Repr. 1968).

## Abbreviations for Modern Titles

| | | |
|---|---|---|
| *BORI* | : | *Bhandarkar Oriental Research Institute.* |
| *ABORI :* | | *Annals of the Bhandarkar Oriental Research Institute.* |
| *BV* | : | *Bhāratīya Vidyā.* |
| *Die. Sup.* | : | *Die Suparṇasage.* |
| *Encl. Brit.* | : | *Encyclopaedia Brittanica.* |
| *Encl. Rel. E.* | : | *Encyclopaedia of Religion and Ethics.* |
| *Epic. Myth.* | : | *Epic Mythology.* |
| *HOS* | : | *Harward Oriental Series.* |
| *Hist. Skt. Lit.* | : | *History of Sanskrit Literature.* |
| *Hist. Dh. Śa.* | : | *History of Dharmaśāstra.* |
| *Hist. Ind.* | : | *History of India.* |
| *Ind. S. (Ser.) L.* | : | *Indian Serpent Lore.* |
| *JUB.* | : | *Journal of the University of Bombay.* |
| *JRAS* | : | *Journal of the Royal Asiatic Society.* |
| *JAOS* | : | *Journal of the American Oriental Society.* |
| *JBORS* | : | *Journal of the Bihar and Orissa Research Society.* |

# INDEX